The Dog Lady of Mexico

A NOVEL BY
Alison Sawyer Current

ISBN: 978-0-578-41380-8

Published by Alison Sawyer Current | Isla Animals, Isla Mujeres, QRoo, Mexico

www.islaanimals.org

Endorsements

A heartwarming story of hope, sacrifice and survival but most of all, it's a tale of love. Inspiring and engaging, The Dog Lady of Mexico is a terrific read!

Teresa Kruze - Broadcaster, Best-selling Author, Speaker

Rose's story is a powerful testament to the human capacity for love. Her passion and commitment to the animals is inspiring. Her writing connects you so closely that you may even bring a dog home for yourself.

Janet Rouss - Best-selling Author, Brand Engineer

Simply inspiring! More than a story about saving dogs. Rose is a selfless woman who makes a positive impact in a community despite countless obstacles. Rich in dog tales and Mexican culture!

Anna Krallis, Adoption and Transport Coordinator, Isla Animals

Preface

It has taken ten years to write this down. Originally, I thought a book of short stories would fit the material well but quickly realized it had to be a novel. A fiction based on some of the more gripping tales of my experiences.

Starting a dog rescue was never part of our plans when we moved to Mexico. We were seeking a beautiful ocean setting, in a laid back community, far from big cities and fast-paced living. The rescue just HAD to happen, it was impossible to ignore the countless dogs in dire need of food, medical attention and love. With no high volume, low cost and continual spay and neuter clinics available, there were literally puppies everywhere.

I started with no animal rescue training or veterinarian experience and had to learn quickly as sick puppies and dogs came under my care. It was crucial to learn how to fund-raise, organize enormous spay and neuter clinics and work with all kinds of people.

I have fallen under a spell that I still do not understand. How did this happen? What makes one drop everything at the sight of a dog or puppy needing help? I thought that writing this book would make it clearer but sometimes a door just opens and will never shut again.

In THE DOG LADY OF MEXICO I have tried to convey the intensity of the situation that inescapably took over our lives. To explain the miserable existence of the dogs, the sadness I felt for their neglect and abuse and the joy in having the opportunity to help them. The issues were never simple, as we struggled to understand and respect the culture we were immersed in.

Ultimately these events have renewed my faith in human nature as the rescue gained the support of animal lovers worldwide. I am grateful for the thousands of homes that opened their arms, welcoming and loving our dogs.

This has been a long and emotional journey.

I want to thank my husband, Jeff, for his unwavering faith in my ability to put this down on paper as it was often hard to continue writing. I'm grateful to him and to our children who have done so much to accommodate this unexpected venture.

Contents

Prologue
November 2000

The first time Rose talked to Rudi she didn't like him. He couldn't have been more than fifteen on the day that he waved her over to the black tar shack he lived in. He had something to show her. It was moving on the ground by his feet—a rat. Rudi had ruthlessly tied a string around its tail and attached the other end to his doorpost and he thought it was great entertainment to watch the poor thing fight for its freedom. Rose stood for a moment, mesmerized, watching the rat struggle.

"That's not funny," she snapped before turning her back to him. What are we doing here with people like this? She asked herself, looking at their half-built cinder block house. How did things get this bad? Rose let her bitterness run free as she kept up a steady pace around bags of sand and piles of wood. There were a dozen or so of the construction workers sitting inside the rock wall that surrounded her and her husband Brad's half acre of property, and she knew they were watching her. They don't care, she thought, our house is just another link in the chain that fills the time in their slow, unchallenged passage from birth to death.

Bitter sarcasm was not an innate part of Rose's disposition but this was not how their dream was supposed to unfold. These people, these attitudes, were not what she'd expected. She was feeling as homeless as the dogs that she passed on the beaches, slowly being emptied out like their emaciated bodies. The same apathetic attitude towards the animals echoed in the unfinished walls of her skeletal home. She knew she shouldn't complain; people had warned them about moving to Mexico. And there was Rudi. Wasn't he living in a trap, as helplessly tied to his life as that rat was tied to the door post? It shouldn't have to be this way, Rose told herself.

She passed through the opening that would be their front door and unlocked their one finished room. It wasn't easy to find her scissors amongst the stacks of containers that held everything they'd brought to Mexico, but she did, and marched back to the tar shack to cut the line that held the rat. Rudi and Rose watched the rat run under the gate with the string still attached to its tail.

"Solo es un raton," said Rudi. "Prefiero perros."

This was their beginning.

Chapter 1
The Beginning -1999

Dog rescue had never been part of their Mexican plan. Rose and her husband Brad simply loved Isla Mujeres. Every special occasion was considered a reason to buy a ticket from Colorado to the five-mile-long isle of sand and coral. This trip was their honeymoon and to celebrate, they'd arranged a month long stay at a friend's condominium.

It was Kat who introduced Rose to the world of animal rescue. She was part of their condominium package. Early each morning Kat would arrive and quietly slip into her office, which was set up in the smallest of the condo's two bedrooms, and the reason why Brad and Rose were only required to pay the utilities to stay there. The place was available but not private. If they hadn't already lived together for ten years it might have seemed an invasion of what should've been an intimate celebration. But Rose enjoyed Kat's company and Brad was working long hours at their new restaurant, The Fishbone Bar and Grill.

Rose had been raised as a hard worker. If any of the four children in her family were caught sitting down, something was found for them to do.

They were expected to be thin and clever and succeed. Rose was the youngest. She was a teenager in the 1960's and her world was shifting from Elvis Presley to Jimmy Hendrix. It made her different. She had to admit that she had taken odd routes and without a conscious effort managed to reject the paths that were expected of her. Mexico was a perfect destination. Even the scary negative publicity did not deter her. By the end of their first week Rose had read two books, re-arranged all the furniture, cleaned every surface and dish and needed something else to do. When Kat arrived, as usual, at eight in the morning, Rose was setting up a sewing machine on the dining room table.

"I'm not going to be in your way, am I? Do you ever use this table?" Rose asked Kat.

"No, not at all, I only use the desk in the bedroom. I never work out here. Mrs. Lange used to do all the reservations, so she'd already set up the office in the condo." Kat looped the strap of her bag over the back of a chair. "When I took over her job, we left the office where it was. When they're here, on the island, they're usually gone during the days, so it works well."

Rose figured Kat to be in her early thirties. She was tall and lean with long brown hair framing a sharp but attractive face. Her personality matched her features. Not that Kat was mean or rigid; it was more like she'd learned to set her boundaries at a young age, and that determination had etched itself into the curves around her mouth and eyes.

"Want some coffee? I just made a second pot," said Rose.

"Great." Kat found a mug, filled it and stirred in some cream before joining Rose at the table.

"Shit," said Rose, she was struggling to load a bobbin into Emma Lange's sewing machine. Kat stretched out her long legs and watched Rose's frustration in silence.

"I actually wanted to ask you something," Kat said as she twisted her hair into a knot on top of her head and stuck her pencil through it. "I mean, if you have a minute?" She asked.

"What's up?" Rose dropped the bobbin on the table. "I give up."

"There's a cat that needs help."

"What's wrong with it?" Rose asked.

"It needs to be spayed." Kat explained. "Usually I work with dogs. They're a bigger problem here, especially when they pack up. I'm sure you've seen them on the beaches?" Rose nodded in reply as she started to leaf through the sewing machines manual. "Well, those packs are not the kind of dogs that you and I grew up with. They're wild, I mean like they've never been pets. They live to be dogs like a deer lives to be a deer, and we're the enemy." Kat sipped her coffee and watched Rose fumble with the bobbin once again. "They hunt for food, whether it's an iguana or garbage, and they'll fight over it if they get hungry enough."

"They do seem different. When I see them on the beach, they move away if I get too close," said Rose. "A few of them look okay but most of them are bone thin."

"Right! Did you notice the mange, the bite wounds?"

"Yeah!" Rose shoved the manual across the table and turned to the front windows. The beach was still deserted, too early in the day for sunbathers. "They looked bad." She said.

"So bad that they scare the tourists and sometimes they file complaints."

"Does the government help?" Rose asked.

"No, it's pretty much left up to soft-hearted foreigners like us."

"So, what are we going to do with the cat?" asked Rose, pleased to join the "soft-hearted foreigners" crowd. As Kat continued to describe the problem Rose grew increasingly ashamed of how casually she'd observed their sad state. She'd owned animals all of her life, but had never worked in a rescue. She would not have complained about them but she hadn't been moved enough to do anything helpful about it, either. She'd already accepted them as part of the Island scenery, like the garbage in the streets, or the poverty, those things people gloss over in order to enjoy the better parts of Mexico. Kat's words surprised her, and not in a good way.

Kat continuing to explain while walking into her office. "The cat's pregnant, but she's not eating well, and she's just so tiny." Kat reappeared with a trap and a can of tuna and she'd exchanged her jeans for a tight pair of short shorts.

"Let's go," agreed Rose, trying to remember the last time she'd worn shorts like that.

Finding the cat was easy. She was a few feet from the door of Brad's restaurant, lounging in a spot where the sun was streaming through a break in the shade trees. She was tiny and grey, with eyes the color of the ocean on a clear day, and those eyes seemed far too big for her head. The pregnant part was obvious, and as they approached she stayed where she was.

"These restaurant cats aren't afraid of people," Kat said. "But if you tried to pick her up, she'd scratch her way free." Kat put the trap on the ground. "Okay," she said, "I'll lead her to the cage with the tuna. When she goes in, you shut the door." It was easy, a perfect plan. The cat walked right into the cage under the spell of tuna fish. Rose closed the door and they had her. Feeling very clever they went back upstairs to call the vet to tell him they were on their way.

When they returned to pick up the trap, it was empty. "Where's the cat?" asked Rose.

"There she is," Kat pointed. She was lying in the same spot where they'd first seen her. "Oh my god, we forgot to latch the back door," Kat said, flashing her wonderfully white teeth. "We're good."

"Have you used one of these traps before?" asked Rose, trying not to laugh.

Kat nodded. "Never mind, one point for the cat." Then she went back upstairs for another can of tuna. Their second attempt was easy since the cat wasn't worried about getting trapped. Kat made sure that the back door was locked before she picked it up and started towards the parking lot.

"You're going to have to ride on my moto and hold the cage. Is that a problem?" Kat asked, pointing at a rundown red scooter.

"I'm not riding on that." Rose said, lifting her chin in the direction of Kat's decrepit moto. Rose had never been a fan of any kind of motorcycle. Her father had warned her against them. He'd ridden them in World War II and loved giving Rose all the blood-and-guts details of horrible accidents and it had worked; she'd avoided anything that was motorized with two wheels.

"That's all we have."

"I'll take a Taxi. That thing looks older than dirt," said Rose, putting her hands on her hips.

"Good luck. They won't pick you up with a cat and I can't drive the moto and carry the trap at the same time."

Rose moved in to have a closer look. "Where are the helmets?"

"You're kidding, right? Have you seen anyone here with a helmet?"

Rose gave up. Moto's were the island's main form of transportation other than taxis and Kat did manage to make it to work every day. "Okay, but drive slowly. Is it far?"

"Nah, just a few minutes." Kat handed Rose the trap and climbed on. She rolled the moto forward to push the kickstand back and turned the key. The old engine made an odd clicking noise, and then slowly came to life.

Reluctantly, Rose climbed on the back and took her time positioning the trap in front of her.

"Don't go until I'm ready," she said. "Okay, I'm ready." The moto jerked forward, making Rose clutch Kat tightly. The driveway to the Condominiums was covered with sand blown over from the beach that it bordered, so Kat held her feet out on each side to keep them balanced as they skidded along. Rose was grateful when they reached the bricks that paved the main street.

"We've got to spay every animal we can get our hands on," yelled Kat over her shoulder. "The best way to deal with street cats and dogs is to prevent them from being born in the first place. Have you seen the sad little kittens in the gardens? Who needs more of those?"

Rose had seen the kittens. They were skinny, dirty and many of them had eye infections. She'd tried to get close to them with food but they always ran off and a bigger cat would eat whatever she'd left on the ground.

Paolo, the veterinarian, was waiting for them. Rose was surprised to see him take Kat's hand and kiss her on both cheeks, she couldn't remember any vets in Colorado greeting her with such intimate enthusiasm.

"Paolo moved here from Bolivia, just a few months ago," said Kat, introducing them.

"Santa Cruz de la Sierra," he said as he took the caged animal and turned towards his door.

Rose thought it unusual to be led through his living room into the small office at the back of his house. With shelves against one wall and a table in the middle, it felt cramped once they were all inside. Paolo placed the trap on the table, measured something into a syringe, and gave the cat an injection in the thigh through the bars of the cage. "You can pick her up tomorrow," he told Kat in Spanish.

"Pobrecita was only going to have one kitten," said Paolo the next day when they returned, "and this wasn't her first litter. And, she couldn't eat because she doesn't have any teeth." Paolo explained that this was quite common.

"When cats have their first litter too young it sucks up all the calcium they need to develop their own young bodies." Paolo pulled the trap from the corner and handed it to Kat. "Very sad," he said.

"How do you pay for this?" asked Rose.

"This thing? It was so cheap I bought it with cash," she said.

"Not the moto, the vet, Paolo, where does the money come from to pay for the surgery?" asked Rose.

"Oh, that." Kat reached in her pocket for the key. "He does it for me for free. Don't you think he's handsome?" Kat turned around and winked at Rose. Rose thought about it. He was handsome. Rose realized and not having noticed made her feel old.

After they let the little grey cat go, they mashed up all her food and stood guard as she ate. In her weakened condition, the other cats could easily have shoved her aside and helped themselves.

That night Rose told Brad all about it and was surprised when he confessed to leaving restaurant scraps out for the cats.

"You never told me that," said Rose.

"Well, I sort of have to hide it. The first time I fed some cats in front of the groundskeeper he literally charged at me, waving his arms. I couldn't understand everything he said, but it was obvious he didn't want the cats around or me feeding them."

Rose gave her husband a hug. "You never stop surprising me," she said.

A week later Kat arrived with another plea for help. She led Rose downstairs to show her a litter of twelve puppies underneath the cement steps. It was just a few feet from where they'd captured the cat.

"She must think these bushes will hide them," said Kat, indicating the foliage along a path. Rose got on her knees and peered into the cement cave. The pups were so young; they looked like big balls of different-colored cotton. The mother, who had moved a short distance away, was a mix best described as an Irish setter with short legs. She was so skinny she looked like a backbone with two rows of swollen tits hanging almost to the ground. And she wasn't friendly.

"She must have moved them here last night," said Kat. "I only found them because I always look when I see a nursing mother nearby."

"That is one ugly dog," said Rose, moving aside to give Kat space to check on the wiggling mass of puppy fur. "What do we do?"

"Okay, we start by giving the mom lots of food and water." Kat stood up and walked towards the restaurant. Rose followed her into the kitchen and waited while Kat explained to the cook in Spanish what she needed. At first the cook pretended that he didn't understand and started to walk away, but Kat caught him by the arm and pointed to some big cans on the upper shelves. The cook shrugged and waved his arm toward the back door of the kitchen. "What a jerk," said Kat when they got outside. She reached into one of the big trash bins and pulled out two large cans with red sauce spilling out of them. "These will be perfect. No one will steal them. We just need to clean them up. One for water and the other I can fill with the kibble I have in my office.

"Red—that's what I called the mom—will be fine," Kat was climbing two stairs in front of Rose. "But we'll have to keep the kids and other dogs away from those puppies. I tried to get near to Red this morning, no chance, someone's gonna get bitten and then there'll be big trouble."

After cleaning the cans they made signs in English and Spanish warning people to stay away. They hoped that people would give Red the space she needed.

Rose loved her new family.

"Did you check the pups on your way in today?" Rose asked while she poured them both coffee. "They're starting to look like puppies, what a difference in just two weeks." She handed Kat her mug. "But I think we should put something in front of the stairs. Now that they're moving around, I mean."

Kat sat down with both hands around her mug. She had braided her hair to one side and her t-shirt was so tight Rose wondered how she moved her arms. Would Brad like it if I wore a t-shirt like that? She glanced down at her oversized twenty-year-old Mickey Mouse t-shirt and let it go.

Later that day they wrapped a cardboard barrier around the opening. Red was getting used to them, not enough to let them touch her, but enough to accept their minor adjustments. Rose continued to check on them three to four times a day. She didn't trust the cat-hating grounds keeper or any of the staff that worked at the condos and the restaurant.

Rose's next concern was Red who was spending less and less time with her pups. "She's hardly nursing them at all," she told Kat. Another week had passed and every morning, after Brad left for the restaurant, Rose found herself impatiently waiting for Kat to arrive so they could discuss new developments. Their morning coffee had become a comfortable routine and a time that Rose valued as they learned more about each other.

"This always happens with the wild dogs. I don't know why. I'll have to ask

Paulo," Kat said with her usual wink, she finally confessed that she and Paolo sort of had a "thing." And from other stories Rose was beginning to suspect that Latin men were one of the major reasons Kat was living in Mexico. That and to get away from her B-movie-star mother who was getting less selective about the roles she took on as she grew older. Kat spared no details when she talked about her lonely childhood. She'd left home young and was never going back.

"Then I guess it's time to take them to the bookstore."

"Really, so soon? I'm going to miss them."

"There are plenty more, I promise you," said Kat. She handed Rose a box which they loaded up with the pups.

Chapter 2
The Bookstore

They hauled the box into town. The streets were lined with stores and as they passed by venders yelled to them trying to sell their merchandise. Rose wondered how they could make any money, they all sold the same things. T-shirts, jewelry, and colorful pottery were displayed on tables outside each shop. "Hey lady, come on in, we have what you want, cheaper than Walmart." Rose hated being called lady.

"How do Gretchen and Jennifer know how to take care of these animals?"

"They work closely with Paulo. If there's a problem he'll take the animal to his clinic."

"And who pays for all of this?" asked Rose. She'd stopped to switch her hands to the corner of the box in order to maneuver around some tourist who had stopped to shop.

"Jennifer is always doing one kind of fundraiser or another. They manage. I'd help more if I had any money."

"How long have they been here?" asked Rose, trying to get a feel for the women who would be caring for her puppies.

"A year, I think. Jennifer arrived first and then Gretchen showed up." Kat had set the box down and was rubbing one of the puppies on her cheek. "Jennifer's some sort of social worker and Gretchen's a teacher. That's why there are always so many kids in the store. Oh, these little fur balls are so soft. They're from Wisconsin, or something like that, grew up together. I think their moms were friends. We don't really hang out."

Once they arrived at the bookstore it was hard to get through the door—so many children were crowding around to see the pups. "This is why the mom didn't follow us," said Kat. "Street dogs don't like kids." Kat pushed the children away from the box in a manner that suggested she felt the same way as the street dogs.

"Is this them?" asked a slim, dark-haired woman after they made it through the door. She had a huge mass of dark curly hair held back with a colorful bandana.

"All twelve, Gretchen," said Kat.

"You're kidding, right?" said a tall blond. "There aren't really twelve in there." Rose backed up so the woman, Jennifer, could get a look. Gretchen already had one in each hand but Jennifer just stood and stared.

Gretchen guided them to the back corner where there was a wooden playpen divided in half and filled with towels and toys. There were already bigger puppies in one side so they put the smaller ones in the empty space. "Do they eat kibble, yet?" Gretchen asked.

"They've started to. I've been giving them a little more each day. I'm Rose, by the way."

"So nice to meet you. I'm Gretchen and she," Gretchen tilted her head towards Jennifer, "is Jennifer.

"Gretchen goes brain dead around puppies," said Jennifer.

"That's not true ..." started Gretchen.

"I have to get back to work," said Kat. "I'll see you all later."

Rose watched Kat head towards the door. Jennifer had closed it temporarily to keep the kids out while they settled the puppies in. They were lined up outside and Kat had raised her arms, wading through the children like they were diseased. Definitely not into kids, thought Rose.

"This is the most we've ever had at one time," Jennifer was saying to Gretchen when Rose turned back to the pups.

"I'd love to help," Rose said, addressing them both. "I've already been watching over them for weeks."

"That's great," said Gretchen, "but these guys are so cute we'll have homes for them in no time."

"Not too soon, I hope," said Rose. "They're still so small." Jennifer walked back to her desk. "I can help with all the pups," Rose repeated.

The next day Rose spent the morning at the book store cleaning and feeding the puppies. She was surprised by how much she'd missed them living under the steps. But the puppies were safer now even if it was such a small area. To compensate, she piled six of them into a basket and walked to an empty lot where she sat on some coral and watch them roll around and play.

The number of children at the bookstore worried Rose. They showed up every day for the fun and art projects but the puppies were a huge draw and the children were rough. When she decided to talk about it, she found Gretchen in the middle of an animated conversation with a customer so she wandered through the book shelves to pass the time. Most of the books were fiction, which made perfect sense for vacation reading, but on one of the back racks was a section dedicated to Mexico. She was pleased that some of the books had English titles: The Mayan World, Life in Mexico. A book called Mayan Legends caught her attention. It looked worn so she pulled it gently off the shelf and settled into the couch that divided the room in half.

The spine of the book crackled when she opened it as if it hadn't been disturbed in a long time. The pages were stiff and some of them stuck together. In the middle she found a legend called The Animal King. The lettering in the title was sculpted out of wild cats and birds and underlined with interwoven snakes. Beneath that there were two dogs' heads, not exactly the same but similar. Rose ran her fingers over the artwork, which was slightly raised, wondering who had done it. She could hear Gretchen still talking to her customer, so Rose started to read.

THE ANIMAL KING

A long, long time ago there was a wise King. He had ruled his land well for many years but he was saddened to see his people, who had enjoyed a good life in his kingdom become languid. There was plenty of food, for the land was fertile and the sky was kind. Fruits and vegetables grew year-round. Twice a year the people would hunt deer and kill only what they needed.

The wise King had two sons, Ek Chauh and Itzamna, and two dogs, Pec-Ah-Puck and Pec-Nicteha. He loved his sons because they were his, and he loved his dogs for their loyalty and companionship. Both his sons and dogs filled him with joy as he honored all living creatures.

As time passed, the King saw the people in his kingdom grow lazier and lazier. His wise man advised him that life in the King's wondrous kingdom had become too easy. He said that working the body and the mind makes men happy. So the King commanded his people to build a shelter for the animals. He wanted to protect all his creatures and share the kingdom's good fortune. He ordered his sons, the princes Ek Chauh and Itzamna, to watch over the work and to ensure that his people built the shelter to match his kingdom, making it a place of wonder.

Sadly, as the people labored the King saw that they did not put all of their hearts into the work and instead of feeding the animals all the good food that was available, they gave them scraps or sometimes forgot to feed them at all.

The disheartened King walked through his village asking his people why they treated the animals this way. They told him that they were smarter and more important than the animals. This the King did not understand. He grew angry. His sons, Ek Chuah and Itzamna, had let this transpire.

The King returned to his wise man. "How can I teach my people to honor the animals?" The wise man replied that he must show them how the animals feel. So the King turned all of his village people into different animals of the forest. Then he turned his sons into dogs and his dogs into men. He ordered his sons, now dogs, to care for all the dogs in the world because his sons were princes and would someday be Kings. The men that were once his dogs became his best companions and advisors on how to care for the rest of animals in his village.

Now, the King was happy and his sons were happy to take care of the other dogs. No longer were they lazy because their biggest joy, like all dogs, was to love and honor their King.

"Hey Gretchen," Rose said looking up from the book. "Do you have a dictionary?"

"What do you need?" The customer had left. "I have one on my computer."

"Well, what exactly is a legend?"

Gretchen turned to her computer. After a few clicks she began reading. "It says here it's a story that has been passed down for generations, and is often presented as history but is unlikely to be true."

"Unlikely?" asked Rose. "What does that mean? That some of it's true and some of it isn't or the whole thing is made up?"

"I don't know," said Gretchen. "I guess I always thought of a legend as a story that probably started as truth and then got more fantastic and whimsical with each telling until someone finally wrote it down. Why?"

"I was just looking at this book of Mayan legends."

"Oh, there it is." Gretchen got up from her desk and joined Rose on the couch. "Jennifer must have put it on the shelf but I never intended to sell it. My friend Miguel's grandmother died and he brought it to me from her house. I haven't had time to even look at it."

"Do you mind if I take it home? I'd like to read more of the legends. Look at this," Rose said, turning the book in Gretchen's direction. "The artwork is beautiful. I'll take really good care of it."

"That's fine," said Gretchen. "I probably won't get to it for a while anyway."

Rose took the book home and put it on her desk. She tried to answer her emails but soon realized that she wasn't registering what she read. Instead her mind was full of the story of the ancient dog Princes. What would they do if they lived in present times? If their kingdom was Isla Mujeres, what would their solution be for the sad neglected dogs?

She imagined them as greyhounds, tall and regal, but heavier. They would need to be sturdy. Maybe the younger one would have a brilliant, shiny, black coat and the older brother would have rich, golden fur and a white chest. What would they be saying to her or anyone who cared about the dogs? How would they help the people know what their father knew?

Rose let her mind wonder, imagining the conversation they would have.

"Are you seeing this?" Ek Chauh would ask. "Somebody cares." Rose pictured the young princes lying next to each other.

"I've been watching her just like you." Itzamna would answer. "I think she wants to help."

"We really need someone," Ek Chauh would say. They would know the sad state of the dogs and see it the way I see it now, thought Rose.

"There are too many puppies." Itzamna would always be worrying about the puppies.

"We've tried people before," Ek Chauh might warn.

"Well it hasn't been enough. Mexico is changing, people moving into cities. The dogs were safer on farms." The brothers would knew this.

Rose wanted Ek Chauh to say. "She could be good. There is something about her."

She then laughed to herself, such a silly fantasy. How she so badly wanted the princes to be real, she wanted to feel their presence. There was so much working against the dogs, nothing short of mythologized saviors could help. She wanted equal company in her concerns—to share her struggle on how to help, even if it was in her own mind. Then she laughed again. Mexico is making me crazy, she thought.

Chapter 3
Rose's First Rescue

Behind the property where Rose and Brad were staying was a large pile of logs. Another remnant of the abandoned building projects that were everywhere. Rose had avoided it, worried about scorpions and other unfamiliar bugs, until the day a strange noise drew her attention. She stopped to check, thinking that it might be one of those huge iguanas that were everywhere. She never tired of watching their long bodies and how fast they were on their stubby legs. Getting closer she spotted something moving, but it was too tiny to be an iguana. "Probably a mouse," she said out loud without meaning to.

"No, it's a puppy," said someone behind her. She turned and saw a good-looking young man sitting on the wall that served as a barrier between the beach and the sandy road that Kat had skidded along with Rose and the pregnant cat. "I've been watching it, wondering what to do," he said.

"How big is it?" Rose asked.

"A little bigger than a baseball with fur," he said, pushing back the brown curls that had fallen over his sunglasses.

"Did you just see one?"

"Only one," he said. Then jumped down off of the wall.

Rose moved around to the back side of the pile. She squatted to get a view under the curve of the log, and there was the tiny pup. Remembering Kat's warnings about defensive canine mothers, she looked around before she reached for it. "Oh, look at you," she said, touching the little bundle. By then the young man had moved closer.

"There must be more," he said. "There's rarely just one."

"How do you know?"

"I work with animals. I'm a vet tech—veterinarian technician."

"So, how old do you think this pup is?" said Rose.

"Let me have a look at its teeth." He took the puppy and lifted its upper lip, uncovering a solid line of sharp teeth just poking through the gums. "Maybe five weeks old, and it's a male," he said after turning it over.

"You want to help me look for more?" asked Rose, taking the puppy back.

"Sure, that's what I was watching for, to see if any more appeared."

"Ok," Rose said, circling the pile. "But don't move anything. I'm afraid they could get trapped or crushed."

"Hey, my name's Greer, by the way." Greer reached out and Rose accepted his hand shake. He stood a head taller than Rose's five feet eight inches, the same height as her husband, and was wearing a T-shirt and jeans.

"I'm Rose, nice to meet you. Why don't you start at that end and I'll start over here?" They both got on their hands and knees and started to search.

"I hear something," said Greer, his head next to a lower logs. "Are there scorpions here?" he asked, pulling away.

"I think so," said Rose, "but I've never seen one."

Greer leaned forward and reached into an opening and pulled out a puppy. "Oh," said Rose, amazed that he'd been right. He reached back in and pulled out two more, handing them off to Rose.

"That's it," he said. But Rose worried he might have missed one, moved closer and reached into the den.

"You're right, there's no more. Let's take them back to my condo where we can check them over." Rose indicated the direction with her elbow.

"Great, I'm staying there, too," said Greer.

Rose was excited to show Kat the pups but she imagined Greer would be a nice treat, as well. "Kat?" She called as they entered the condo, "Kat, are you here?"

"Back here in my cave." Rose found Kat at her desk, her long legs sprawled out in front of her as she held a paper in each hand. Her shorts were longer today but her top was lower. It was one or the other, as if Kat had a certain amount of space on her body to cover. One day the space was higher up, higher neckline, shorter shorts, and the next day it was lower, longer shorts but a low-cut t-shirt.

"We found four puppies in that pile of logs at the end of the road," Rose told her.

"Who's we?"

"Oh, sorry. Kat," Rose signaled Greer to join her at the open doorway. "This is Greer, and Greer, this is Kat." Kat flashed him one of her wonderful white smiles.

"Hi, I think I've seen you around," Kat said, looking Greer straight in the eyes. Not a shy bone in her body, thought Rose.

"Probably, I'm staying here." Kat reached out to shake his hand but he gave her a puppy instead. "We just found these."

"What should we do?" asked Rose, feeling like she'd disappeared as the other two grinned at each other.

Kat stood up slowly and gracefully. Usually she jumped from her chair but Greer was watching. She handed the puppy back and picked up a box of towels, which she emptied and lined with newspaper. "Let see if they're thirsty," she suggested, putting the box on the dining room table and brushing past Greer to get to the kitchen. He was still watching her, a pup in each hand, as she reached into the cabinet for a cup.

"They're so little," said Rose, lowering her pups into the box. Then she reached for Greer's pups. He seemed to have forgotten that he was holding them.

"Is that all of them?" asked Kat.

"That's it," said Rose. "I double-checked."

Kat picked one up and rubbed a bit of water she'd put in the cup under its nose. When it showed interest, she tilted the cup just enough so he could drink. She repeated this with each one, then suggested that they take them to Paulo. "He has flea shampoos. Want to come?" she asked Greer sweetly.

But Greer shook his head, "I've got some friends on the beach. They're probably wondering what happened to me. Hopefully I'll get to see you later. You can tell me how it goes."

"Okay, I'll let you know." Kat turned to Rose with a big smile. "It's time for the scooter."

Paulo, the vet, had recently decided he needed more room and had rented a space away from his house. It was bigger and better equipped. Using a deep sink in one corner, he showed Rose and Kat how to bathe the pups in special tick-and-flea-killing shampoo. It had to be left on for ten minutes, so after they were lathered up the pups slid comically around on the clinic floor. When they were ready, Rose and Kat rinsed them off before taking them outside into the sun to finish the job with a flea comb. By then the puppies were tired and easily picked at. They sleepily sank into the curves of Rose and Kat's bare legs in the afternoon warmth.

Meanwhile, Paulo softened some dog chow, which the puppies devoured before flopping down on the cool tiles, their back and front legs splayed in opposite directions. For Rose it was enormously gratifying seeing them clean, fed, and safe. Paulo had to wade through them to get to his examining table when someone brought in a cat for treatment, but he still insisted on keeping them at the clinic for a few days.

Kat went back to work but Rose hung around a little longer to watch over them. She then hailed a taxi. A nice safe taxi.

After paying the driver, she strolled along the sandy road towards the condos but she couldn't pass the logs without checking one more time. She knelt down and stuck her arm in the hole determined to feel the end of the tunnel or the back wall of a cave or whatever the space was that had housed those puppies. Lying on her side she stretched her arm in as far as she could and then wiggled her fingers from side to side. Feeling something to the right, she pushed in harder, sending a smaller log rolling off the side of the pile. There was something warm, she could feel some fur. Gently, she pulled the puppy out; it was a female, a tiny golden orb.

"Oh, you poor little mud pie," she said. "You must have wondered where everyone went." Holding the pup firmly to her chest she sat on the logs for a few minutes, as that familiar feeling kindled and grew at the thought of the scared and lonely pup left behind. But it was more than that—it was all of them, the hundreds of litters in hundreds of holes that were left to fend for themselves. The thought of it made her feel like she hadn't eaten for days so Rose took a few deep breaths until she felt better, enjoying the puppy's warmth next to her body.

Thank you, Itzamna, thought Rose. You knew she was there. Rose gently placed the pup in her pocket, fleas and all, and hailed a taxi back to the clinic.

Chapter 4

The Island's First Spay And Neuter Clinic

On Roses next trip to the island, two months later, Gretchen asked her to help at a spay and neuter clinic that she and Jennifer were planning.

"I've already enlisted Paulo to handle the medical side," she said. "Kat's on board and we're looking for volunteers."

Rose placed her latest basket of puppies on the floor and sat in the chair beside Gretchen's desk. "I'd love to," she said. "I'm not sure what I have to offer but I'll be glad to do whatever I can."

"Terrific," said Gretchen, "we're having a meeting next door in an hour."

"At the restaurant?" asked Rose.

"Yup, I thought we could have lunch while we talked."

"Perfect! That gives me time to clean up the pups and take a few of them outside." Rose picked up her basket, she was now officially in charge of the pups at the book store during the days that she was on the island. Gretchen did it whenever Rose was back in Colorado.

It was still early for lunch when Rose arrived at the restaurant. Jennifer and Gretchen waved her over to their table by the window.

"Hey, we're just getting started," said Gretchen, pulling out the empty chair next to her. "I'm so glad you're here."

Rose sat down and hooked her bag over the back of the chair, then pulled herself closer to the table. "I'm ready for whatever you've got," she said.

"This is going to be different from any veterinarian experience you've ever had," said Gretchen.

"Shocked the hell out of me the first time," said Jennifer, as she rearranged the condiments and napkins in the middle of the table. "I mean, we're talking blood and guts."

"Didn't bother me a bit." Gretchen's face lit up. "I loved it, being able to watch the surgery was amazing. I was sorry we were only there for two days." Gretchen spread her arms to indicate the size of her dismay. Rose had noticed that she punctuated her conversations with great, flourishing arm movement. It was obviously hard for her to sit still. Even running four miles every morning didn't use up the abundance of energy that was her daily allotment.

"You've lost me, what are you talking about?" said Rose.

"Sorry, Gretchen and I volunteered at a spay and neuter clinic in Tulum," said Jennifer. "It's a small coastal town on the Mayan Riviera south of Playa del Carmen. I told Gretchen that I wouldn't help her plan a clinic for this island until we'd actually seen what it was like."

"So, we went down there about a month ago," said Gretchen, twisted in her chair, looking for a waiter. She quickly spotted one and flagged him over. "I'm starved and I know exactly what I want. I have the same thing every time we eat here," she told Rose.

As soon as the waiter arrived with a pad and pencil, Gretchen ordered. "I'll have the chicken fajitas," she said, "less chicken, more veggies and lots of guac…por favor."

"Same for me," said Jennifer, "but I want flour tortillas."

"You're in Mexico, Jennifer. You should have the corn tortillas, they make them here."

"I don't care where I am, I don't like corn tortillas." The waiter continued writing and then looked at Rose.

"I'll have the same. Sounds great! But sorry," Rose said to Gretchen. "I'd like flour tortillas, too."

Gretchen shook her head.

"Algo para tomar?" asked the waiter.

"Water's good, no ice," said Jennifer.

"I'll have water too, extra ice," said Gretchen shaking her head at Jennifer.

"A Diet Coke for me," said Rose, amused by the old friends poking at each other. It made her feel homesick for the people that she had the same type of a familiar history with.

After the waiter left, Jennifer moved her chair back from the table, reached around and pulled a pad and pencil out of her tote bag. "I'm going to stick to the paperwork this time," she said, "since I get to choose my job. In Tulum, they put me in recovery. Ugh, blood and drool everywhere. It was disgusting."

"You're better at organizing anyway," Gretchen said, before turning to Rose. "She does all that stuff at the book store. When we were in school, she got better grades than me but I was better at sports and tried to show her how to have fun. That's why we work so well together. I loosen her up and she drags me down." Gretchen winked at Rose.

"Really," said Jennifer, raising her eyebrows. "I thought I was helping you."

"How long have you two known each other?" asked Rose.

"Forever," said Jennifer. "We grew up on the same street in Madison. But I'm younger."

"One year," said Gretchen. "But then Jennifer skipped grade three so we were in the same grade."

"There's Kat," said Jennifer, who was facing the door. "Hey!" Kat crossed the room towards them and plopped onto the fourth chair.

"We just ordered. Do you want something?" asked Jennifer, waving the waiter over again.

"I can't stay long. I have to get back to work. What did you all order?" asked Kat, reaching for a menu.

"We're all having chicken fajitas," said Rose.

"Great, I'll just have some of yours, they always serve way too much here."

The waiter reappeared with two waters and a Diet Coke. Kat asked for an extra plate and ordered a beer.

"So, we were just talking about who should do what at the clinic," Jennifer said after the waiter left.

"We were telling Rose all about the clinic we went to," Gretchen explained to Kat. "You remember, we went with my friend from Tulum." Kat nodded and took a sip of Rose's coke. "I was about to tell Rose that the vet team in Tulum wanted to work in other parts of Mexico."

"And Gretchen's wanted to do a spay and neuter clinic on the island forever," said Jennifer.

"We've been working on it since we got back." Gretchen said. She took a long drink of her water. "Ah, so cool and refreshing." She jiggled the glass before putting it down to reinforce the advantage of ice.

Jennifer ignored her and took over the story. "The vets told us when they could return to Mexico and gave us a list of what we needed to do,"

"They'll be on the island for seven days." Gretchen said, pulling Jennifer's pad and pen across the table. "They want one day to set up, five days to operate and one day to tear down. After then the head vet wants to give her team some time at the beach."

The waiter returned with Kat's beer and deposited knives and forks wrapped in paper napkins in the middle of the table.

"It's grueling work," said Gretchen. "And most of the vets use their vacation time to come down here. They deserve a break."

"It's true," said Jennifer dropping a roll of cutlery in front of each of them. "I mean, everyone else can take a break, work different shifts, move around, but the vets have to stay in the operating room doing surgery after surgery."

Gretchen watched Kat take a long swig of her beer and waved the waiter over. "Una cerveza, por favor. That just looks too good."

"Kat, have you called Greer about coming?" asked Rose.

"I did, he's not sure about it yet."

Gretchen's beer, arrived quickly. She wrapped one hand around it. "Ice cold, how wonderful." She took a long drink before continuing to explain the clinic. Two waiters arrived with their food. The first carrying a tray with three sizzling black frying pans piled high with chicken, peppers, and onions. Behind him a younger waiter carried two round baskets, a bowl of salsa and a bowl of guacamole, and plates all expertly balanced in both of his arms.

"Buen provecho, algo mas?" the first waiter asked.

"This looks wonderful," said Rose.

Jennifer checked the baskets and pulled the one with the flour tortillas between herself and Rose. Gretchen grabbed the other one and shared it with Kat. They made more plans, talked about possible volunteers.

Rose let the conversation continue around her. She was trying to imagine the clinic and wondered where she could be the most help. Plus, having seen the average dog on the island, just one short step up from the mangy and wounded wild beach dogs, she worried that five long days of exposure would be too much for her. It was Gretchen who brought her back, touching her arm to get her attention. They all needed to agree on the time for their next meeting.

Rose and Kat had signed up to clean the site the day before the clinic began. The only rent-free place Gretchen could find was a small, decrepit, three-room house that had been abandoned for months, maybe longer. It was next to the ocean on the Caribbean side of the island, sitting on a cliff that dropped off dramatically. The waves rolled in from the open ocean and battered the coral wall with such force that Rose could feel the pounding in her legs if she stood too close to the cliff's edge.

"This is a norte," explained Kat, gesturing at the cloudy sky. "They typically last three days long. I hope it doesn't make problems for the clinic."

"Does it usually mean rain?" asked Rose.

"Not necessarily but lots of wind for sure cloudy that might be nice!" Standing in the small space behind the house and looking back into the crowded room they'd come through, Kat decided they should move everything outside. That included broken furniture, dirty piles of disintegrating boxes, newspapers, old dirty blankets and more. At first they carefully moved things out to the small yard, but after boxes broke apart and bugs scurried out from under all the clutter they started to shove and fling things out of the house.

"This is nothing but garbage." said Kat, wrinkling her nose as the dust and mold filled the air. "Someone else can sort through this shit." Then they scrubbed. Rose was mopping the ceiling when Kat charged out of the bathroom.

"Oh my god, this is disgusting!" Kat said, brushing at her clothes.

"Don't worry, I'll do the bathroom. I'm a poop cleaning expert. I did have kids in my first life, and all the puppies, not much bothers me."

"Thanks," said Kat. "I was starting to gag. Really! I mean the water's been off and bugs are crawling up the drain. Worst of all, I can't go near that toilet, no way."

"The bugs under the boxes were harder for me. We have cockroaches in Colorado but these roaches are huge."

"Well, you'll be okay in the bathroom then, the bugs are smaller," said Kat, grabbing Rose's mop and moving to the other side of the room.

Later that day they helped assemble tables and chairs. "Where did these plastic Coke tables come from?" asked Rose. She was pushing the legs into the corners of each table top. "They're so flimsy."

"We borrowed them from the restaurant where we meet, they're just for check in," said Kat. One room had just enough space for three operating tables. The room next to it was for recovery and the front room was set up to prep the animals for surgery.

It bothered Rose that there was no door to the bathroom, just a curtain. "We'll just have to stand guard for each other," Kat said when Rose mentioned it. Obviously it didn't bother Kat at all.

The next morning the volunteers showed up at seven for a briefing. "The goal," Jennifer explained, getting right to it, "is to keep the vets and their techs busy from eight a.m. to six p.m. That's the way to get the maximum number of animals done."

Stationed in recovery, Rose spread towels on the floor with four other volunteers. Norma, the head vet, instructed them all on how to give shots, check gum color, and clean the blood around the incisions. One side of the recovery room was designated for cats. Rose and Kat were on the side allocated for dogs.

"Can you believe that they want us to give shots? Have you ever done that before?" asked Rose.

"Never," Kat told her.

"I just think it's cool, it makes me feel like Dr. Kildare."

"Like who?"

"Never mind, I'm dating myself. Do you know any of the cat people?" Rose asked Kat as she sorted Q-tips and cotton balls.

"I've seen the lady with the hat before, but not the other two. I'm sure we'll know more than we'll ever want to know about them by the end of the week." Rose elbowed Kat disapprovingly, but still laughed.

Each recovery volunteer was given tweezers, scissors, a small bottle of hydrogen peroxide, cotton balls, gauze, a thermometer, ear cleaner, Q-tips, and the bottom half of a one-gallon Clorox bottle to arrange them in.

Since the surgeries hadn't started Rose went outside and sat in the shade. She watched Jennifer, instruct her volunteers. "Every dog or cat has to be assigned a number," she told them, and pointed to a pile of ropes hung over the back of the chair next to her. "We've already cut them and wrapped a piece of duct tape around each one. Very few animals will have collars, so it's important to make sure that you write the number that's on the paperwork on the duct tape and tie it around their necks. And make sure you fill in all the information. You'd be amazed at how messed up it can get if we aren't careful." Everyone nodded and watched as Jennifer checked in the first dog to arrive.

"Your name?" she asked the owner.

"Roberto Manuel Rodrigues," he answered. Jennifer wrote this down.

"Your address?"

"Across from the Comex and down two houses," he told her.

Jennifer turned to her volunteers, "This is the kind of address you'll get, just write down exactly what they say."

"Telephone number?" she asked, turning back to the dog owner.

"No."

"Not many of the islanders have phones but I want you to ask them for a number anyway, just in case, okay?" The volunteers nodded.

"Your dog's name?" Jennifer asked.

"Blanca," the owner answered, without looking at his dog.

"Okay, this is precisely why it's important to get that number on each animal," said Jennifer. "They all have the same names: Blanca meaning white, Negro meaning black, Canela meaning cinnamon, Mancha meaning Spot, and Champion which is pronounced more like chomp-y-yawn."

"Male or female?" Jennifer asked Roberto.

"Female."

"Age?"

Roberto had to think about this. "Maybe two," he finally answered.

"Vaccinations?" Jennifer asked.

"Yes," Roberto answered proudly.

"Rabies?"

"Yes, last month with the government."

"Any other shots?" Roberto looked confused by this question, and Jennifer explained this to her volunteers.

"This is something that you'll have to make sure is very clear," she said. "There are two places for shots on this form; one is for rabies and the other is for the four or five-way vaccinations. Four or five-way just means that it covers four or five different diseases or viruses like Parvovirus, Distemper, Hepatitis, Coronavirus or respiratory infections. What can cause misunderstandings is that most people here get their dogs vaccinated for rabies because it's free from the government. It's a program that was started to protect the population since rabies kills people as well as dogs and it's been very successful."

"You mean they don't have rabies here anymore?" asked a tall blond volunteer.

"Yes, I mean no, the Yucatan is pretty much a rabies-free zone, but it isn't official. But it makes it tricky for us because the dog owners think it means their dogs are totally vaccinated. Parvo and distemper are a huge problem and ideally, the dogs should be vaccinated against those diseases as well."

"Why don't people vaccinate for both?" asked another volunteer.

"Because most people don't know that they need more than one kind of vaccination, or they just can't afford it, or, believe it or not, they don't know that such a vaccination exists. Their dogs die and they don't know why because they never see a vet. I could go on and on," she said, but instead turned her attention back to Roberto.

"Has your dog been sick lately?"

"No."

"Vomiting, diarrhea?"

"No."

"Okay, please read this and sign at the bottom." Jennifer turned the paper around and pushed it across the table. As the man looked over the form Jennifer explained what it said to the volunteers. "On the bottom it explains that all surgeries can be dangerous, but most of them go well. We want people to understand the risk before they allow us to operate. This avoids problems if something goes wrong." The man signed the paper and pushed it back towards Jennifer.

"Ha," she said to him, "your dog's number one." With that Jennifer wrote the number on the duct tape and handed it to the man. "Be sure to get the owner to tie these numbers on their animals. Many of these dogs are not used to being handled and they're already stressed out just being here. I don't want anyone to get bitten. Okay, any questions?"

"What if they can't read? What do we do about the consent form, then?" A tall blond volunteer asked.

"Good question. There should always be at least one Spanish speaker at this desk. Just explain what the form says and ask the owner to make any kind of mark they can on the form. Okay?"

"How about two people who can kind of speak Spanish?" asked the same volunteer?

"That'll work. If you need help, just ask."

Jennifer got up from the check-in table and offered her chair to the tall blond volunteer. Then she stood by and watched her check in the second dog. Satisfied that they could handle it, Jennifer went into the front room where a vet tech was examining number one. Rose followed her inside. She already knew the tech's job was to make sure the dog was healthy enough for surgery, but Rose wanted to see each procedure necessary to get an animal all the way through the process. The vet tech was asking Roberto, the owner, to stand on the scale alone and then to do it again while holding his dog. As the dog struggled in Roberto's arms it was difficult to read the quivering needle, so Rose knelt down to get a closer look. "Twenty-two kilos," she told the tech, who nodded gratefully and recorded the weight.

"Sorry," the tech explained in Spanish to the owner, "but the weight is very important in determining how much anesthesia will be necessary." The owner practically dropped the dog before he got off the scale. The poor thing staggered to stay on its feet. It was obvious that Roberto was put out by having to handle his dog that much.

When the next owner was ushered inside with dog number two, Rose helped the tech read the weight and then followed Jennifer back outside.

"When Cory, the dog trapper, arrives," Jennifer told her volunteers, "can one of you please come and find me? The process is different for the animals she has."

"I will," offered the tall blonde volunteer at the check in table. "I met Cory yesterday, I know who she is."

"What's your name?" asked Jennifer.

"Meaghan."

"Great, thanks, you let me know, okay?" Meaghan nodded.

Jennifer and Gretchen had told Rose that they were determined to spay and neuter the street dogs and even the wild beach dogs if they could get them. Cory, a woman they'd met at the clinic in Tulum, was able to trap dogs that no one else could get close to. Gretchen, who was particularity impressed by Cory, had described her arriving once or twice a day in the back of an old truck surrounded by an array of dogs, some in traps and some tied to the side of the truck bed.

Each of Cory's dogs would be a different level of feral. So instead of weighing them the technicians guessed their weight, and instead of having a number around their necks their size and color was carefully recorded. After that they took first place in line for surgery. The faster they were in and out of the clinic the less chance there was of someone getting bitten. For recovery they were put back in a crate, still asleep, and taken outside where they were watched closely until they were alert enough to be set free again. At the end of the day Cory would take them back to where she trapped or found them.

The first time Rose saw her, Cory was sitting on the curb smoking a cigarette. She was wearing tan overalls and a man's undershirt and rubbing the back of her neck with a red scarf. Rose guessed that she must cut her own hair because it was so uneven and headed off in all different directions. Her whole look said, "I don't care". She was explaining to the volunteers who had approached her truck that the dogs were hers, no one else was allowed to handle them.

"How do you do it—catch them, I mean?" asked a volunteer.

"What's your name?" asked Cory.

"Charlene," answered the volunteer, drawing out her name in two parts.

"Well Char-lene," said Cory, pronouncing her name the same way it was given, "in the morning I boil three or four whole chickens and then break them into pieces for bait."

"I thought we weren't supposed to give dogs chicken bones?" Charlene said.

Cory snorted. "That's what all the dogs eat around here—garbage, full of chicken bones and everything else that we've been told not to feed dogs."

Cory was a serious woman, but Gretchen said she was friendly, and completely dedicated to animal welfare. She'd told Rose about the afternoon she'd seen Cory sitting on the ground with one of the dogs she'd captured, one of the ones that no one else could approach. The dog was sitting in her lap looking like a house pet that had lived with her for years. Cory loved them all and they knew it. Gretchen thought she was magic.

Finally there were dogs in recovery. Rose was sitting on a rolled-up towel but what she really wanted was knee pads. She'd recovered two dogs so far, numbers two and four, and spent most of her time kneeling over them to clean their ears and cut their nails. "These ears are disgusting," she complained to Kat, who was doing the same thing.

"It's the fungal and yeast infections that they get here from the humidity. The poor things, I've seen them scratch the fur right off their ears, it can get that itchy. Just think of what a great favor you're doing them."

"Yuck, it's greasy and smells like dirty socks," said Rose.

"You'd better toughen up, it's going to get a lot dirtier and a lot smellier before we're done," said Kat, grinning.

"Well thanks, there's something to look forward to." Said Rose. She gently moved her dog around so she could clean its other ear. "I can't believe it, but I'm actually getting hungry. You'd think this stuff would kill your appetite."

"That's proof that you're just whining," said Kat. "Jeannie and Addy are bringing lunch every day, so it should be terrific."

"Jeannie's the one in the muumuus, right?" asked Rose.

"Yup, she's really big and very British."

Rose enjoyed Kat's unfiltered dialogue. She knew it bothered other people, but Rose got tired of polite conversations. "So, who's Addy?"

"Well that's the big mystery. She showed up last year. The first time I saw her she was already working at Jeannie's bed and breakfast. They seem to know each other but they never talk about it. Everybody has a different idea of what the connection is, but no one really knows."

Rose had picked up her nail clippers and was holding her dog's paw. "Oh my God, look at this nail."

Kat leaned over to see what Rose was talking about.

"That's the dew claw. I've seen that before, they grow in a circle and if they aren't cut they grow right back into the dog's foot. Usually, I just cut it. Let me ask the vet tech in the front room. Nan? Is that her name?"

"Yeah, I'm pretty sure. I'll watch your dog," said Rose.

Kat passed Addy coming the other way carrying a big basket with both hands. Addy was small and thin with dark hair that hung lethargically around her childlike face. She looked pale and unfed and unsure of herself and every time Rose saw her she had an overwhelming urge to hug her. Jennifer followed her into the room and then squeezed past her to cover the little table that was reserved for food.

"Are you really expecting us to eat right there, with blood and shit everywhere?" Rose asked Jennifer. Addy, who was emptying her basket, stopped and stared at Rose, looking worried.

"You can eat it outside if you want," said Jennifer, nodding at Addy to continue. "But the vets wanted the food right here so they could grab a bite and keep working. You'll get used to it. I did."

"Maybe I'll lose some weight," said Rose, smiling at Addy, trying to make up for worrying her.

"Hey, if I can eat there, anyone can," said Jennifer.

Rose did manage to eat and was back on the floor for her afternoon shift. But she was completely caught off guard by the next dog placed in front of her.

It was actually a puppy, maybe four or five months old, but what she saw was a pile of bones, with mangy fur infested with ticks and fleas, scabs and scars. She checked his papers. There was a dash where his name should have been. The papers had an owner's name and a strange address that she couldn't identify. How could this happen to such a young dog? Rose thought as she stroked his body, running her fingers over each rib. She could see the fleas darting in and out of the few furry spots that still remained. His ears were full of ticks, which she started to remove with the tweezers until so much blood oozed from every bite that she couldn't see what she was doing. Appalled and determined, she kept wiping and picking until there were no bugs left and then checked his feet. There were ticks between his toes, between his foot pads, and actually falling off of his legs. Rose kept at it, even picking up the ticks that fell on the floor so they wouldn't climb up her own legs. She took pleasure in dropping them into the cup of rubbing alcohol.

Rose wiped her hands with some wipes she had in her purse. After cleaning herself up tried to wipe some of the dirt off of the bald spots on puppy's back.

"Don't do that," said Norma, the head vet, who was standing over Rose eating a sandwich.

"What?"

"Don't wipe that pup with that wet cloth," said Norma. "We have to keep their body temperature up after surgery. If he's wet he could get cold."

Rose had been so completely focused on the tragic puppy in front of her that Norma caught her by surprise. Suddenly, Rose's eyes filled with tears. "He's just so dirty. How did this happen? And he's so young, I thought it took a long time for a dog to get this bad." Rose wiped her nose and face on her sleeve. "I've never seen anything like this."

Norma squatted down in front of her and looked at the pup. "I did the surgery on this guy. Good thing it was a male or I wouldn't have done it. The surgery is less invasive on the males. We saw puppies like this in Tulum. It's incredible." Norma lowered herself to the floor and sat cross legged. "I'm sorry, I don't mean to sound harsh."

"No," said Rose. "I want to do everything right. I don't' know what's wrong with me, I can't even fathom how someone could see this and not do something. I mean, this puppy has an owner." The puppy stirred and Rose picked him up and settled him in her lap.

"Is this your first clinic?" asked Norma. Rose nodded. "I'm sorry."

"Norma! Norma!" It was a call from the operating room. Norma stood up, looked down at the pup and touched Rose on the shoulder before she left.

The pups back at the book store were plump, and generally in good health. Is this what her pups were being adopted into? She had assumed they were going into loving homes. But this.

Rose placed the pup on the floor and slowly unfolded her legs. She'd been sitting for too long and endured a painful moment straightening herself into a standing position. When she picked the pup up again he was lighter than she'd expected and his blood was dripping onto the floor and soaking into her shirt. His feet were bleeding from the tick bites. Rose didn't care. She flipped his towel up under his legs and walked outside. She'd already decided he wasn't going back to whatever neglectful place he'd come from.

She spotted a volunteer standing idly by the check-in table and asked if she would take Rose's place in recovery. Then sat in the shade to wait for Gretchen, whose car was gone.

It wasn't long before Gretchen bounced down the pitted road in her old jeep. As soon as she stopped there were two volunteers next to the car ready to unload the cases of soda. Rose waited and then waved her over.

She handed her the check-in papers for the puppy. "Do you know anything about this pup?" Rose asked.

"Wait," Gretchen said and grabbed an empty chair. "Ah, this is nice," she said. She closed her eyes, took a deep breath and then looked at the paper. "I know this one. We weren't sure if he was fit enough for surgery."

"This puppy isn't going back," said Rose, shaking her head. "I'd keep him if I lived here."

Gretchen looked at her for a moment. Rose waited.

"No worries," Gretchen finally said, "he's not going back. The lady told me that she'd found him. Whether that's true or not, I don't know." Rose was so relieved she almost started to cry again. "We'll talk to Norma about it."

Norma suggested they keep him at the clinic so she could monitor him during the day and offered to take him home each night. She sent Rose to get a big crate they'd stowed beside the house. The door was missing so they couldn't use it. Relieved, Rose pulled it into the recovery room, lined it with towels, and then sat where she could see him, while tending to her next dog.

Chapter 5
Claws And Teeth

The third day of the clinic was busy and hot. The Norte had passed over, and the windows only provided a light ocean breeze. It was sadly inadequate at cooling down a room full of hardworking people and panting animals. The surgery room was the worst. It was the smallest space and fans couldn't be used as they would jeopardize the sterile environment, which was already a challenge to maintain. Stirring up old dust and germs was the last thing they needed, even if it would have provided a small bit of relief.

Rose had found it hard to get out of bed that morning. Apparently, her duties at the clinic were tapping into new sets of muscles. But when Kat arrived at the clinic looking worse than Rose felt, she didn't mention her own aches and pains. Wednesday had been designated for the wild cats, and after Rose had gone to bed the night before, she knew that Kat had gone out trapping. The vets were still spaying and neutering any dogs brought into the clinic by their owners, but Cory had the day off.

Kat plopped on the floor beside her, missing the towel Rose had rolled up for her. "You look like shit," Rose told her.

"Shut up, I'm just a little hung over," said Kat, repositioning herself on the towel.

"I thought you were trapping cats last night?"

"I was, but trapping cats is like fishing. You set up the trap and then you wait." Kat winked and leaned back against the wall. "What do you think we did while we waited?"

"You got drunk?"

"Actually, we all didn't get drunk. But Greer flew in yesterday and the two other women left when he arrived, and by then we'd only trapped four cats." Kat rubbed her eyes. "So Greer went and bought us some beer and chips and we had a little party while we trapped seven more."

"Wow, good job. Is Greer coming to the clinic today?"

"No, the jerk's probably sleeping in. We didn't finish until 2:30 in the morning. Actually, after a while Greer did most of it. I was too drunk."

"So, did you have fun?" asked Rose. Kat smiled for the first time since she'd walked in.

"It was great." Kat slid further down the wall and closed her eyes. Rose could see sweat glistening on Kat's forehead and placed a wet wipe in her hand. Kat smiled and cleaned her whole face.

"I hope it's not too hot today," said Rose. "I felt disgusting when I got home last night."

"How about your nails? I swear there's blood caked under my nails and it's hard to get out," said Kat, holding her hand in front of her face.

"Could one of you help me with this?" asked Nan, peering through the doorway from the prep room. Rose looked at Kat and got to her feet.

 "Sure, what do you need?" said Rose.

"I need to give this cat an injection but the other tech went outside," Nan explained. "This guy is really pissed off." The cat was spinning around in her cage hissing at Nan. "Can you push the cat to the back of the trap so I can get her in the rump? Have you seen this done?"

"I saw someone do it twice yesterday. Where's the towel?" asked Rose.

"Right here on the floor." Nan reached down and handed Rose the towel. Rose rolled it up and slowly raised the trap door, shoving the thick wad of towel up underneath at the hissing cat. Meanwhile, Nan was filling a syringe with the sedative Acepromazine or Ace, as they called it. At the same time, a volunteer staggered into the room clinging to the leash of a terrified dog. As she struggled to control the dog she bumped Nan and knocked the bottle out of her hand. In a desperate attempt to keep the sedative from breaking on the cement floor, Nan lunged for it, hit the leg of the plastic coke table they were using and knocked it out of its corner socket. The table collapsed immediately, taking the cat trap with it. Rose had the trap door open so she could get the towel inside, and the terrified cat leapt out the door before the trap hit the floor.

"Cat!" screamed Nan. That was the protocol. Whenever a cat got loose, feral or not, someone was supposed to yell, "Cat!" as a warning to close all the windows and doors and then watch out. It was especially important in a small space. One scratch or bite from a feral cat could cause an infection or severe blood poisoning.

"Shut the doors!" screamed three or four other people in unison. With nowhere to escape, the cat was literally climbing the walls. Everyone in the recovery room, except for Kat, was screaming and trying to keep out of the cat's way. Luckily there were only two dogs in recovery, and they had just come out of surgery and were completely sedated. In fact, the cat bounced off of the larger dog two or three times on route to different walls before jumping onto the only window in the room, where she attached herself to the screen like she was being sucked from the other side.

"Throw me that blanket!" yelled Rose. She was the closest one to the window.

"Get a crate ready so she can drop the cat inside," ordered Nan.

Rose folded the blanket in half for better protection, got hold of the cat and managed to pull it off of the screen, but as it writhed in the blanket, the layers slipped and Rose temporarily lost her grip. The cat landed on the ground, still partly under the blanket. Rose tried to grab her again but misjudged which part of the cat she had. Unfortunately, it was only the back half and the cat spun around and chomped on Rose's Achilles tendon. The frantic feline got a nice chew on the back of Rose's ankle before two more blankets were thrown down and the cat was subdued. Someone had found Nan a larger cage and they dropped the cat in, blankets and all, and slammed the door shut.

Norma, the head vet, had heard all the screaming and came into the recovery room to see what was going on. Quickly assessing the situation, she instructed Nan to take Rose outside and scrub the bite with iodine.

"Make sure she gets some antibiotics and starts them today," said Norma.

"No problem," said Nan. "Come on, let's get you outside." Nan grabbed some iodine before instructing another volunteer to ask the vet what the best antibiotics were. "It's those damn tables," said Nan. She positioned herself on the ground and started to scrub Rose's ankle. "Those tables are old. They're meant for parties. We have to use them everywhere we go. There's never enough good tables for these clinics, but really, it's not safe." Rose was too stunned by the incident to take part in a conversation.

There were eleven wild cats to do that day, and the escapee was only number two. By midafternoon they had three cats left. Gretchen was helping Nan while Rose was back on the floor, sitting quietly on a blanket, keeping an eye on her puppy. That was all they would allow her to do. Rose was embarrassed, but refused to leave.

Nan had already sedated the next cat and it was sleeping quietly.

"Gretchen, number ten is ready—could you get a weight on her?" asked Nan.

"No problem," said Gretchen, who had just come through the door with the last owned dog. She handed the leash to a volunteer.

"Bring the cat back here," said Nan, "so I can finish her chart and figure her dosing for surgery."

"Got it." Gretchen pulled the sleeping cat out of the trap and turned towards the front room where the scale was. Unfortunately, the volunteer who had taken Gretchen's dog was chatting with the woman next to her holding the end of the leash giving the dog to much slack. When it saw Gretchen with the cat, it lunged, barking loudly. The stimulation woke the cat up, and as it struggled to get free, Gretchen held on tight.

"Drop it!" yelled Nan. But it was too late. Before Gretchen could react, the cat had badly scratched and bitten her hands and then escaped out the front door. Nan grabbed the gauze and iodine as she escorted Gretchen outside.

Rose's puppy wasn't coming out of its crate so after they had the lunging, barking dog checked in she found a red-eyed Gretchen sitting in the sun. Her hands were orange from the iodine scrub and she was holding two inflated rubber gloves. It was a standard practice to freeze water filled exam gloves in case of sudden fevers.

"How're you doing?" asked Rose.

"Feeling stupid," said Gretchen. "I held on tight when I was supposed to drop."

"I know what you mean," said Rose, pointing to her ankle. "But I didn't get the cool frozen gloves." Gretchen didn't laugh.

They found Gretchen's cat asleep in the tree in front of the clinic. It had had just enough energy to climb to the first branch before giving in to the anesthetic once again.

Both Rose and Gretchen learned that night how much cat bites really hurt. They hurt when it happens, and then much more later on. These were wild cats. There was no way to know what kind of repulsive fish or rotten rat they'd eaten last. Most likely it had been some yummy morsel teeming with bacteria.

Undaunted by their injuries, both Gretchen and Rose kept working at the clinic. Gretchen wore gloves and Rose kept her ankle wrapped. "How are your hands?" Rose asked Gretchen when they stopped for lunch the next day.

"I think they're better. The gloves help and I've been putting antibiotic cream on the worst scratches. How's your ankle?"

"I have to admit it's pretty sore. I'm sure it'll be fine," she said. But as they wrapped the clinic up that day Rose was finding it harder and harder to walk. The pain kept her up most of that night. She was relieved when it felt better the next morning. Brad drove her to the clinic and lectured her to take it easy.

"You okay to do recovery today?" Nan asked, when Rose limped through the front door.

"I'll be fine. It's much better. I think the worst is over,"

"Okay, but I want you to stay in one place," said Nan. "Sit and keep that foot elevated."

"Hey, Addy!" Nan called, "Would you please bring Rose the dogs so she doesn't have to get up and down? I want her to rest that ankle."

"Should you be here?" Addy asked, watching Rose limp to her place in the recovery room. Her sad puppy had been brought back for the day so she sat next to him and made herself comfortable on some of the soft towels piled against the wall. She noticed Addy staring at her and flashed a big smile and a thumbs-up.

By midafternoon, Rose had to go the bathroom so badly that she couldn't wait any longer and asked Addy, who had been hovering around her, to find Kat.

"What's going on?" Kat asked, as she stepped gingerly over sleeping animals to get to Rose.

"I have to use the bathroom," Rose told her.

"You called me in here to watch the curtain?" Kat looked around, "There's only women in here!"

Rose looked Kat right in the eyes. "We promised, remember?" she said, pronouncing each word deliberately and held up a hand. "I think my foot's asleep. Can you help me up?" Kat helped Rose to her feet and continued to support her all the way to the bathroom.

"People are going to think we're gay," complained Kat, until she noticed Rose's face. "Are you okay?" Rose closed the curtain.

"My ankle is killing me," she said. "I didn't want to ask Addy for help. If she thought my ankle was bad she'd probably start to cry and I couldn't handle that."

"But are you going to be all right?"

"I'm sure that once the antibiotics start working I'll be fine. But I was wrong when I thought the worst of it was over last night."

"Why don't you go home?" Kat said, as she pushed the curtain aside. She was surprised at how much support Rose needed to walk the few feet across the recovery room.

"And do what, sit around thinking about the pain in my ankle?" Rose said. "Forget it. But do me a favor, just come by every once in a while." Rose sat back down on the floor and fussed with the towel that was her cushion, then fidgeted with her hair clip, so she could pull the hair away from the sweat on the back of her neck. Kat watched her for a minute and went back to her duties.

That afternoon passed without any problems. The vets and the volunteers had a routine, each knowing exactly what they needed to do.

By Friday, Rose suspected that she was in trouble. She couldn't put any weight on her foot and had started to feel nauseous, so before lunch she called Brad to come and pick her up. She gathered her belongings and asked Kat to walk her out to the curb. "I'm just getting tired, I think I'll go home and put this stupid foot up," she told her. Kat knew how much Rose hated to leave and assured her that everything would be handled well in recovery because Greer was working that afternoon.

"Wow, I've been so preoccupied I haven't even asked you about Greer," Rose said.

"Don't worry, I'll tell you everything later." Kat winked and went back inside.

Brad arrived a few minutes later. He had to help Rose into the car and she could tell that he was mad. "It just got really bad all of a sudden," she said, defensively. "But I'm feeling kind of weird."

"You're such an idiot. Why'd you let this go so far?"

"I thought the antibiotics needed time to work," she said wearily pulling on the seat belt. "Hell, I've been bitten before. I just need to go home and put my foot up."

"Shit, I should've watched you more closely." Brad didn't say anything more, he was talking to himself. Rose laid her head back and closed her eyes.

Brad often bragged about being the perfect support for what he referred to as, "Rose's overenthusiastic activities." He was her self-preservation. His purpose in life, he would joke, was to stop Rose before her overstimulated work ethic destroyed her.

He'd come from a big family and had learned to get along or get out of the way. The seven children did everything together, so he was accustomed to mayhem and had perfected the ability to find humor in situations that were dangerously in need of comic relief. Rose called it unpredictable, said he could turn down the angst in any situation.

At home, he set her up in bed with pillows under her foot and a book. She knew he was irritated and did everything he asked. "If you're not better in a few hours I'm going to call the doctor," he told her.

Rose read for a while and then dozed off. The next thing that she remembered was swimming. Brad was swimming with her but she couldn't reach him. She was being pushed around by wave after wave, but she could hear his voice.

"Rose, can you hear me, Rose?" Rose opened her eyes and looked at her husband. "Hey, there you are," he said gently. Rose closed her eyes again.

The next time Rose opened her eyes there was someone else standing next to Brad.

"Who's that?" she asked.

"Ah, she speaks," the man said with a smile. "Can you sit up?" Brad pulled Rose to a sitting position and stuffed some pillows behind her. "I've got jello," he said with a huge grin. Rose looked around the room. It was a light green color with one small painting on a big wall, and nothing was familiar.

"Am I in the hospital?"

"Yup."

"What happened?"

"I couldn't wake you up," Brad explained. "I couldn't wake you up after you came back from the clinic so I called the doctor. He came right over, and I told him everything that had happened. He looked at your leg and you had red streaks running up towards your knee, for Christ's sake."

"Are we in Cancun?"

"Yup, we had to hire a boat. Too bad you didn't get to see it. We didn't have a stretcher so we stacked two plastic Coke chairs together and sat you in them. We tilted you back and while I held your head, three of us walked you along the pier to a boat. The doctor arranged the whole thing. He had an ambulance waiting for us on the Cancun side."

"No way!"

"Yeah, way." Brad said. "You scared the shit out of me."

Rose stayed in the hospital on an IV antibiotic drip. She felt much better after the first twenty-four hours but they insisted she stay for two more days and those quiet days gave her time to think about the clinic. She decided that other than her injury, she'd loved every minute of it. From the first day when they let her watch a surgery, to learning how to care for the animals in recovery. It had all been wonderful.

There were only two things that she didn't like. The first was the sad condition of the dogs. It made her want to learn more so she could do more. The other thing was returning the dogs or puppies to their owners at the end of each day.

In recovery, the volunteers had watched every animal carefully until they were awake and well enough to leave. They cut their nails, cleaned their ears, removed ticks and fleas, and tended to any wounds. It was probably the best treatment these animals had ever experienced. But the clinic was small and space was an issue, so some animals had to be sent home as soon as they could walk.

Rose had helped Gretchen take some of them home at the end of the first day. The vets had provided them with a stack of sheets explaining in Spanish the significance of keeping the dog or cat warm and dry and the importance of watching the incisions for any signs of infection.

"Bueno." Gretchen would yell, standing at a front door. "Bueno." She usually had to repeat herself before she caught someone's attention. There were no door bells and sometimes there wasn't even a door. After a while children would appear, followed by an adult.

"Si?"

"We have your dog here." Gretchen would say in Spanish.

"Si."

"Well, I have a sheet with directions on how to care for your dog since she's just had surgery." If the person at the door didn't reach for the sheet, Gretchen would assume that they couldn't read and would read it to them. She was very perceptive, and made it look as if that was the norm, so as not to embarrass anyone.

"What you need to do," she would start, "is keep your dog dry and warm and quiet for a few days, just a little food and water tonight."

"Put it over there," people often replied, pointing to a patch of dirt next to the house.

Rose wanted to take every single one of the puppies home. The older dogs could find places to get some rest but the puppies were helpless. The children played with them like rag dolls.

Rose hoped that someday she wouldn't have to take these puppies home. She didn't know how, but seeing them treated so poorly was heartbreaking.

While Rose was still in the hospital, Kat called her. "I have something to make you feel better."

"I already feel better, but what is it?"

"Norma is taking the puppy home."

"What puppy?"

"You know, the one that was in such bad shape. She said she just couldn't leave him behind."

Rose was thrilled and thanked Kat for telling her. She wished she could thank Norma and planned to call her and ask for pictures. She wanted to see this pup looking the way a puppy should look.

There are so many more just like that, she thought. "What are you going to do about it?" She imagined Itzamna asking her.

"I need help," thought Rose.

"Just start." Rose liked to think of Itzamna pushing these thoughts at her, like a partner. He'd remind her, "Don't forget what you've seen and how it made you feel."

Chapter 6
The North Point

Over the next 10 months Brad and Rose returned to Isla Mujeres as often as they could, always staying in a different condominium at the same Casa Mar complex. It was an ideal place. Brad's restaurant was next door, and all of the buildings were fronted by a beach where the sand sloped gradually into the ocean. Going north, this same beach continued to wrap its broad band around the island's northern point before giving way to the rough shoreline on the eastern side. Here, the coral met the water and was filled with shining pools constantly refreshed by waves rolling in from the open sea, it was here that they found the property that convinced them to build a house on Isla Mujeres.

They'd eaten breakfast and decided to go for a walk. After strolling along the beach they stopped to put their sandals on before stepping onto the jagged coral. There it was, an empty lot with a 'For Sale' sign. The land was perfectly positioned—surrounded by water on three sides. They made an offer that day.

They simply bought it and agreed to wait on any big decisions. But when the city of Boulder made the announcement about their use of power lines, it all became clear.

"The whole thing is coming together." Rose told Kat, Gretchen, and Jennifer one afternoon at the Fishbone Bar and Grill. She and Brad had returned to the island to sign the final papers on the land. "It was those power lines that made our move possible, what a funny thing."

"Okay, this is the second time I've heard about the power lines. Could you please tell us what the hell you're talking about?" demanded Kat.

"Sorry. Here's what happened. We've been living in this great house in Colorado that we bought ten years ago. We got an incredible deal on it because it was built under power lines before all of the research had come out about power lines causing cancer. I never believe that sort of stuff, anyway. Hell, the week before they said alfalfa sprouts did something horrible. Every week it's something new. Anyway, when the research hit the press, the owner didn't want to live there anymore and no one wanted to buy it, so we did. It was beautiful. Then a few months ago they officially stopped using those lines and the house tripled in value overnight."

"So now you're rich and you have a brain tumor," said Jennifer.

"They hardly used those power lines anyway." Rose said. "We checked." Jennifer looked unconvinced. "Well, I never worried about it and now Brad's sold his restaurant and that's it, we're here. It all happened so fast, just boom, boom, it's almost…freaky. Brad's been trying to sell the restaurant for a while and then it sold, almost right after we bought the island property. Don't you think that's weird?"

"It's because I put it out there," said Gretchen. "Send me an obsessive dog person, I asked. It's the universe answering my call."

"Wait until I tell Brad that is was you who sold his restaurant. I'm sure he'll have other things for you to wish for," said Rose, smiling at her friends. This feels like home, she thought. "You know, this island has always had a familiarity, like it was more than just a place that we visited. And now it's actually going to be our home." Rose spread her arms as if the whole island was now hers.

"Welcome aboard," said Kat. "That makes you one of the crazies."

"I'm ordering a beer," said Gretchen. "Anyone else?"

"One's my limit until after work," said Kat. Jennifer shook her head no.

"Solo una," Gretchen called out to the waiter before he reached the table. Kat lifted up her beer so he could see what Gretchen wanted.

"I remember moving here," said Jennifer, touching Rose's arm, "everything just sort of sparkled for a while."

"It is amazing that first time you don't have a return ticket hanging over your head," said Gretchen. "You just hold on to that feeling. Keep it coming for as long as you can."

"So you're going to build on the property?" asked Jennifer.

"They're going to break ground before we leave. Ha—break sand." Kat rolled her eyes.

"Well then this is a celebration," said Gretchen. "I now have a full-on partner in crime and that lets you off the hook, Jennifer."

Jennifer grinned and raised her arms to the sky. "Hallelujah! Then maybe I can have my book store back for books and kids."

"Just your half," countered Gretchen, taking a drink from the beer the waiter had placed in front of her.

"When will you move?" Kat asked, rolling her cold beer across her forehead.

"Hopefully this fall. We'll need the summer to get everything else worked out," Rose replied.

They all heard a yelp and turned to see Addy on the beach. Some kids were chasing her with a big crab. "Those little punks," said Kat. She jumped up, apparently to help Addy, and then changed her mind and sat back down. "What's the point of saving her? It's just going to happen again."

"I still don't know anything about her," said Gretchen. "Do you think she's related to Jeannie?"

"Isn't Jeannie from London?" asked Rose, reaching for a chip.

"Yeah, and supposedly Addy's from Vermont or something like that," said Gretchen.

"Then what makes you think they're related?" said Rose. "UGH." She said after the salsa ran off of her chip and splashed on the table in front of her plate. Rose reached for more napkins but the waiter beat her to it with a cloth.

"It's just the way they are. Addy always seems so sad and fragile, and Jeannie's always taking care of her." Gretchen pulled the chips and salsa closer to her side of the table and took a handful before she pushed the chips back. "I'll keep the salsa over here," she said to Rose. "Besides it's too hot for all you wimps."

"Jeannie takes care of everyone," said Jennifer. "She's a nanny to the world."

Brad walked over to the table and stood behind Rose's chair. "Are you guys getting everything you need?" he asked. "Has Rose told you the news?"

"I've told them that we'll be neighbors in the fall," said Rose.

"That might be a bit optimistic," said Brad, giving his wife a condescending pat on the shoulder, "but it'll be soon." Rose elbowed him in the thigh.

"Don't you have a daughter?" Jennifer asked.

"Yes, but she's married and has a life of her own," said Rose. "She lives near her dad, and if she needs me I can be there in four hours."

"She thrilled, she thinks she's getting a free vacation spot," said Brad. "It didn't seem to bother her a bit. We'll go back and forth and probably see her as much as we do now."

"Hey, girls!" They all looked up at the sound of Jeannie's voice. "Have you seen Addy?" Jeannie's muumuu was purple and pink with enormous flowers flowing all the way to the floor.

"We just did," said Kat. "She was on the beach and some little shit kids were chasing her with a crab. Want to join us?" Kat pulled out the chair next to her.

"Sure, for a sec." Jeannie scanned the beach and then sat down. "Was she okay about it?"

"We heard her shriek but the next time I looked she was ignoring them," Kat said. "I was going to give those horrible brats shit if they didn't leave her alone. I hate that family. They come here every year with that bunch of snotty kids and never watch them. One of these times—"

"It's a celebration," Jennifer interrupted. "Brad and Rose have just closed on their property and they're moving here in the fall."

"Splendid, that's great news," Jeannie said. "I think we should have a toast. Does anyone know where we can get some wine around here?" She winked at Brad.

"Coming right up," he agreed good-naturedly.

Six glasses of wine arrived and Jeannie stood up, raising hers for a toast. "Here's to President Vicente Fox. May he fulfill all of his promises, clean up Mexico, alleviate corruption and make life better for everyone who lives here, including our new neighbors." They all stood up and toasted, clinking their glasses. Other customers in the restaurant joined in the toast, yelling in agreement and clapping.

Chapter 7
On The Move

Rose's summer, as she had predicted, was a whirlwind of packing, selling, and moving. Finally, after the car was loaded and the trailer was full, Brad and Rose hooked it all together and drove south, out of Colorado. It took five days to get to the Mexican border. Brad nervously approached the immigration office. The amount of documentation necessary was overwhelming. They were directed to five different windowed booths inside a crummy building full of noisy fans and people standing in lines. After four hours everything was stamped and approved and they drove into Mexico.

It took three more days to drive around the Gulf of Mexico. The landscape along the west side of the Gulf reminded Rose of an enormous bowl of tropical fruit. In the orange-growing part of the country, the highway was built along an old river bed that zigzagged between low hills striped with rows of round, green, trees. From a distance the tops of the trees appeared so perfectly cylindrical, they looked like green lollipops. After that were fields of pineapples, their spiky tops low to the ground. Then there were banana trees bowing gracefully, weighed down heavily with long bunches of bananas wrapped in plastic bags and slowly ripening, shaded by their enormous leaves. Between the fields of fruit were boxes of honeybees. These were stacked neatly a small distance from the road and the honey was sold in recycled plastic pop bottles that dangled from tree branches next to the highway. In the shade beneath, venders sat behind tables covered with smaller jars of bee pollen and other things that Rose didn't recognize. "What do you think those are?" she asked Brad.

"I can't tell from here," he said, squinting at the tables. "The bigger bottles are obviously honey but the other stuff looks weird."

"Do you want to stop and check it out?'

"Not today," said Brad, who was usually a good sport about stopping to see things, but he knew this was going to be a long day. The guide book had warned him about this section of highway being slow due to the number of small towns with ridiculously enormous speed bumps, what it didn't tell them was that they stretched out for a quarter of a mile. Approaching the first town, the bumps, called topes, were spread out in front of them like a thick, inconvenient, lumpy, welcoming mat. The topes that gradually rose and declined were the easiest but there were also smaller ones that were like six-inch tubes of cement. These jolted the car no matter how slowly Brad drove. Another thing that the guide book failed to elaborate on was the women and children who swarmed the car every time they were forced to slow down. They were selling bags of cut-up fruit and bottles of juice. It was the worst in the towns where the children felt it necessary to bang on the side of the car, as if the occupants could possibly have not seen them.

"We're not buying any of that," said Rose, irritated by the assault. She and Brad had already agreed—no street food.

"I wasn't going to," said Brad defensively.

"I can't imagine where that fruit was cut up. Forget it." Rose lay her head back and shut her eyes. Watching the adults sell their produce was fine but seeing the children desperately banging on the cars was upsetting.

Brad continued to follow the line on the map up and down isolated mountain ranges and over roads that could easily dislodge a tire on a car less sturdy than theirs. He'd commented on how the streets of the cities were crowded with busy mechanic shops. Now he understood why.

Rose's excitement grew as they turned north and drove up the east side of the Gulf. Passing through the historic town of Merida meant there were only four hours left before they'd reach Cancun. When they drove up to Punta Sam and got in line for the car ferry, Rose couldn't stand the waiting anymore. She jumped out of the car to get a better look at the island. "Brad, its right there, right there, oh my God, look, it's right there, OUR Island." She dragged him down to the water and they watched the car ferry pull in.

The ferry ride was difficult. They couldn't get out of the car. The boat was full; in fact, the people in the back of the line didn't make it on board. Men in orange overalls directed the cars and trucks on and off of the ferry, cramming the vehicles so close it was impossible to open the doors.

"This is excruciating," complained Rose.

"Well, you live on an island now and this is part of it."

"You make it sound like it was my idea to move here and not yours."

"I'm just telling you that you'll have to put up with stuff like this, now." Rose made a face at him.

"I'm not riding this ferry if I can't get out of the car," she said reaching for the watch on Brad's wrist. "How long has it been?" He pulled his arm away.

"We should be there soon. Next you'll be telling me that you have to go to the bathroom," he said.

"I do have to go to the bathroom."

"Well you'll have to wait."

"I know that, you jerk," Rose said.

"Why am I a jerk because you can't get out to the car to go to the bathroom?"

Rose decided to change the subject. "Look, that driver is getting back in his truck." The trucks had such high doors, even with the ferry packed tight they could get in and out. "This must mean we're almost there." Rose grinned, leaned over and gave Brad a kiss on the cheek. The ferry jerked and vibrated as it hit the dock and finally it was their turn to drive down the ramp. It took a while for their eyes to adjust to the light. Then they were there, on their island which generously served up all the feelings of joy, excitement, and relief they'd hoped for.

Brad had rented a small apartment for the month to fill in the time before their home was scheduled to be completed.

"You won't believe how slow they are," Brad told Rose a few days after they'd arrived. He'd been going to the house every day and always came away grumpy. "Everything's done by hand. Even digging the foundation in the sand is done with shovels and buckets."

They were having lunch at Brad's restaurant.

"I thought they were done with the foundation a long time ago!" Rose said, pulling the straw out of her Diet Coke before she took a drink.

"They were—this is for the garage. You just can't imagine it. Men are down in the hole, digging. They have these buckets with ropes tied to the handles and they fill them with sand, and then another worker hauls the buckets up and away. We now have new sand dunes near our one palm tree. They're going to kill it; that sand will shift, I just know it."

"I just can't believe they don't have more modern equipment than that. My god, it's not like we're in Siberia. It doesn't make any sense. There are tall buildings on this island, and you can't tell me that all those foundations were dug by hand." Rose rubbed her temples like the thought of it was giving her a headache. "Was there someone there you could talk to?"

"Not today, just the workers. I'm sure they'll quit early with no one there to stop them. I'll bet you their tools are already back in that tar shack."

Kat and Jeannie came into the restaurant and Rose waved them over. "Hi, hi, so glad you're here," she said, relieved to have a distraction—anything to brighten Brad's mood before it dragged them both down. It was why Rose stayed away from the building site—she needed to stay positive. All the delays, any small detail that threatened their dream reminded her of how vulnerable there were. One of them had to deal with the construction and one had to keep their hopes energized.

Kat and Jeannie settled in their chairs and Brad signaled a waiter. "We were just talking about the construction being slow."

"What about that wall? Did you measure it?" Jeannie asked Brad. Having renovated her bed and breakfast, she was familiar with construction in Mexico.

"I did," he told her. "It's okay, at least twenty meters back from any water."

"What does that matter?" asked Kat.

"The rock wall has to be twenty meters from the sea," explained Brad. A waiter arrived and Brad asked Jeannie and Kat if they wanted anything.

"A lemonade would be heaven," said Jeannie.

"Diet Coke's perfect for me," Kat told the waiter.

"I'll take a refill," Brad said, and then looked at his wife.

"I'm fine, thanks," said Rose, sipping her drink. "What's Jeannie talking about?"

"Owners with property next to the ocean have to be twenty meters back from the water," Brad said. "This area is called the Federal Zone and nobody owns it, but if you live next to it you have to pay taxes on it. And worse than that," Brad was talking to Kat, "foreigners aren't allowed to own property within twenty-five kilometers of the coast. The deed to our land has to be held by the bank in a trust called a Fideo Comiso. It makes me nervous, but everyone, including Jeannie here, assured me that it's safe. She'd just warned me to measure the distance from the water."

"Wow, I never knew that. Renting will be just fine for me." Kat turned to Rose after accepting her Diet Coke from the waiter. "So are you going crazy waiting to get into the house?"

Rose laughed, "You'll love this: we're living out of garbage cans."

"Why? You own a restaurant?" Kat chuckled. She knew that Rose meant it a different way.

"What are you talking about?" asked Jeannie. "You've all gone a bit off the head."

"We bought a bunch of big garbage cans," Rose explained. "Hey Brad, do you think we could order more chips and salsa?" Brad asked the waiter and then made an exaggerated display of taking a napkin from the middle of the table and placing it under the lemonade in front of Jeannie. The waiter got the message 'napkins under drinks,' and left to bring more chips and salsa. "We'll need them at the house anyway, but in the meantime I've unpacked everything we need into the cans. There's one for the kitchen stuff, one for the bathroom stuff. We have six of them in all."

"I just think it's so funny," said Kat. "Move to Mexico, go for your dream, and live out of garbage cans."

"You would think that was funny," said Rose. "I'm just trying to get organized. The house is almost finished enough for us to move into one room."

"Is that legal?" asked Jeannie.

"Absolutely not," said Brad. "But I'm learning a lot about what's not legal and how many people don't care." He turned around and impatiently scanned the restaurant for the waiter that he'd sent off for the chips.

A few days later, Rose and Brad arrived with their six large garbage cans and moved into the one completed bedroom of their house. Even though it was not how they'd planned things, it was an exciting day. Their friends showed up the next morning with balloons and mimosas, and the waiting, moving, and selling all drifted away in a dusty cement cloud of homecoming.

There were, however, a few problems. Every morning the workers arrived and surrounded their small abode, making them feel like fish in a bowl. The noise and dust were tough to get used to, but the lack of electricity and water was much harder. Candles were romantic; even going to bed when darkness fell was acceptable. But crawling into bed covered with cement dust on a hot night without a shower was edging on the far side of a manageable challenge.

After two weeks Brad bought a generator. "We can only run it for a few hours every day," he warned Rose. "I don't want to piss off our neighbors right away. It's pretty noisy." The generator was loud and smelly, but for Brad and Rose, it was one step towards normalcy. In those two powered-up hours they recharged all their batteries, showered, and then filled three of the garbage cans with water. That water would have to last them at least twenty-two hours. Most days it was enough to fill the back of the toilet, wash clothes, cook, clean, and take care of anything else that came up. Rose was amazed at how much water she used now that she nervously watched the levels go down in her garbage cans.

Their kitchen consisted of a cooler and a coffee maker. Their clothes were stuffed onto two plastic shelves with a broom handle suspended between them for hangers. "Ta-Da! A closet!" Announced Rose. She sat on their bed to admire her handiwork, then lay on her back and stared at the ceiling. "We're just doing this for a little while, right?" she asked Brad, trying to sound casual.

"I don't have the answers anymore," he responded glumly.

As he feared, the work continued at an unhurried pace but as the months passed their paper plans took shape in cement. Windows and doors were added. Electricity was hooked up and water flowed through the pipes. Rose and Brad were excited by and grateful for anything that brought them closer to completion. Meaning a time when they wouldn't have to pay for, or be dependent upon people who would let them down, cheat them or simply not to show up. They were especially excited to see the building lose its cinder block signature as cement was covered with stucco and then painted and the debris was cleared away. With these achievements, the project ceased to be the entire focus of their new life.

Rose had missed working with the dogs during all the moving months and then throughout the time she'd been occupied with the house construction. The many Island visits when she'd helped Kat, Jennifer, and Gretchen with the animals had modified her Mexican dream, so she was ready to do more.

Chapter 8
Peewee

The puppies Rose had helped rescue had been young and quick to trust humans. The litters were easily plumped up and mostly healthy, so it caught Rose's attention when she saw an emaciated three-month-old puppy alone in the street. After the clinic, Rose had made herself a promise—she would never walk away or allow a sad dog to fade into the scenery as an accepted part of the culture she was living in.

So, she followed the pup but when it sensed the attention, the little creature squeezed through a dilapidated fence at the side of the road. Rose walked along the fence until she found an opening that led into a wide field behind it. There was a mechanic shop on the right but no one appeared to mind her being there so she kept going, circling around behind the building in search of the spot where the pup had come through. Finally, there he was with three other puppies. Rose's arrival sent them flying in different directions; one dove under bits of old building material and two dashed behind a nearby shack.

The shack was made of vertical sticks tied together with fishing line. The roof was sheets of tarpaper and the whole structure leaned slightly to the right. Rose doubted that anyone had lived there for a long time.

This hidden gap of land appeared to be one of those forgotten places that was too small to build on, but just big enough to entice anyone with junk to relocate. It was inconspicuously nestled between a hotel on the beach and the mechanic shop, and just a short walk from Rose's house.

That first afternoon she returned with dry food and spread it on the ground where the pups could see it and then sat against the back of the mechanic's shop waiting for them to eat. But they didn't. The next day she took dry food and two cans of wet food, located a Styrofoam plate amongst the debris, mixed the two together and returned to her spot by the wall. This they couldn't resist. The biggest and obviously bravest of the puppies approached the food first, moving closer and then popping back, but narrowing the gap each time. Soon, he was at the plate and after one last sniff, he started to devour the mixture. Two more pups quickly joined him but Rose's original little dog wouldn't come out.

The next day she brought an old plastic bowl and a bottle of water with the food. The brave one went through the same wary dance but it didn't take as long and the others joined him right away. They ate everything she brought and then lapped up the water. It took a week before the scrawny one would join in. Rose called him Peewee for obvious reasons. His short black fur clung to his ribs and his legs had swirls of black and brown stripes. Each pup was completely different: one was solid black, one was white with a bit of tan on his back, and the brave one was vaguely brindled from head to toe.

After two weeks the brave pup, who she named Lately, finally let her touch him. He earned his name because if she missed a day, he would bark at her as if to say, "Where've you been, lately?" The white pup she named Blanco, which is Spanish for white, and sadly, the black one disappeared before she gave him a name. She searched everywhere, willing him to return, but he never did. She hoped that someone had adopted him. Islanders were accustomed to seeing stray pups and periodically took them home.

On some mornings, the pups were joined by an older black female that Rose assumed was the mother. She looked like a lab and was friendly and agreed to be touched, but not fondled. Eventually another female showed up who wasn't friendly and who would not eat the food if Rose was nearby. The workers in the mechanic's shop now waved at her when she arrived and the dogs were genuinely glad to see her.

After two months of visiting, Rose rounded the corner to the mechanic's shop and was surprised to find Jeannie Tull talking to the men. Rose almost ran right into her.

"Oh, I'm sorry. I should watch where I'm going." Rose apologized.

"No problem luv, I never look where I'm going, I mean you can't miss me, people usually make room." Jeannie pulled at her muumuu to accentuate her point. "I'm just trying to find someone to fix my stupid golf cart," she explained.

Rose held up her bundle of wet and dry dog food, "I'm here feeding my dogs."

"I heard you were helping out some of the strays," Jeannie said, and smiled approvingly.

"Did Gretchen tell you that?"

"No. I'm just that way. I know everybody and everything. Where are these dogs of yours?" she asked. "Hiding in the spinney, no doubt." Rose looked at her quizzically. "Oh, sorry," Jeannie said, "You know, the bushes."

"My little family's around the corner," Rose said. "I've been feeding them for over two months now. Come on, I'll show you." They circled around behind the shop. Jeannie hung back while Rose set the food dish on the dirt. Blanco and Lately started to eat right away but Peewee wasn't coming out. Secretly, Rose wasn't surprised that something as large and colorful as Jeannie Tull would keep this shy pup from his food. After filling the water dish, Rose suggested that they leave so Peewee would eat something.

They strolled along the street together. "You've been spending a lot of time at the book store, as well, I hear?" Jeannie said.

"Gretchen and I have been doing some dog stuff together and I just love helping with the puppies," said Rose.

The road they were on ended. They could go to the beach on the right, straight ahead to an old hotel, or left led into town. They turned left. The street sand, and the buildings on the right side became more dilapidated the further they walked from the beach. On the other side was a huge auditorium that had been built by the government, called "Centro de Convention," and it had been painted a terrible shade of baby blue. Apparently the last mayor of the island had been a woman and it was her favorite color. What Rose found the most interesting was that they had only painted the front and two sides of the building but the back wall was still the original dull red color.

So many things had surprised Rose since moving to the island. A disappointing façade was becoming apparent. Who left the back of a building unpainted? Who left paint splatters on the windows? To Rose it screamed—don't look too close. They'd never cleaned the paint off the windows at her house. The workers had smiled and agreed to do it but never did. It was the same with the grouting in her bathrooms. It was so sloppy. Each item seemed just a few steps from done, the steps that showed you cared. For Rose, she compared it to the work that she was doing with the dogs, it showed in the work, the homes, through everything. The standards were very different.

Rose realized that Jeannie was talking to her. "Hey, where did you go just then?" Jeannie was saying. "I just asked you if you wanted to go for lunch."

Rose gave Jeannie a huge hug. "You know, I would just love that. Didn't you tell me that you knew everything?" Jeannie nodded, looking suspicious. "I think I need to understand more about how things are done here, what the locals are like. Can you help me with that?"

"Are you kidding?" said Jeannie, smiling broadly. "I run a business. Your husband is probably learning more about it than you are. Let me fill you in."

Chapter 9
Puppy Camp

The morning after Rose had lunch with Jeannie she decided to go to the bookstore before feeding Peewee's family. She loved helping Jennifer and Gretchen, not just for the dogs, but for the human company. There was always something going on. Jennifer had her hand in everything. Her background was in community development and she was involved in different projects for the children and their mothers. Hildy, a friend of Gretchen's, had opened a coffee shop across the street and Hildy's boyfriend started a pizza-by-the-slice stand next to that. With a youth hostel in the next block, all four establishments were constantly full of young backpackers, tourists, and island children.

People of all ages loved the island for the same reason Rose and Brad did. It offered a laid-back atmosphere that appealed to casual guests looking to spend less money and experience more Mexican culture. The streets were sand, most restaurants didn't take credit cards, and there wasn't an event that warranted fancy clothes. And you could still watch the local fisherman pull their boats up on the beach to clean and sell their catch of the day.

Jennifer and Gretchen were just about to hit their thirties but to Rose, they were "the girls." Nevertheless, the three of them chatted away like dorm-room buddies even though Rose was twenty years older. What truly illustrated the difference in their ages was the girls' never-ending energy.

Rose went to bed around nine but the girls partied late and were still up and ready to go the next day. And while Rose was happily married, the girls were dealing with a stream of new relationships, bad relationships, old relationships, recovery time, and then new relationships all over again. Rose was amazed by their stamina.

"Are there two more pups in here today?" asked Rose, as she started to clean one side of the pen.

"Yup," said Gretchen. "Someone found them last night."

"Where do they keep coming from?" Rose sighed. "It's just never-ending."

Gretchen turned back to the customer she was talking to at the counter. "The book is 65 pesos but if you bring it back we'll give you 20 pesos' credit towards another book." After the customer went in search of something new to read Gretchen walked over to the puppy pens. "First," she said, talking to Rose, "we have more people finding them. Secondly, so many of the islanders like their animals as long as they're no trouble and they still don't want to spay or neuter them. Some say it's for religious reasons but I think that it's more complicated than that. We still have lots of educating to do."

"The men don't want to neuter their big, huge, watch dogs, right?" Rose said sarcastically. She'd seen many macho examples of this island trend.

"That, and they don't think it matters or they just can't be bothered or they can't or don't want to afford the surgery even though Paulo doesn't charge the locals that much. Anyway, that's why most families prefer male dogs. If there's a litter born, then it's someone else's litter—someone else's problem. Some families think it's fun to have litters."

Jennifer noticed a box of books on the floor and started to go through them, placing them on the shelves where they belonged. "It's entertaining to watch the puppies when they're really young and the mom does everything. She feeds them, cleans them and even cleans up the poop, but as soon as they're weaned and need extra food or care, the puppies are boxed up and dropped off in a vacant lot a long way from the house."

"That's just so cruel. How can people do that?"

"Luckily, it's not all of the islanders. It's just the 'bad dog owner' islanders. There are bad dog owners in every country."

Rose picked up one of the pups and rubbed its ears. "Yeah, yeah, I get it. You can stop reminding me. I've heard it enough to get the idea. It's not the Mexicans; it's the "bad dog owner Mexicans." It's me you're talking to, remember? You can save your "social work" sensitivities for the rest of the world. You know I don't care who they are, but I'll always have a stone-cold heart for people who don't take care of their animals."

"You just have to watch how you say it, that's all. I mean, we live here." Rose hugged her puppy a little closer. She was sick of Jennifer lecturing her every time Rose said something bad about Mexicans. Jennifer knew what Rose was talking about, she was talking about the people around her, the same as she would talk about people no matter where she was, so why did she always have to remind her of the necessity for such tiring "politically correct" lingo?

Jennifer returned to the main desk to get another stack of books, then stopped and leaned on the back of her chair. "Oh my God, this store smells. I swear, it wears me out just trying to pretend it doesn't," she said.

"It's hard to keep them in the corner," said Rose as she watched one of the new pups produce a large pile of diarrhea on the newspaper. Gretchen came through the front door waving her hand in front of her nose, "Wow that stinks. Are those new pups?"

"Yeah," answered Rose, grabbing some clean newspaper and a bleach spray bottle.

"Poor little things," said Gretchen. "There's just too much going on - all new food, new people. No wonder their tummies are upset. Who knows what they've been through?"

"I agree, it is sad, but this week has been the worst," said Jennifer. "Ten diarrhea-producing puppies, and we're scaring the customers away, and then two more come in. That smell—I wouldn't come in here if I didn't have to." Jennifer looked around the empty book store. "We have to do something about this."

"Look, I've got an idea," said Rose. And then she voiced a plan that had started forming several weeks before. "I was going to mention this anyway. We have a storeroom over the garage. It has windows and a separate entrance. For now we don't really have that much stuff to store up there, so why don't we keep the pups there at night? I can bring a few in each day and we can post pictures of the rest of them on your board over there with descriptions. What do you think?"

"I think you may have just saved our business," said Jennifer with an enormous smile. "Can we start today?"

Rose smiled back at her. She so wanted to be a bigger part of their puppy rescue, and she knew she could do a good job because that would be all she did. There would be no conflicts of interest with customers and smells and over-zealous children. "Sure, if one of you can help me get it ready before we take the pups over."

Gretchen volunteered and went to the house with Rose to inspect the room. She immediately pronounced it perfect. The next step was getting Rudi to help.

He was living at the house with Brad and Rose. When the construction had slowed to almost nothing around Christmas, Rudi had knocked on their bedroom door. He was upset, saying that he hadn't been paid for six weeks and just couldn't stay any longer.

"No!" Brad and Rose had cried in unison. "Please stay. We'll pay what's owed to you."

"We need security," Brad said. "Maybe you could work for us?"

Rudi had happily agreed. When the tar shack that he'd been staying in was torn down, he turned the little room under the garage, the half that wasn't a septic tank, into a livable space. The builders had dug so far down in the sand to get to hard rock or coral that they'd essentially dug out a basement. It seemed a waste to just fill it back in, so Brad had told them to finish it as a storage room. The problem was that the climate on the island was so humid that the small, closed space became a mold factory. It did, however, have half windows, so they added an air conditioner and built a door for the top of the stairs. Rudi tiled the floors and walls with left-over and broken tiles from the construction, hung a hammock, and moved in. He said it was the first time in his life he'd had a room of his own, and even though Rose and Brad couldn't imagine staying there, he loved it and was grateful for a job and a place to live.

Rudi was part Mayan, square and powerful, with a round open friendly face, and he was so young that Rose felt more like she'd adopted a son than hired a worker. She made his meals and did everything she could to make him feel at home. She'd never forgotten that Rudi had told her he liked dogs—it had been on her mind when she offered her storage room for the puppies. So they enlisted his help in clearing the room at the top of the stairs.

"I really need to unpack these things anyway," Rose explained, standing in front of the boxes that Rudi had relocated to the garage. "But there's no hurry because we can't actually put a car in here. The septic tank was supposed to go under the front door but the workers dug it out halfway under the garage. Now we're afraid the floor won't support a car."

"You're kidding?" said Gretchen.

"Nope, Brad's worried about what other things are going to show up."

"You got newspaper?" asked Gretchen, trying to deflect Rose from one of her 'house building' rants.

"There's a big pile under the stairs to the kitchen."

Gretchen headed to the stairs and Rose turned to Rudi. "Can you please take up the cinder blocks? They're beside the house." Gretchen passed Rudi on his way out and dropped a pile of newspapers on the floor. "We are so lucky to have Rudi," said Rose. "I swear he can lift anything and he's excited about the puppies. I want him to be part of this." Rudi came back up the stairs carrying cinderblocks, stacked three high. While he made five trips, Rose and Gretchen covered the floor with the newspaper, then used the blocks as dividers so that they could separate the pups by size.

Starting puppy camp meant Rose swapped a bucket and mop for her morning crossword puzzles. Now, she poured herself a cup of coffee and cleaned up shit for the first hour and half of every day. Her casserole dishes made perfect puppy bowls. The sides were low and offered enough space for four or five pups around each dish. Her reward after all the cleaning was putting the food on the floor. The room would go silent but for the slurping and lip smacking and the most rewarding part was that a good appetite meant a healthy puppy. The younger pups usually walked through the gruel a few times and then pawed the goop onto their littermates, so after the dishes were licked clean, Rose loaded puppies, five at a time, into a laundry basket and carried them down the stairs to play on the driveway. Then it was Rudi's turn to clean the room—the food would be everywhere.

Watching them play was bliss. They were all different colors and sizes and provided a comical theater of rolling, bumping, and waddling fur balls. Rose imagined them climbing over Ek Chauh as Itzamna watched for any signs of illness. The thought that her newly developing instincts were backed up by an experienced observer, even an imaginary one, edged her forward to read and learn as much as she could.

They started taking three or four of the healthiest pups to the bookstore every day with the hope that they might charm someone into to taking them home. The best adoptions were tourists who took them back to the US or Canada, but a few were adopted by local families. Rose soon discovered that some of those puppies would eventually be found back in the street, sicker and skinnier than when they had first arrived at puppy camp. It was these times that Rose wished she was in charge. She'd learned more about their care since that sad puppy came into the spay and neuter clinic. Norma, the head vet, had taken that pup home and the pictures that she sent Rose barely looked like the same dog. Now he was covered with shiny fur, no ribs showing, and you couldn't see any traces of his former sad state. Things could be done for these animals, she could make a difference.

Once the puppies were at the house she appreciated every one individually and loved seeing each different personality emerge. During the first months, Rose called Paulo every day, always apologizing for the inconvenience but desperate for information. He started training her to recognize significant symptoms and behaviors, and set her up with medicines and doses so she could treat the puppies herself. Paulo sometimes worked on the mainland and didn't want her to wait if something was needed. Puppies were difficult, he'd explained, the younger ones could dehydrate and die in 24 hours if not treated. He had never charged Kat, Gretchen, or Jennifer anything other than for supplies if he had to, and he did the same for Rose. Paulo made Rose feel more like a partner than a customer. Everything interested her and she was willing to try anything. The more she learned, the more she enjoyed the work, as well as overcoming some of the angst she felt when Paulo wasn't available.

Watching the positive results of her treatments made up for any inconvenience that caring for them caused. And if Rudi wasn't busy with a house project he would work alongside of her. At first he didn't like the needles, but he got used to it. Each pup had to have three vaccinations, and often medicines were injectable. One of the biggest causes of puppy death was dehydration from diarrhea, so Rose quickly learned how to set up intravenous lines or give fluids under the skin. Soon, she was using the internet to look things up on her own, and emailing questions to the vets who had come to the island for the clinic.

Eventually she started seeing things about newly arrived pups that other people didn't notice: wobbly legs – calcium deficiency, white gums – anemia, red patches under the skin – ehrlichia, which was a tick-borne disease and very common. With the experience came a confidence and a deeper connection to the whole project. Rose was excited about all she was learning. And that search for information, even on such a small scale, was like a sparkler that never fizzled out.

At night she often thought about the princes Itzamna and Ek Chauh, and sometimes she would dream about them alive and working beside her. Or if she was alone while treating a sick puppy she would visualize them, the brothers wrapping themselves around the pup's tiny body and willing it to survive. She visualized them as proud of her and these thoughts kept her company as she moved farther into a world, month after month, that was all dog.

Rose and Rudi alternated mornings, carrying two or three pups back to the book store. As the heat of May increased, Rose would be sweating by the time she arrived. One morning she found Jennifer waiting for her in the doorway. She'd shaved her blond hair down to less than half an inch long and Rose, who was a few inches taller, found it hard to resist rubbing Jennifer's fuzzy head.

"Bonnie's back," Jennifer told her, referring to a little brown pup that they'd adopted out the month before.

"Where is she? How does she look?" Rose asked.

"You're not going to like it," Jennifer said. "She's in the pen." Rose walked over, lowered the puppies she carried gently into the corral, and couldn't believe what she saw. Bonnie had been adopted by one of the local girls who worked in the bookstore, someone who should've known better. What Rose found in the pen was all bones with green goop crusted in the corners of her eyes and she was cowering behind the basket full of toys.

"Oh my God. Come here, sweet heart." Rose lifted her up. "You're filthy." She turned to Jennifer. "Where is she, where's Anna?"

"I don't know. Someone else brought Bonnie in." Jennifer looked worried.

Gretchen appeared at the door, "What's up?" she asked. "New pup?"

"Does she look familiar?" Rose asked, holding the skinny thing up for inspection. Gretchen eyed Bonnie, then took hold of her. She turned her from side to side and looked in her mouth. Bonnie was light brown with black brindle striping that covered her entire body, and her face was shaped like a heart that framed her big dark eyes. She had been one of the most distinctive pups they'd had; everyone had wanted her, but still, in this condition, she was not easily recognized.

"This pup must be related to that one we had last month. Remember her? Bonnie. That was her name, right?" Gretchen concluded after her inspection.

"This is Bonnie!" Rose said with disgust.

Gretchen drew a quick breath. "What did Anna say?"

Rose left it to Jennifer to explain. "She's not here. Someone else brought the puppy in." Rose took Bonnie from Gretchen and started to clean her eyes. The puppy tucked her tail between her legs and sank her head into Rose's shoulder, looking for a place to hide.

"Gretchen, I'm too mad to talk to Anna. Will you find out what happened and come over later? I'm going to take this baby home and give her a bath and some food."

"Maybe Anna lost her," Jennifer suggested, "and was too afraid to tell us."

"Well then, she must have lost her a long time ago for her to get this skinny." Rose walked out of the bookstore holding Bonnie close to her heart. She felt as though she'd let her down. Bonnie had been sick and thin when she first came in and they'd let her suffer again. They'd taught Bonnie to trust people and then allowed her to be abused. As always, Rose wanted to talk to the dog, to somehow explain, but all she could do was gently hug her.

Her house was just a short walk away. She passed shops and restaurants, then crossed the road just after the youth hostel, where the surface changed from pavers to sand and ran alongside the jungle that sheltered their house from town. The trees and underbrush were a hundred different shades of vibrant green but Rose hardly saw them. Finding Bonnie in such bad shape reminded her that, in this place where she lived, a dog's life meant nothing. These reminders came so often that cynicism was beginning to pop up in places where humor or forgiveness might have existed before.

Rose was almost home and deep in thought when she spotted Leanora. Not today, she thought. But it was too late. The woman was waddling happily towards her. Lenora was a neighbor. She owned one of the properties between the town and Rose's house. Rose liked Leanora—it was the energy that was required to speak to her that Rose wanted to avoid. Rose was always studying Spanish. Even though she realized that she didn't have a knack for it, she determinedly tried to use the little she had learned by talking to the locals. Conversations with Leanora had left her extremely frustrated until Rudi told her Leanora was speaking a mixture of Spanish and Mayan, and actually, he admitted, it was more Mayan than Spanish. So Rose tried to keep these conversations short by pretending she understood, often drawing on hand gestures and attitude to fake it.

Every once in a while it would get her into trouble, like the time she agreed to give Leanora a loan without realizing it. She discovered her mistake the next day when Leanora showed up for her money. Brad and Rose had already learned the hard way that in Mexico, personal loans are rarely paid back; it's a façade to even call them loans. Luckily, Leanora never asked for very much.

She was a pleasant woman, short and heavy and always wearing the traditional dress of the older island women: a simple, midi-length white shift with colorful embroidery around the neck and the hem. Occasionally, Leanora would bring them young palm trees or aloe plants or sometimes baked goods that Brad complained left a bad taste in his mouth.

"Hola, Leanora," Rose said, trying to look pleased to see her.

"Blah blah blah perro (dog) blah blah blah blah casa (house)," said Leanora.

"Yes, this puppy is sick," replied Rose. She was hoping that this might be a good answer after deciding from the inflection in Leanora's voice that she'd been asked a question.

"Blah blah blah, ojala," said Leanora. 'Ojala' is an Arabic word, meaning 'God willing'. The Spaniards picked it up from the Moors and took it with them to everywhere they settled in the world.

"I'm going to work hard to make her better," Rose said, assuming that Leanora was saying that the puppy will survive, God willing.

Then Leanora turned. "Ven, ven," she said, beckoning with her arm, as she waddled back to her property. She lived on a half-acre square plot of sand covered with trees. There was stuff everywhere that Leanora must have thought useful or possibly useful one day. On the outer edge were two small, decrepit shacks.

Leanora had made it clear that she loved the place; she'd inherited it from her father, and from her perspective she had everything she needed. Her grandson lived with her, his mother visited occasionally, and Leanora made money feeding laborers in the middle of their work day. She did all the cooking over an open fire, and as her customers sat eating on red plastic chairs that matched the red plastic Coca-Cola tables, she joined them and chattered away.

Leanora returned with two coconuts, each sprouting a young palm tree. She glowed with anticipation as she showed Rose her gift.

We do need trees, thought Rose, smiling gratefully. She shifted Bonnie under one arm and held her other arm next to her body, creating a ledge. Obviously, Leanora didn't think this was too much to handle and gently placed the coconuts, sprout side up, on her arm.

"Muchas Gracias, ellos son bonita." Rose said, turning quickly towards her house, avoiding any further conversation.

Later that afternoon, Gretchen came over as had been requested. Rose was sitting in her courtyard with Bonnie on her lap wrapped in a towel. She'd fed and washed her and then patiently picked every tick off her tiny body. Bonnie was so much happier and even gave Gretchen a little wag of her tail.

"I talked to Anna," Gretchen announced, coming through the door.

"What did she tell you? Let me guess, the dog was perfectly fine this morning, right?"

"No, she said that her friend's puppy had died so she'd loaned her Bonnie to help her feel better." Rose attempted to assimilate Anna's explanation. There were so many things wrong with this excuse Rose didn't even know where to start. "She said she hadn't seen the pup for a while," Gretchen added.

"Let me see," Rose finally spoke after removing a few more ticks from Bonnie. "I'm not sure where to begin. First, who loans out their new puppy? And I wonder if she even bothered to ask why her friend's other pup had died? She's lying."

"Probably," was all Gretchen could say. "Want some wine? I'll bring some down for both of us." Jennifer and Gretchen loved Rose's free wine. A used bookstore on a small Mexican island barely covered their living expenses and they were always too broke to buy their own. They loved that Rose was happy to share.

"That would be great," Rose replied, and then returned her attention to Bonnie. Deciding the pup was finally tick free, she opened the towel to let Bonnie explore. She'd definitely suffered in the past month. There was a deep groove between each rib, and when she walked Rose noticed a tremor in her front legs, which she knew meant a calcium deficiency. She had bald patches on her belly and behind her shoulders, and one ear was split at the end; probably another dog had bitten her in a food fight.

"That's the last family on the island that gets one of my pups," Rose told Gretchen when she returned. "I think we've already filled all the good homes."

"I know there are a lot more responsible dog owners on the island," Gretchen said defensively.

"Okay, maybe you're right, but when it goes wrong it's so heartbreaking," Rose said.

"What are you going to do?" Gretchen handed Rose a glass of wine. "You can't send every dog off of Isla Mujeres." They both sipped their wine silently.

"Well, this baby isn't going back on the streets, she's staying with us. We'll just have to find more volunteers to help take care of the dogs until the perfect home comes up for each one."

That night the princes were in Rose's dreams. They were worried too.

They were on the beach watching the puppies play in the surf. Ek chauh was chasing the puppies and then he would lie nearby and let them crawl all over him. Rose was sitting on a piece of driftwood and itzamna was lying next to her. His beautiful golden fur was just a bit darker than the sand.

"What are we going to do with all these puppies?" Rose asked itzamna.

"The pupppies are at the end of the problem," he told her, wagging his tail as he watched his brother play. "We have to start at the beginning. They should never be born."

Rose lowered herself to the sand so that she could be closer to itzamna. And as they continued to watch ek chauh, the puppies started to disappear.

Chapter 10
Trapping By Morons

Rose sat next to Jeannie in the restaurant that had become their regular meeting place. They were there to organize themselves into a formal group and coordinate their volunteer efforts. After the incident with Bonnie, the neglected pup, Rose had taken a bigger role in how the puppies were handled at the book store. She'd told Gretchen and Jennifer that she wanted to have more say over where her pups went, and that had prompted Jennifer to arrange a meeting for anyone interested in helping.

Things had changed. The pups had become Rose's pups. She no longer felt like a volunteer. She knew what they needed and where they should go.

While they waited for the others to arrive, Jeannie told Rose how impressed she was by the people who stayed at her bed and breakfast. They'd been voicing their concerns for the sad cats and dogs on the island and asking her how they could help.

"I thought we should set up a donation box at the front desk with a poster describing how we're trying to change things."

"I love the idea," said Rose. "I already have tons of pictures of the pups, I'll put something together. One thing I was going to mention today was that I'd be happy to head up this group, I mean, if we're forming an actual group, and since everyone else has a job, I have the most time."

"Splendid idea," agreed Jeannie.

"I'm a little concerned about stepping on any toes," said Rose. "I'm the newest one here and the girls really started this all in their book store."

"Well, let's see, we've got Gretchen, Jennifer, Kat, and Addy. I wonder—" Before Jeannie could finish, Gretchen and Jennifer joined them at the table. "Hey, girls, so good to see you," said Jeannie. "Oh, by the way, I forgot to mention that Addy's not coming and, Kat said she'd try to make it but she wasn't sure. So if you don't mind, let's go ahead and order. I'm famished."

After they told the waiter what they wanted, Rose explained what she and Jeannie had already discussed. Jennifer, who was by nature an organizational person, had brought notes on setting up a formal rescue. "It doesn't bother me who we put at the top except that I'll need information for this paperwork."

"How do you feel about me heading up the group, Gretchen?" asked Rose. "I figure it should be you or me since we do most of the hands-on part of this."

Gretchen gave Rose a huge smile. "I couldn't be happier, I'm always feeling conflicted between the animals and the bookstore. Now I can have both without worrying." Gretchen put her hand on Rose's back, "You will be so great at this. I've never met anyone who cares about the dogs the way you do." She turned to face Jennifer, "And now I can be more help in the book store. It's perfect."

Lunch arrived with so many dishes that Jennifer had to put her note pad away. They had ordered fajitas, their usual, with hot black skillets of meat and vegetables, two kinds of salsa, a bowl of hot peppers, guacamole, and baskets of tortillas, plus drinks and more plates. As usual Jennifer organized the mess so everything fit, and then eating involved a lot of picking and rolling and dipping, so it was a few minutes before they continued their discussion.

Rose mentioned the cost of the medicine and food, and Jennifer pointed out that people would be more interested in donating money if they could get a tax write-off. Rose couldn't imagine anyone donating enough money to need a tax write-off but they all agreed, they needed a name and a non-profit status could only be a good thing.

Towards the end of the meeting, Kat dropped in to say that she couldn't stay but she was happy to be part of the group and she wanted to help when she could.

"This is all good news," said Rose. "And I already have a project for you and me Gretchen, when you have the time. That momma dog that I've been feeding needs to be spayed. A few weeks ago she had a whole pack of horn dogs after her."

"You mean the one in your little family by the garage?" asked Gretchen. Rose nodded. "I thought you spayed her already."

"I did. I took the friendly one to Paulo last month but I can't get near the other one."

"Okay," said Gretchen. "How about tomorrow? Can you do it then?"

"Sure," agreed Rose.

"You and I can trap her. I'll get some tranquilizers from Paulo."

"That would be great," said Rose. "I can meet you at the mechanic's shop at nine."

The next morning the first question Rose had for Gretchen was if she'd remembered the tranquilizers.

"Yup, and some hot dogs," said Gretchen, holding out a plastic bag from the store.

Rose took the bag and pointed at the dogs. "They're all in their usual spot. And yesterday, after lunch, one of Jeannie's guests gave her a thousand pesos so we can actually pay Paulo to do three spays."

"That's great," said Gretchen. "Paulo didn't charge me for the tranquilizers, but I told him we're bringing in a dog so it'll be nice to be able to pay him for a change."

Gretchen set a dish of food on the sand and moved away. As Rose had anticipated, the puppies charged right in and licked the plate clean. They hoped that after eating, the puppies would be too full to get in the way. And they did just that, they trotted off to a hole in the sand under a piece of driftwood and snuggle together for a nap.

Their plan was to wait until the unfriendly dog came close enough for them to toss the laced hot dog in her direction. This female was the wariest of the pack and they knew she would take her time approaching anything they put out.

After the puppies moved off, Rose loaded up another plate of food and then she and Gretchen sat in the shade and watched. The black momma had been eyeing them and the food. "Here she comes," said Gretchen. "Try not to move too much. I'll wait until she starts eating and then roll the hot dog towards her." After the dog had taken a few bites Gretchen rolled the bait in her direction. When the hot dog hit the plate the startled dog jumped back and looked around. She paused and then satisfied that she wasn't in danger, began eating again until the aroma of the hot dog caught her attention. She barely sniffed it before swallowing it whole. Rose and Gretchen quietly "high-fived" so they didn't scare her off.

"How long do you think it'll take?" Rose asked. She was rearranging her towel on the sand, trying to get more comfortable.

"Maybe twenty minutes," Gretchen speculated.

So they waited. Momma finished the plate of food then wandered around the open space looking for a spot to rest. Her stalkers were up immediately. They kept their distance, but never took their eyes off of her. Sadly, their expectations were based on what they wanted to happen, not anything that experience had taught them. They'd hoped she would eat the tranquilizer and fall into a deep sleep after twenty minutes, at which time they could pick her up and put her in the back of Rose's car and drive to the vet clinic. They were so wrong.

They waited. After forty-five minutes she finally put her head down. But when the ladies approached her, she got up and moved away. When another hour and a half had passed they decided she wasn't going to fall over as planned but now they had a problem.

"I can't believe this," said Gretchen, sitting against a palm tree. "What're we going to do now?"

"I don't know," said Rose, settling on the sand next to her. "We can't leave her wandering around half-tranquilized. I've seen these dogs fight."

"I guess we'll just have to keep following her. Maybe she'll tire more and we can get her with the pole. You brought it, right?"

"Yup, it's in the car. Do you know how to use it?" asked Rose as she stood up.

"You just loop the wire around her neck and then pull it tight." Gretchen mimed the motion of dropping the loop and pulling the wire out through the other end of the pole. "Once you've got her you have to push the pole towards the ground to keep her steady."

Rose retrieved the pole and they continued to stalk the momma down the beach. The dog was leading them in circles. Twice they found themselves back where they'd started. Her awareness of them was obviously keeping her on her feet. Occasionally her pace abated slightly, but if they attempted to close the gap she would take off again. After two more hours the dog must have decided that they weren't much of a threat, and she settled in a shady spot just in front of a parked car.

"This is our chance," said Rose. She surveyed the area to determine what their best options were in the space they had. "Okay, you stay out in front of the car and keep her watching you. I'll go around behind the car, and see if I can get the loop over her head from behind." Rose was hoping there would be just enough street noise to distract the dog until she could lower the wire.

It worked perfectly. Rose moved closer, concealed by the side of the car. And then in one swift motion she dropped the loop over the dog's head and pulled the wire tight.

"Oh my God, you got her!" cried Gretchen, but there was no time for celebration. At the last minute, the dog had leapt up enough to get one of her front legs in the loop, and she was going ballistic, rolling over and over, and attempting to rub the line off of her neck, gyrating and screeching so loudly people stopped to watch. They seemed concerned, so Gretchen explained what they were doing.

"We're going to have her spayed, everything's fine," she repeated twice.

The dog continued to spin around Rose, one way and then the other. She was biting at the pole and writhing in fear and Rose was worried she'd crack a tooth or the wire would cut through her skin. The number of spectators had grown. Finally, it was sound of Jeannie Tull's English drawl that helped to calm the situation.

"Don't you worry about a thing, folks, these girls know what they're doing," assured Jeannie. Not likely, thought Rose.

Beside Jeannie was Addy. Rose knew that Addy couldn't stand the sight of a mouse trap. She cried when the fishermen cut the heads off their daily catch. They had all seen that death or suffering of any kind would bring forth rivers of tears. So when Rose heard Addy sniffling it tightened the knot that was already twisting in her belly. Oh my God, she thought, what am I doing?

After what seemed like an eternity, the dog tired. She finally stopped writhing when she hit the wheel of the parked car. Rose felt stupid and embarrassed. Gretchen gave her a look that said, "What the hell do we do now?" The crowd was still growing and Jeannie continued to assure everyone that things were just as they should be. "There, you see, the dog's just fine now," she said.

"Okay, Gretchen, you take the pole now," said Rose. "I'm going to the house to get a big blanket. I'll bring Rudi back to help us. I'll go as fast as I can.

You can't leave me here, was written on Gretchen's face.

But what Gretchen said was, "Okay, don't take too long," and she reluctantly took over the handle of the pole.

Rose raced to her house, yelling for Rudi the minute she was through the gate. He was there. He was always right there. "You have to come with me now," she yelled as she grabbed a big blanket out of the garage. They were back with Gretchen within minutes.

Rose had learned that covering a dog's head will usually make it give up. "Remember GONE WITH THE WIND," someone had explained to her, "when Rhett Butler covered the horse's head so that the horse wouldn't panic as they escaped past the burning warehouses? Well, it's the same for dogs."

Rudi quickly assessed the situation. As Gretchen kept the dog down with the pole he draped the blanket over the dog's head. By then Rose could see that it wasn't necessary. It was obvious that she was done, lying there by the tire, looking around but not moving.

Rudi wrapped the blanket around the momma's whole body and held on tightly while Gretchen slipped a muzzle over her nose and clipped the strap behind her ears. Now they were able to release the loop and completely wrap her up. Rudi climbed into the back of the car holding the poor traumatized dog in his lap, muzzled with her head still covered. She didn't even struggle.

They arrived at the clinic feeling tired and stupid but proud. Paulo came out to the car and gave the momma dog a shot to calm her down so they could safely get her into a crate. He agreed to operate on her right away. Rose was watching the dog closely. She knew how terrified she was and when they unwrapped her head there was still a wild look in her eyes. Rose was worried about Rudi getting bitten. This female was a strong dog and Rose was sure that she'd have a fierce bite.

"I don't think she's tranquilized enough," Rose told Paulo when he brought a crate out to the car.

"You tranquilized her, right?" he asked.

"We put it in a hot dog about three hours ago," she said.

"That should be enough," he assured her. "I'll check her again." It was three o'clock and everyone was looking tired. After a quick glance he pronounced her sufficiently drugged.

"Okay," Rose reluctantly agreed. The dog didn't look calm but he was the vet. "Rudi, esta bien." Rose turned to the vet. "Should we remove her muzzle?"

"Por favor," he said, on his way back into his clinic. "The dog needs clear airways." Rudi loosened his grip on the momma and removed her muzzle. Rose stood by the rear bumper, preparing to shut the door and follow them inside. What came next happened so fast that Rose didn't realize it had happened until it was over. As Rudi was working his way closer to the back door of the car, the dog pushed forward off of Rudi's chest and bit Rose's arm, above the elbow. Rudi instantly whipped part of the dangling blanket back over the dog's head and held her tightly against his chest. Rose was startled by the dog's quick actions and had felt the pressure on her arm but had no idea that she'd been bitten.

"Take the dog inside," Rose told Rudi. "I'll find Gretchen." Rose didn't have to look for Gretchen, she was suddenly beside her. Without realizing it, Rose had yelped and Gretchen, who'd been helping set up for surgery, had raced back outside. By then Rose had felt the blood running down her arm. The whole day had been so emotional. "Gretchen, I've got to si—" she started to say but before she finished talking she was down on the curb. She hadn't fainted, she'd simply stopped standing.

The two of them sat in stunned silence as the blood ran onto the pavement. It was a few minutes before Gretchen finally checked the wound. It was on the outside of Rose's arm, a few inches above her elbow.

"It's a perfect bite," Gretchen told her. "You can see all the teeth marks."

"I feel so much better about it now," replied Rose as she tried to look at it over her shoulder.

"There's one big tear that doesn't look too good, though," Gretchen said. "I think we're supposed to let it bleed. It washes the wound, right?"

"Shit, I don't know, it doesn't seem to be stopping, anyway." Rose was looking at the large puddle of blood accumulating next to her feet.

By this time the vet had put the dog in a crate and come back outside to see what was going on. He looked at the two of them sitting side by side on the curb with blood on their shirts and shook his head.

"Take her to Dr. Rita," he said unsympathetically. He'd seen these girls bitten and bruised before. Rose wanted to say something about his telling her that the dog was drugged enough but couldn't be bothered. Her ears were ringing and the sight of her own blood on the road was starting to make her woozy.

"You drive," Paulo told Gretchen before going back inside. He returned with a towel to wrap up Rose's arm. "Is that one of your dog towels?" Gretchen asked.

"It's fine," he said. Avoiding the answer, thought Rose. He helped her into the car and shut the door.

"Rudi can help you for now," said Rose and Paulo nodded as they drove away.

Rita was an Irish doctor who worked at the Red Cross Clinic. She took them in immediately and instructed the nurse to scrub the wound with iodine for ten minutes. She didn't stitch the nastier parts of torn skin, explaining that dog bites often get infected and need to stay open to drain. While Rose was being scrubbed, Jennifer walked into the clinic.

"Paulo said I'd find you here. He's in surgery so I didn't ask him which one of you bozos was hurt." Jennifer was talking to the curtain between the beds so she couldn't see who was being tended to by the nurse. "I swear you both go brain-dead when it comes to dogs."

"You can't talk to me like that," said Rose sheepishly. "I'm older than you."

"I sure can. You're the one sitting there with," Jennifer leaned in to see what the nurse was scrubbing, "an enormous dog bite."

"You can see all the teeth marks," Gretchen pointed out. Jennifer just shook her head.

"I want you to take these for 10 days, just in case," said Dr. Rita handing Rose a bottle of antibiotics. "Keep that bite clean and come back if there's problems."

"Rita, tell them to stop playing with wild dogs," said Jennifer.

"I would," said Dr. Rita lifting her arms and shoulders. "But I know it won't do any good." Dr. Rita was shaking her head as she walked away.

"This is nothing," said Rose as the nurse taped gauze over the wound. Rose was suddenly feeling much better and slid off of the hospital bed smiling, completely undaunted by the multiple scoldings. Gretchen was smiling back at her; they'd become co-conspirators with a worthy mission.

"It's just a little bite, for heaven's sake," Rose told Brad later that night when they finally had time to discuss it. They'd eaten at the restaurant which meant that Rose ate alone for most of the meal. There was no way for Brad to sit at the restaurant and not be called on when something came up and something always came up. Rose ate quickly and they returned home early.

"Really," said Brad, "first blood poisoning and then this. I suppose Gretchen got hurt, too?"

"Not this time," Rose said as she removed her shoes. "Besides, it wasn't my fault."

"Oh, that makes it okay?" said Brad. He sat on the bed, leaned back against the pillows, and watched Rose pull the old t-shirt she slept in over her head.

"No, I just mean that I'm being careful," said Rose. She didn't want another lecture and tried to change the subject. "Oh my God, you should see Jennifer. She's cut her hair to less than an inch long." Brad was not amused.

"That's because she's the practical one, not nuts like you and Gretchen. Really, Rose, what are we going to do about this?"

"I'll be more careful, I promise." Rose climbed across her side of the bed and snuggled in next to Brad. She laid her head on his shoulder and felt safe and hoped nothing else would happen in the near future.

Napoleon watching over the puppies

Chapter 11

A Sad Reminder

The wound healed quickly. And Rose continued to feed her dogs almost every day for the next two months—until the day that she couldn't find them. She'd arrived later than usual and was expecting some attitude from Lately but there were no dogs next to the hut. In a panic she began to shove the trash around and then checked the beach and the field nearby. Finally, she located them in a group of palm trees back from the sand. Peewee was shaking and none of them would come close to the food that she offered. She returned to the mechanic's shop and asked them, in her broken Spanish, what had happened.

"Que pasa?" she asked. At first they tried to ignore her, but she persisted. They told her that the owner of shop and the shed thought that the dogs were spreading fleas and had instructed the workers to get rid of the animals. The mechanics had proudly announced that they'd only used rocks, as if that was the kindest thing they could have done. Rose wondered what their alternative to rocks was.

Looking back at her bruised family, she noticed the friendly mother walk with a limp to a new place in the shade. She wished that she could talk to them, explain that not all people were bad. She wanted to apologize for the world that they lived in and separate herself from the cruelty.

She felt responsible. Her care hadn't helped them. Instead it had lulled them into a false sense of security and made them more vulnerable. She'd heard people talk about the complexities of the island's dog situation. They had explained how some of their best efforts had gone awry. One woman had gone from one end of the island to the other putting collars on every street dog, or any dog that she could approach. Since the "ecologia" picked up strays, the woman thought that all the dogs would appear to have owners. It didn't take long before the dog catchers were picking up all of the dogs with or without collars since they could no longer differentiate between strays and owned animals. It turned out to be a disaster for dog owners when they couldn't afford the fines to get their dogs back. Obviously, solutions were not simple.

Rose hated these frequent and blunt reminders that this was a different world. The warm tropical sun she usually enjoyed was searing the top of her head. The correlation between helping and hopelessness was making her feel guilty and uncomfortable. How could she care so much and other people care so little?

She walked slowly back to the palm trees but didn't try to get too close to the dogs. Sliding down a sturdy palm to settle in the sand, she sat listening to the nearby ocean, her mind shifting between sympathy for the dogs and planning acts of revenge. Trying to calm herself down, she imagined the brothers sitting next to her. She wanted Itzamna to tell her that at least she was trying. She wanted Ek Chauh to nuzzle into her and tell her that he knew it wasn't easy, but that it would be okay. Rose stayed that way for a while, drawing on the comforts of her imagination, not ready to leave her family of dogs unprotected.

On the way back to the road, Rose approached the mechanics. She tried to explain that they could have relocated the dogs with food or they could have asked her for help. They just stared at her like she was out of her mind. Why would they need some silly, dog-feeding gringa to take care of such a little thing? She thought when she finally gave up. Rocks were easy; they'd always used them.

Their indifference reminded Rose that this wasn't a single incident. This was a culture. Rose turned and walked quickly home. She felt like an alien, she needed like-minded company. The men had seemed nice enough but they were from a different world: raised with different sensibilities, different everything. People aren't the same, she thought. The same feelings weren't there, the same cares, the same things didn't make them happy. Dogs clearly showed their emotions, fear, pain, happiness, loyalty and affection. How could they miss that?

After that day, she fed the group at the end of the field, sitting a little closer and talking to them while they ate. The mechanics were leaving the dogs alone in their new location. Rose assumed that the situation had been resolved but the truce didn't last. A few weeks later she arrived with her food and found Peewee staggering aimlessly. He didn't seem to know where he was. He actually brushed her leg which was extraordinary since he'd never allowed her to touch him. Without any struggle, she easily wrapped him up in the towel she'd brought to sit on, and hurried home. Rushing along the road, she saw Manuel, a friend. "Can you give me a ride to the clinic?" she asked. "There's something wrong with this puppy."

"Well," Manuel replied, "I need to do some stuff, if you can wait—"

"What are you talking about? This animal is sick."

"But I have an appointment, it's—" She never heard where his stupid appointment was. She ran on to the house instead. From there, she and Rudi rushed to the clinic.

"Paulo, there's something wrong with Peewee," Rose said, racing through the clinic's open door. She lay Peewee on Paulo's examining table, which was a regular kitchen table with a towel over it. As she stroked Peewee's head the doctor hooked him up to an IV with fluids. After Rose explained that he'd been staggering, that he'd vomited on the way to the clinic, and now he couldn't stand at all, Paulo said it looked like Peewee had been poisoned.

"I thought they would leave him alone," said Rose to no one in particular.

"Who?"

"These men who work at a mechanic's shop near my house."

"What makes you think they did it?"

"They've hurt them before," Rose told him, watching the fluids drip into the top of the IV line.

Paulo nodded knowingly. He'd told her that the attitude toward the animals was much the same in Bolivia. "We just have to wait," he said, looking at Peewee.

Rose stayed with Peewee for a while, then went back to the other dogs. She watched them for similar signs of illness but they seemed fine.

Rose knew it was silly, but she couldn't stop herself from yelling at the mechanics. "Que es su problema?" Even if they'd put out the poison they only did it because they were told to. Once again, they looked at her like she was an alien and tried to ignore her.

Rose's cheeks were wet with tears and she was so frustrated that her toes were curling up the fronts of her sandals. She continued to shout at them. "What's the point? You don't care...do you...do you?" They continued to ignore her, looking up occasionally, hoping that she would disappear. "What's the matter with you? These are living things!"

Rose was out of words. She'd spend so much time in this field around this shop that it had become familiar. In front of the building, there was a broken down old truck with its hood open. Vines had grown around the engine and through the bumpers and wheel wells and often there would be an iguana sunning itself on the roof. Nearby was a wooden boat tilted to one side to accommodate its V-hull, and similar vines crawled through its broken windows and spread out over the rotting wood of its front deck. Previously, Rose had taken pictures, thinking it was charming. Today, it all looked like ugly garbage: everything looked ugly.

She decided to move her dog family closer to her house for safety. Rudi helped her relocate an old wooden canoe that was part of the debris they'd slept under in their first place by the fence. They leaned the boat next to her rock wall, and then Rudi went with Rose and carried Lately to the new spot while the others followed at a distance. They put food and water under the canoe and quickly left. The next morning, Rose woke up early to check on her brood. They were gone. She found them back at the beach by the mechanic's shop.

Peewee survived the poison, but was very thin and frail. They kept him in the clinic and fed him vitamins for a week. When Paulo thought it was safe, he neutered him. Rose visited daily, trying to decide what to do. His life was so dangerous. Should she put him back with his family? Maybe he would get comfortable with people. Maybe Brad would like him. Every day she watched him for signs that could help her decide. When she opened the door to his crate, he would cower at the back. When she did pull him out, he would go straight to the wall and edge around the room looking for something to hide under. No amount of coaxing or soft talking would generate a shred of trust. So, after his incision healed and he didn't need to stay at the clinic any longer, Rose decided to take him back to his family.

Peewee leapt with joy when he saw them. He jumped his greetings next to them, onto their bodies, twirling around and around, then leaping up on them again. The momma would lick him if he stood still for a moment, and the other pups joined in on the dance. The answer Rose needed was the joy this shy puppy so energetically displayed.

When Brad got home from the restaurant the following day Rose was all grins.

"You're not going to believe this," she told him. "The most wonderful thing has happened." Rose sat on one of the kitchen stools and then jumped up again and went over to the kitchen window.

"It must be really good," he said, taking off his sunglasses. "What?"

"So this morning I'm in the kitchen and I look out the window," Rose indicated the window in front of her like Vanna White showing prizes in The Price is Right, "and guess who I saw?"

"I can't," said Brad.

"My little family. You know, Peewee's family."

"Is that unusual?"

Rose huffed indignantly. Brad was not sharing her excitement and she was determined that he should. "No," Rose moved to the next window so she could point to the exact place that she had seen the dogs, "but what happened after that was."

"What?" asked Brad?

"So I saw them all trotting along the shore line." Rose pointed to the spot and Brad tried to look interested.

"Rose, get to the point."

She ignored him. "I was so excited. I opened the window and called them. It was really cool. They looked up and wagged their tails when they saw me. God, it felt good. Anyway, I put some food together and ran

110

downstairs and out the front gate. They were still there, so I showed them the food and they actually followed me."

Brad couldn't resist poking at Rose. She looked as excited as a ten-year-old. "There's a surprise, a street dog following someone with food."

Rose put her hands on her hips. He was taking all the fun out of it.

Brad saw the change. "Okay, where are they now?"

"Well that's the thing, I put the food and water down by the boat that Rudi and I moved here. They settled in. I kept checking all afternoon to see if they were still there and they've stayed."

"I didn't see them when I came in," said Brad.

"None of them?"

"No."

Rose raced outside. Brad watched her run along the driveway, and then peek around the open gate. She turned around, smiling. "They're still here," she mouthed, smiling and pointing.

Chapter 12
Sol

When Brad and Rose bought into The Fishbone Bar and Grill they'd bought out a silent partner's shares with the understanding that they didn't have to live on the island to own half of the business. Brad liked the idea of being a consultant.

They were already friends with Luca, their new partner. But everything changed when Luca started to take more trips home to Morocco to care for his sick mother. Grudgingly, Brad had to work more hours than he had originally planned on.

The building had a huge palapa roof and the walls on the ocean side were only waist high, offering an atmosphere of ocean breezes and sunshine. Facing the surf were three steps leading down to the sand, and just to the right of the steps was a free-standing beach bar with swings instead of stools. People loved the swings.

It had been two years since the house had been completed and Brad was still searching for a restaurant manager he could trust. He went through the first group quickly and painfully. When Pedro was recommended, he looked good; he had a great deal of restaurant experience.

Pedro started well. He got everyone working hard and business was good. He ran the restaurant while Brad and Rose were in Colorado visiting Rose's daughter. Things didn't start to unravel until Luca went back to Morocco again. After that, when Brad returned to the island, there was no money and worse: very few bills had been paid. Sadly, it turned out that Pedro had a cocaine habit that he was supporting with the restaurant's profits.

Next, Brad learned too late that a common mistake in the Mexican restaurant business was to hire more than one member of the same family. One of his cooks recommended his brother, Pablo, so Brad brought him on as manager. He was a charmer, charming, like a smiling snake, and he and his brother cheated Brad in every way possible. But that wasn't even what Brad fired him for. During the snake's last month of work Brad received a ridiculously high phone bill and was sure there'd been a mistake. It was two thousand dollars. When he checked with the company, most of the calls were to 900 numbers. As it turned out the little snake had been sneaking back into the restaurant at night and making sex calls. Either he liked a lot of sex or it took a lot of calls to satisfy him. They didn't want to know. He was out.

Unfortunately, there's no unemployment insurance on the island so if you fire someone you have to pay them off. The only way to avoid this is to file a legal complaint with three witnesses. In other words, it's impossible; there are never any witnesses. So they had to pay the smiling snake off after paying the two-thousand-dollar phone bill. Consequently, it didn't take long for Brad to hate the Mexican restaurant business.

The next manager Brad hired waited until Brad left the restaurant in the late afternoons and then locked himself in the office with a bottle of booze and an ice bucket to urinate in. After that, Brad tried a female manager, but she kept necking with the waiters in the storage room. She ultimately got fired for having a naked swimming party on the beach in front of the restaurant after hours.

Finally, after the sex-calling smiling snake, the bucket urinator, the coke head and the beach stripper, Brad found someone he could trust. Manuel wasn't perfect, but he was honest and he knew the business, so Brad could relax slightly and try to enjoy the reasons they were in Mexico.

"You're rescue friends are all weirdos," Brad told Rose one night when he got home from work. "They were at the Grill today."

"Who was there?" asked Rose as she worked on the salad that she was making.

"Gretchen, Addy, and Kat."

"That's an odd mix, I must admit."

"Yeah, Gretchen and Kat argued and at one point Addy burst into tears. Luckily, we were crowded so no one seemed to pay any attention."

"Do you really think that rescue people are different than any other group of personalities? I mean look at the weirdo's you've dealt with at the restaurant." Rose added onions and started peeling carrots. "I mean, you've got hard workers, big talkers, some honest, some not so honest, plus the positive and the worriers." Brad sat at the counter with some restaurant work open in front of him. He was X-ing out large portions with his pen and groaning every time he turned a page. "I guess it's possible," said Rose, "that dog people are a bit quirkier than most."

"They're definitely crustier," he said, surprising Rose, she thought he'd stopped listening.

Brad pushed his papers in to one pile and headed out of the kitchen. "Brad, do you think I'm a fanatic?" Rose called after him.

"You're kidding, right?" There was a pause. "Of course you're a fanatic. Do you see any of our neighbors with twenty-five-plus dogs?"

"We don't have twenty-five dogs. We have seventeen puppies, four older dogs and our little family outside the gate."

"Minor detail. The neighbors don't have any dogs at all."

"We don't have any neighbors, just hotels," said Rose.

"Hey, you asked." Brad called from the other room.

"Okay, no one else has seventeen-plus puppies." She put down her peeler and was quiet for a moment, thinking. "I don't know why. I can't help it. How can I say no?" Abandoning the salad, Rose sat on the stool next to the counter and stared out the window. Maybe I am nuts, she thought. She had been shocked at how fast their number of rescue dogs increased.

Time had passed quickly after the house was finished. What had started with puppies had rapidly changed to accommodate any dogs who needed help. There had been adoptions but the numbers kept climbing.

Rose, once again thanked the stars for bringing her Rudi. Without his help it would have been overwhelming.

"It's okay," Brad walked back into the kitchen and kissed Rose on the cheek. "Let's just keep the population down, alright? Want some wine?"

"Sure." Rose pulled the chopping board towards her and continued to peel carrots. She was grateful that Brad had said, "Keep the population down," rather than picking a specific number. If a dog needed help, Rose would help. It was that simple.

She decided to have the next dog meeting at her house instead of at the restaurant. She scheduled it for the following day and for a change, it was going to be later in the afternoon.

Kat arrived first, grinning from ear to ear. "I just talked to Greer. Can we organize another clinic soon?"

"He almost missed the last one," Rose pointed out.

"Yeah but he didn't like me as much then," said Kat.

"Jeannie told me that she saw you on the beach with Ricardo or whatever that other guy's name is. It was just a few days ago."

"Hey, I like Greer, but we're not married. I mean, I'm not dead."

"You will be when Ricardo's new girlfriend gets her hands on you," said Jeannie, who had arrived during their conversation.

"Ppppffftt," sneered Kat.

"You need a mother," countered Jeannie.

"You need a diet," spat Kat, who often got herself into trouble with her quick temper.

"None of my clothes would fit," said Jeannie, completely unfazed by the insult. "You're going to have to come up with something much meaner than that, Kitty Kat."

"Ah shit, sorry," said Kat. She gave Jeannie a hug. "Ricardo's girlfriend just pisses me off. I shouldn't be taking it out on you."

"You can't have them all, you know," said Rose.

"I don't see why not," Kat replied with a laugh. Kat's mother did, thought Rose. Not exactly a great example.

"Hey, Gretchen," called Kat, as Gretchen walked into the courtyard.

"Hi you guys, where's the wine? I need it today."

"You need it every day," said Kat.

"Kat, stop that." Rose said. "Get Gretchen some wine and stop being so ornery."

Jennifer came in next. "Hey, I found Addy on the way." Addy had a long dress on, just like the ones that Jeannie wore, but less colorful.

"Come on in, get some wine," said Rose. "I put some chips on the table if anyone's hungry. Addy, did Jeannie make that dress?"

"Yeah, what do you think?"

"She's so small," said Jeannie, "I couldn't use any of the fabrics I have. There wouldn't be enough space for a pattern to repeat itself."

"That's not true, I'm five foot two," Addy objected, standing up straighter.

"I haven't been your size since I was ten." Jeannie laughed. She'd planted herself in one of the teak lounges with a glass of wine and some chips. "Wake me up when it gets interesting, I've got a loud crowd at the inn right now. I feel like I haven't slept for days."

"Pay attention," Rose said, settling into a chair. "We need you. We have to get the dog population down. My biggest fear is not having room for the dogs that have no other place to go and Brad's already made it clear that we've exceeded his limit."

"Ah, Saint Brad," said Kat.

"I get so tired of hearing what a saint he is," said Rose. "Fanatics get no understanding at all, only the people who put up with them get the credit."

It was the quality of their lives that Rose really worried about. The stress of too many animals changed the atmosphere. She felt guilty and Brad tried not to be impatient. Sometimes they just had to avoid each other and that's when it bothered Rose the most.

She watched her friends as they chatted and drank wine. This was exactly what she'd designed the courtyard for. The rest of the house wrapped around it like a horseshoe; the open end was the front door that led onto the driveway. The closed end of the horseshoe had the ocean view and was all windows. On each side of the courtyard was a guest room, the kitchen and master bedroom were above them on the second floor. Sitting quietly among her friends, Rose decided that the waiting had been worth it. She was feeling at home.

"Brad is awfully understanding about all of this," said Jennifer.

"He has been great," admitted Rose, "But we are near our doggy limit."

"How about we take some of your smaller dogs to our garage sale?" suggested Jennifer, pulling out one of her note pads. "I'm helping the school group put it together this year."

"I don't know," Rose said. "My dogs aren't for sale."

"Listen, are you daft?" Jeannie said. "You can't be so picky or you're going to have to move."

"Look, Rose, you don't have to be there," offered Jennifer, pushing down a pup that had escaped from its corral. "I'll sit with the dogs and talk to people who are interested. I'll get all the information and we can do home checks. I won't let one dog go unless it's a perfect situation." Rose was sensing a conspiracy. They've been talking to Brad, she thought.

"They'll find good homes for them, Rose. I just know they will," assured Addy, who betrayed her words by looking worried. She had picked up the puppy that had worked his way out of the enclosure and was holding it close. Sometimes the group wouldn't tell Addy they were having a meeting if they had some sad things to discuss. No one ever wanted to hurt her or experience her inevitable tears.

"Why don't you take some more pictures of the dogs and I'll add them to the poster at the front desk," said Jeannie. "Addy will make sure everyone has a good look. She goes on about the dog rescue to all our guests anyway." Rose thanked Jeannie and made a mental note to put another poster together while Jennifer was obviously writing it on her pad.

"Is Cally coming anytime soon?" asked Gretchen?

Cally was a new member of their group. She'd helped Rose every morning during her vacation on the island. She was younger than Rose, unmarried, full of energy, and very committed. Every morning she would arrive in a pair of men's shorts and a t-shirt, with a bandana wrapped around her short brown hair, always ready to work and full of ideas.

"She's making plans to come down in a few weeks. We're already trying to decide which dogs she'll take back with her."

"We're lucky to have her help," said Jeannie, popping a chip in her mouth. "I saw pictures of the last pups she took. They all looked so happy, snuggled into their new homes. How many has she taken so far?"

"Five, but it was way too many at one time," said Rose. "This trip I think she should only take three or four, depending on their size. I don't want to burn her out. Plus, I'm not sure what's going on with Mexicana airlines. I heard they were having troubles, and they're the only company that will take that many dogs at once.

"What plots are you all brewing?" asked Brad, entering the courtyard. He was headed for the second guest room which he'd converted into a music room, a place where he could get away and play his guitar. He had to zig zag through the chairs and table to get to the door.

"We're trying to help you out, luv. Shipping off some of your extras here," Jeannie said, pointing to the puppy in Addy's arms.

"They're all extras," quipped Brad good-naturedly.

"You don't mean that," said Jennifer.

"Oh, yes he does," said Rose attempting to tarnish his saintly status. It never worked. Everyone loved Brad. He was that kind of guy.

"Get rid of them all or I'm never coming out of the music room," he said as he ducked into his sanctuary.

"You're so lucky. He's such an easygoing guy," said Gretchen.

"That's because he was raised in a large family. There were eight kids, and you had to get along or get out of the way," Rose said.

"How about the rescue groups on the mainland? Can they take some of your dogs?" asked Jennifer, getting back on subject.

"They're all in the same boat. Too many animals and always more on the way," answered Rose. She scooped up the pup that Addy had just put down.

"Should we take some pups too?" asked Gretchen. Music had started playing in the guest room. It was hard rock, Brad's favorite.

"What a teeny-bopper," said Rose, tilting her head in the direction of the music.

"Everyone wants a pup. If a family wants an older dog, that's a good sign." Rose said. She retrieved the bottle of wine and turned to her friends. "More wine, anyone?"

"No thanks," said Jennifer, getting out of her chair. "We're having a music night tonight." Once a week they had music night in front of the bookstore. It was really just a sing-a-long; another one of their endless fundraisers for the animals and the children. Mostly young travelers took part, but there were usually enough of them to raise thirty or forty dollars, and every penny made a difference.

The day of the garage sale, Gretchen arrived at the house to pick up the dogs. Rose was reluctant to send one of her newest dogs, a scruffy little creature named Scooby Doo. The people who delivered him told her their neighbors were kicking him and it was obvious that he'd been abused. He would cower at loud noises or a raised hand. He reminded Rose of the little 'cockapoo' her family had when she was growing up.

However, Brad and Rose had just adopted a puppy. Someone found him on the beach, a tiny white thing, about the size of a melon. He was too small to put with the other pups so Rose had kept him upstairs. After the usual deworming and good food he'd come alive and started following Brad around the house. It was too funny for Rose, watching this miniscule dot on the floor trailing behind her six-foot-two husband. When she heard Brad calling him Napoleon she knew that the pup was theirs and so when Gretchen arrived to take dogs to the garage sale Rose let her take Scooby Doo, two other dogs and one puppy.

"You remember" she said to Gretchen, "and remind Jennifer, it has to be a very special home and don't let Scooby Doo go until you talk to me."

"I know," said Gretchen rolling her eyes. She'd heard it ten times already.

Halfway through the sale, Gretchen called Rose with the news that an American woman named Heather was interested in adopting Scooby Doo. Rose had met the woman and knew she'd provide a great home, so she let him go.

That evening when Rose saw Gretchen come through the gate without Scooby Doo she felt more upset than she'd expected to be. Usually she was thrilled when a dog got a good home. Two of the younger dogs they'd taken to the bazaar had been adopted as well as Scooby Doo, and she should've been ecstatic, but she wasn't. Brad walked in on her tears. "What's the matter?" he asked. She was sitting on a stool at the kitchen island so he hugged her from behind and waited until she was ready to tell him. She had mentioned her connection to Scoobie Doo but hadn't pushed it.

"This lady at the garage sale adopted Scoobie Doo. It's just that he looked so much like Sally, that scruffy cutie that we had when I was growing up and I just...."

"Go on down and get in the car," said Brad, releasing his hold on her.

"What?" Rose stood and turned around to face him.

"We'll take the car. Do you know where the lady lives?" Brad picked his car keys up off the counter. "I was afraid this would happen," he said, opening the kitchen door for Rose. "It was obvious that you felt different about Scooby Doo and you were sweet not to push it." Brad turned and locked the door behind them. "I was thinking about it this afternoon. Hell, look at the way we live. I mean really—one dog, two dogs, what difference does it make?"

"We've got another little fluffy dog that looks a lot like Scooby Doo. It has incredible green eyes," she said, and gave Brad a grateful hug. "I didn't send him to the garage sale because he needs to be neutered, but I don't have to worry about that with Heather."

"Bring it in the car," Brad said. "You never know." The woman didn't have a phone so they drove down island and called up to her balcony. She came right out.

"Come on up!" she yelled. Rose tucked the shaggy, young dog under her arm and climbed the stairs behind Brad. Heather was standing in her doorway when they reached the fifth floor.

"Heather, this is beautiful," said Rose, admiring the view from the open staircase. She wasn't sure how to start the conversation. She was usually begging people to take dogs not to give them back. Brad bailed her out.

"I brought Rose here because she was so upset about Scooby Doo. It's actually my fault. I underestimated how much she liked him and I kept saying I didn't want another dog."

"Come on in," said Heather, opening her door wider. Scooby Doo rushed towards Rose as she passed through the doorway. Rose handed the other dog to Brad and scooped Scooby up.

"Hi, hi, hi! Oh, I've missed you," she crooned into his fur.

"Please, sit," suggested Heather. Brad and Rose sat on the couch, each with a dog in their lap. Rose was rubbing Scooby Doo's ears while his tail rapidly slapped the cushion next to them.

"He looks just like the dog I grew up with," she started, "I just didn't know I'd miss him so much."

"He certainly seems to like you," Heather acknowledged.

"I know you'd give him a wonderful home. In fact, I brought this other little dog who's so cute. I didn't send him to the garage sale because he isn't neutered yet, but that's easy, we can pick him up any time for that. If it's the size that's important, they are about the same. Look at those green eyes." Rose rambled on. If Heather had something to say Rose wasn't giving her a chance. Finally she shut up and sat there hugging Scooby Doo, thinking what a ridiculous situation it was.

Heather was sitting in a soft chair facing the couch. "Scooby Doo is really cute," she said. Then she looked at the dog on Brad's lap and asked, "What's that dog's name?"

"He doesn't have a name. We just got him...you could pick one."

"Come here, little guy," Heather said. Brad leaned forward and put the dog on the floor.

"There's nothing wrong with him. It's just that Scooby Doo reminds me of our old dog." Brad squeezed her knee. She couldn't help herself. The other nameless, little dog trotted right over to Heather. She picked him up and he started to lick her face. Thank you, thought Rose.

"Well I guess I could try this little guy out. I've only had Scooby Doo for a few hours but we were doing well. Let's see how it goes with … mmmm…. Nash…that would be a good name for him." She looked at him and tried the name out again.

"Nash." He wagged his tail. "Nash." He wagged his tail. "Oh, you are a cutie." Heather rubbed Nash behind the ears. Rose was so relieved. If she was going to name him she was going to keep him.

"Thank you so much. I really, really appreciate this." Rose said quickly, to firm up her assumption.

"Let's get Scooby Doo home." Brad said, jumping up from the couch. "You and Nash can get to know each other." Heather stood up with Nash still in her arms, and walked them to the door.

"I'll come and check on you in a few days." Rose said, knowing she wouldn't. She wasn't going anywhere near the place. She would send someone else. Heather would have to find her if she wanted Scooby Doo back.

She snuggled with him the entire ride home in the car, feeling just a little guilty, but ultimately really pleased. "We absolutely cannot continue to call him Scooby Doo. It's so obnoxious," she said to Brad. Holding him higher, she put her face close to his. "Let's call him Sol."

Chapter 13
Ariel

Getting three dogs out at the garage sale was a big help. Rose made a point of thanking Gretchen for the suggestion after she shared the story of the Scooby Doo/Nash dog exchange with her. Gretchen, who had spent a lot of time adopting out dogs, appreciated the humor in it more than the others did.

Unfortunately, too soon after those three went out Rose was overcrowded again. They kept coming in faster than they were leaving. And there were also those pups that hadn't been adopted. It was sad to have them grow up in a shelter and as adult dogs they require more space, food, and training. Rose had gone from keeping puppies over the garage to dogs in the sandy area on the ocean side of the house and still more dogs in makeshift kennels next to the driveway. Not only was it crowded but the costs were growing as well.

Cally was still flying into Cancun to pick up dogs. It was no big deal to her. She'd fallen in love with a Mexican man and lived there for two years before Rose moved to the island. The experience gave her insights that other volunteers didn't have but what amazed Rose was that she didn't mention any of that until she had already volunteered for a week and returned to Texas.

Cally was different and difficult: so intelligent, that she was habitually engaged in her own mind. Her reaction time in conversations was so fast that she would be onto the next subject before other people had finished articulating their own responses. Rose suspected that most of the time Cally couldn't hide the fact that people bored her and it inescapably made her unlikable.

The trick to getting along with her was to never take her behavior personally. She was a vet tech and her knowledge and dedication were a gold mine. It made her the perfect way station for Rose's pups and dogs, before they went into new homes in the Texas area. Cally knew what illnesses to look for, how to treat them, and how long it would take. She taught Rose how to deal with "street-dog-specific illnesses," something Rose couldn't learn from most Mexican vets. They weren't paid to take care of the street dogs and taking care of domesticated dogs and cats was a fairly new thing.

Additionally, Rose appreciated Cally's love of and commitment to Mexican dogs. Rose didn't have to keep her happy or make excuses for things. They simply worked alongside each other for their own personal reasons. She had become a member of their newly formed group which had they named 'Amigos de los Animales' and Jennifer had set them up as a non-profit in the USA.

When the number of adult dogs increased so did the different personalities and the frequency of conflicts in the packs. For the first time, the older dogs had to be separated into more than two groups. Yet even then there was still only one pack leader, one king of the castle, and that was Ariel. Ariel was a magnificent mix of black Lab and Greyhound, and he figured things out fast. He was an easy dog to read, but hard to control, and Rose was convinced that he had a great sense of humor.

The wooden gate that kept the dogs from getting onto the street had been poorly built. Like many other things at the house, they'd accepted shoddy construction as the price for an ultimate completion. The gate was warped, too heavy for its hinges, and hadn't closed properly for a long time. Ariel had discovered that if he ran at it, and hit just the right spot, it would pop open. The only defense was to push it tightly closed so that its whole weight sat on the raised cement at the beginning of the driveway. Unfortunately, every once in a while someone would forget to give it that extra push and Ariel would charge, leap, and hit it with all his weight, allowing every dog on that side of the house to escape. Depending on how Rudi had divided the dogs that day, it could be as many as fifteen dogs running for the beach and it was worse when it happened in the middle of the day.

It was always the same, when the pack of dogs arrived, all beach activity was disrupted and small children were immediately snatched from the surf. By the time Rose caught up with the stampede, she'd see people standing, angrily shaking out their beach towels or wrapping up their food. It got worse if the dogs did their business on the beach or lifted their leg on someone's tote bag. Rose could never fault the bathers for being mad.

Fortunately, Rudi and Rose knew these dogs so well they could predict who they'd find together and where they'd be. Ariel was always in the ocean. He was a great swimmer. The sandbars were his favorite, where he could leap like a dolphin over the waves, and it was usually his clowning around that saved the day. They already had everyone's attention, all reading, sleeping or eating had been rudely interrupted. Most people were annoyed, especially the Mexicans, who, at that time, had less patience for dogs.

However, their hostilities were no match for Ariel's sheer joy. He'd leap up and spin around, sometimes falling over when he landed. He would splash water into the air with his nose and try to catch it in his mouth, and then chase his tail until he'd spun into deeper water. He barked at the waves before leaping over them or charging into them. What Rose loved the most about his behavior was that he was alone, charging and leaping for the sheer delight of it. No other dog or human was involved; this was between Ariel and the ocean that he loved.

While people watched Ariel, Rudi would gather up the other dogs as quickly as possible. Rose would stay at the beach until the end of the performance. Roo, Ariel's favored companion, would sit beside Rose and watch the show like everyone else. When Ariel tired, Rose would put him on a leash and take him around to meet people. He could charm the most reluctant spectator. Rose was usually pleasantly surprised by the number of people who wanted to touch him. Even the grumpiest sunbathers were wooed by this beautiful, free loving animal. Possibly it was a reminder of what was available to everyone, if they learned how to access it.

Ariel was at the rescue for a year and a half before a woman came by the house, fell in love with him and his buddy Roo, and adopted them both. Rose was so pleased that the new owner lived in Washington State near the ocean, and that she kept in touch, giving updates and sending pictures. Roo adapted to his new home immediately but Ariel took some time. Being king over only one dog was a big adjustment for him.

Four other big dogs were adopted around the same time as Ariel and Roo, reducing the pack to one manageable group again. After too many escapes Rudi built four more kennels beside the driveway, using old doors, bits of wire fencing and cinderblocks. It was not attractive, but Brad was pleased. There were no dogs in the driveway and he could have the front gate repaired without any "great escapes."

Chapter 14
Pokey

Still, the puppies kept coming in. Rose and Gretchen started to name new litters with themes to help keep the records straight. One family consisted of four males so they named them after the Beatles. Another was found by a bar called 'The White House,' so they were named after Presidents and First Ladies. One little guy came in on his own at the same time, they named him Henry Kissinger. There were the Cars with names like Nissan and VW, and then another litter named after the Gods; that group was skinny and weak, so they thought it would give them a boost to have names like Zeus and Apollo.

The average street puppy was going to grow up to be a light brown, medium-sized dog. Somewhat like a small, skinny Lab with big, pointed, Chihuahua ears. And though this was the norm, it was intriguing to see how the prevailing features changed from year to year.

A few months after Ariel was adopted a young traveler brought a whippet to the island. When he left, he just abandoned the little guy at the beach one day and headed off on his travels. Since the dog was intact, meaning he had all of his male parts, in a few months Rose started to see wiry, Whippet-like puppies.

One of the first whippet litters was born behind a local restaurant. The owner put them in a box and instructed one of his waiters to find Rudi or Rose. She was overjoyed that the locals had started to see her as a solution to their dog problems and were actually bringing her the strays rather than taking them to the dump or an empty lot. Of course, they couldn't figure out what she wanted them for; they just figured she was crazy. Rose didn't care. The fact that they brought them to her was an incredible improvement. It was much better to get the puppies before they starved for three weeks or were bitten by bigger dogs or exposed to illnesses like Parvovirus or Distemper.

When the box of whippet puppies arrived, Rose called Gretchen. "Wait until you see the pups I got today," she told her. "There's one male and two females and they're such an odd mix of grey and beige and white. The little females are so pretty, but the male—wait until you see him, it's like everything went wrong. The dark parts are on his head and legs and the light parts are on his torso. He looks like a dog in a children's drawing, everything slightly askew."

"I'll come over later. Have you got some wine for Jennifer and me?"

"You have to ask?" said Rose.

Jennifer and Gretchen arrived with Jeannie Tull later that day. They'd brought some snacks and Rose supplied them with drinks, and they sat in her courtyard watching the pups play.

"That little male's a bit off the norm, isn't he?" Jeannie said, watching him slink along the walls.

"Let's call the girls Laverne and Shirley," suggested Gretchen. She was on one of the benches and was shaking a toy in front of the puppies who were playing underneath. The two little females were taking turns trying to yank it out of her hand.

"Isn't that a little before your time?" said Rose. She was watching the male, trying to decide if she should pick him up or just let him alone.

"Yeah it is, but it was my mom's favorite show."

"That dates me for sure. I guess I asked for it. I'm at least a little younger than your mom, right?" asked Rose.

"No worries. She's got an easy ten years on you," Gretchen assured her. She'd let one of the female pups snag the toy and the other one was chasing her around the courtyard trying to get it back.

"Rose, you shouldn't worry," said Jeannie, "I love getting older. I'm so much smarter and it's not like I'm losing my figure." Everyone laughed. The little male pup had worked his way around the entire courtyard and settled against the wall next to Jeannie's chair. She looked at him and said, "I think you should call the little tyke Pokey. Look at him, he's got his head down and he's just poking around looking for a place to hide."

Rose couldn't resist any longer. She had to pick him up. He cowered as she approached him but didn't move away. She sat back down and put him on her lap where he remained stiff and standing, so she gently stroked him around the neck. "Pokey it is," she said. "Oh my God, speaking of poking around, you should've seen the pups last night. I swear I almost wet my pants. It was about this time of the day and I took some of the puppies to the beach." Pokey finally sat down and Rose started to stroke his back.

"I just parked myself on that big log near the water and watched them play. One little guy dug a hole in the sand, nice and cool to stretch out in, right? Then something distracted him and another pup lay down in the hole. When the first pup turned around he seemed to forget he'd even dug that hole so he'd dig another one. I watched that pup dig three holes before he finally got to lie in one."

"They are too funny," said Gretchen, who had coaxed the two female pups and the toy onto her lap. Their coloring was so similar that when they curled up together they looked like one dog. "I used to watch them at the store when business was slow, which was probably because the smell was so bad. It's like they have short thoughts, each one a tiny spark that fades fast."

"Oh, I forgot to tell you," said Jeannie tracing a huge flower on the front of her muumuu. "I've got some guests that want to come and help. When should I tell them to come?"

"Any time tomorrow after nine," Rose replied. "Unless you think they are the poop scooping kind, then send them earlier."

Word had spread about the rescue and often tourists liked to volunteer— people who missed their own dogs or dog lovers who volunteered at home and wanted the experience. Some of them were a great help, but unfortunately, many of them took up more time than they were worth. Rose had become wary of such visitors, as the hours that she worked every day grew with the number of dogs she had. Plus, she was always asked the same questions: How long have you been here? Did you build this house? How did you get into the rescue business? How many dogs do you have? And on and on. Rose was tempted to write down the answers and make copies to hand out when people first arrived. However, there were those who returned every year. Rose enjoyed their company, but gradually, as the rescue grew there just weren't enough hours in her day to sit and chat.

Laverne and Shirley were easy to find homes for. Soon after they arrived, Rose had to call the plumber to fix a leak under her sink. When the plumber left he took both of them, one for his brother who lived next door. Rose was happy and confident that these would be good homes.

But she worried that shy, ugly Pokey would have a problem charming someone into adopting him. She was wrong. Within two weeks he'd charmed the hell out of Rose and became their third dog, joining Napoleon, the tiny white puppy from the beach, and Sol, whom they'd repossessed from Heather. Pokey grew up lean and wiry and was glued to Rose's side whenever possible, and when he ran, he went so fast he appeared to defy gravity. Undeniably there was some of that poor, abandoned, whippet in him.

One of the best things about Pokey was that he came to Rose as fast as he could whenever she called. Rose didn't even have to use his name. A quiet whistle, sometimes even a cough would bring him to her side, and for reasons unexplained, all the other puppies would follow. Even the older dogs went wherever he went. This meant that Rose could go for a walk with ten or twelve dogs at a time without any leashes. If Pokey stayed nearby, the rest of them stayed nearby and if Pokey wandered a short distance away the others would allow a little space as well. If Rose saw some threat she would merely whistle and Pokey would be at her side with eleven other dogs in tow.

After the sun went down and the beaches were deserted was the perfect time for walks. Waves would spread high up the sandy slope to cool her toes and tease the puppies. They'd chase the waves in and out and then in again. She knew her life had taken a strange turn. The rescue was not something she'd planned, but those walks replenished her. As she strolled along with her beautiful, discarded dogs in the late afternoon sun she often felt a rush of pleasure and satisfaction.

Pokey went everywhere with her. At times, when walking along the main street Rose could hear people's comments and see the concern in their eyes. "Oh, look at that poor skinny dog," they would say, or "don't they feed the dogs here?" But the truth was that Pokey couldn't keep an ounce of fat on his wiry frame.

It became a problem that Pokey was as agile as he was fast. He could leap over their four-foot rock wall without any trouble at all, so if Rose didn't want him to come out with her, she'd have to lock him in the house.

Pokey was six months old when Brad decided it was time for a few days on the mainland. Island fever was not an unusual condition for people who had not been born there. For some, everything would start to crowd around them in an empty way and the only solution was a trip to the mainland. So they left the house and dogs with Rudi.

When they returned, Rose was pleased and assured once again that Rudi could handle the rescue without her. But Pokey was not happy. He must be put out with me for leaving him behind, Rose thought as she carried him into the house and placed him on the couch. He'll feel better in a few hours. After that, Rose busied herself unpacking and tidying her bedroom until it was time to cook dinner. As she passed through the living room on the way to the kitchen she checked on Pokey. He was still where she'd left him except that his head was hanging off the edge of the seat. He opened his eyes when she got closer, but he didn't move. "Hey, you. Are you okay?" she said. He still didn't move. Rose sat on the chair and lifted him onto her lap. His body was limp. He was watching her, moving his eyes, but the rest of him was motionless.

"What is it?" Rose asked Pokey. He continued to stare at her. She picked him up and hurried into the kitchen to call Paulo.

"I'm not at the clinic, I'm at home, but I can meet you there," Paulo told her.

"You have to hurry. Something's really wrong with him," Rose said. And then she dropped the phone without hanging up, grabbed her purse, and ran outside still clutching Pokey.

"Rudi!" she yelled, rushing towards the gate. "Find me a taxi?" He opened the gate and hurried past her.

Having had no time to put her shoes on, she could feel the gravel digging into her feet as she raced down the road. She'd gone a quarter mile before Rudi pulled up beside her in a taxi. On the way to the clinic Pokey closed his eyes and she thought he'd died. After a gentle shake, he opened them again so Rose talked to him, trying to keep him focused. "Can't you go any faster?" she asked the taxi driver. He simply shook his head, totally indifferent to her situation. In fact, he informed her that he didn't usually allow dogs in his taxi. She ignored him and kept her attention on Pokey.

When they arrived at the clinic Paulo wasn't there. Rose had a key and let herself in after sending Rudi home to feed the rest of the dogs. She paced back and forth in the examining room, talking loudly and occasionally giving Pokey a tight hug. How can this be happening, this is my dog?

"Paulo, where are you?" she said over and over again, trying to create some noise in the far too empty room. Finally Paulo arrived. Rose watched impatiently as he inserted a catheter and started Pokey on fluids.

"What is it?" she pleaded.

"It looks to me like he's been poisoned," he said, checking Pokey's eyes and then gently bending his legs.

"What are you talking about? This is my dog." The possibility of poison had occurred to her in the cab. She'd dismissed it. Pokey had been at the house when they got home. He was not the kind of dog to wander off.

"He must have gotten into something." Paulo said. "We just have to wait. He doesn't seem as stiff as when I first got here."

"God, what if the other dogs got into it?"

Paulo put his hand on her shoulder and said, "He's looking good. I'll stay with him, you go home, check the other dogs."

Pokey opened his eyes when Rose said goodbye so she left feeling positive about his recovery.

"Rudi, was Pokey anywhere different today?" she asked when she got home.

"Si, he's been on the road in front of the gate. I thought he was waiting for you so I left him alone. I'd already kept him in the house for two days."

"Is anyone else sick?" Rose asked.

"I checked when I got back to the house," said Rudi, "and all the other dogs are okay."

It was six o'clock in the evening. Rose went inside and poured herself a glass of wine. She told Brad what had happened and was on her way to call the clinic when the phone rang.

It was Paulo. "Rose," he said, and then he paused. "Pokey died. It was just too late."

She wasn't prepared for this. "NO! It's not possible! NO!" was all she could say. Brad took the phone from her and she stood next to him in a daze. The shock of the news flitted about for a while and then it landed on her chest like a truck, a big Mack truck that was driving over her. She couldn't breathe. She dropped on to the nearest chair, almost missing it entirely. There was something working its way up the back of her throat. It was crawling through her, spreading quickly. Didn't they kill enough dogs?

Dogs are like rats to these people. All the brutality, the callous indifference to suffering animals, everything she'd seen since moving to Mexico joined forces and fueled her fury.

Rose jumped up from the chair and rushed out the door, so mad that she didn't know what she was going to do. "Someone should have stopped me," she admitted to Brad later. She charged barefoot down the road to the nearest group of hotels. She went into the first one and demanded to speak to the owner.

"He's not here," said the startled man behind the counter.

"You liar!" She growled at him. As she headed for the next hotel, she yelled over her shoulder, "He's afraid to come out."

Rose approached the second front desk. "Where is he? Where's Raul?" The poor man behind the counter was clearly shaken. His eyes were wide and she had his full attention.

"He's not here," he said.

"He killed my dog! I will talk to him!"

"He's not here," the man repeated.

"I know he's here, he's always here! He has to face up to what he's done!" A few people had stopped in the front lobby to watch. Everyone could hear the crazy lady in the foyer.

Rose spun around, "They kill dogs here! They poison them!" She spat out at anyone who was listening. "They killed my dog! They poisoned Pokey!" Some of the guests stopped to listen to her and some of them walked around her trying to escape an ugly scene. "They kill all the dogs!" She said again.

Gradually the world around her started to come into focus. Rage that huge was hard to maintain. She was running out of steam. "They killed my dog," she said again, and would have gone on but she felt someone touch her elbow and turned around.

"Come on," said Brad, and he led her out of the building. He walked her along the road towards the house as she cried for Pokey and for all the dogs that had been unwanted, kicked, and poisoned. "We're supposed to take care of them," she said, feeling exhausted.

"We do the best we can." Brad told her. Rose went to bed. She needed her Princes, and they lay with her as she fell asleep. She slept poorly.

The following day they dug a hole next to the driveway and lowered Pokey into it wrapped in a towel. Rose wanted to look at him one more time. He didn't look dead if you didn't look closely. They buried him. Jeanne Tull, Jennifer, Gretchen, Kat, and even Leanora came over. They stood by the grave and talked about Pokey for a while and then everyone went home.

A few hours later Rudi came into the kitchen and told Rose that someone was at the gate and wanted to talk to her. "Not now," she said, but he persisted, saying that she'd better go down and see. So she dragged her thousand-pound body to the front gate and opened the door. It was the hotel owners, of course. Oh, where's Brad? She thought. Then she remembered that he'd gone to the store. There were three hotels, three owners, and all of them were standing in the open sandy area outside her gate.

"Please come out here and talk to us," one of them said stiffly.

"Why don't you come in," said Rose, feeling guilty about her outburst the night before.

"No, we can talk here," said Raul. "You've insulted us. Accused us of poisoning dogs. We have a business here. You can't come to the hotels and behave like that."

"You poisoned my dog," she said, starting to cry.

"We didn't poison your dog. I don't know what happened." Raul said, totally unfazed by Rose's tears.

If I look weak he'll just feel more power, thought Rose. She tried to stop crying but couldn't keep her chin from quivering as she talked. "Yes you did, that's what you do. I'm trying to help the dogs. You don't need to poison them."

"We didn't poison your dog." One of the other owners said. Rose couldn't remember his name. "The dogs are a problem. They scare people at night when they're returning to the hotels. Something has to be done."

"So you poison them. I know you do it, that's the way you've always done it." It was hard to talk and it was getting harder to breath normally.

"You can't come to our hotel yelling like that, acting like some sort of crazed dog lady." Raul repeated angrily. Perhaps he expected an apology but she knew they'd done it. They all knew that, it wasn't the point. She was a foreigner, this was their country and she'd made a big scene over something of no importance to them. "I come from a very powerful family," said Raul, standing taller. The other owners nodded as if to assure Rose it was true. "I could have you deported for such behavior." Rose hadn't expected this, and the threat temporarily replaced her sorrow with outrage.

"What are you talking about? You can have me deported for yelling at your stupid hotel and no one cares who's killing innocent dogs?"

Oh my god, she thought. This is useless. She knew she couldn't change them but making enemies wasn't going to help either.

"I'm sorry I created a scene," she said. "I was upset, my dog had just died. You can't poison the dogs, it's cruel." The men just looked at her as if she hadn't said anything. "There are other ways to do this."

"Why don't you help with the children on the island? There are lots of children that need help," suggested Raul, with condescension.

"Why don't you help us with the dogs?" she said, raising her voice. They think I'm stupid, she thought. Stay calm. "We want to solve the problem. You don't have to poison them." The look on his face only reminded her further that their cultural differences were mutually unbendable. He could no more understand her love for the dogs than she could fathom kicking one.

"I'm aware of the problem," said Raul. "I donated the electrocution machine to the island for the street dogs." The other owners nodded, acknowledging this as a generous contribution.

Rose started to cry again. That gap between them was too enormous. How could she ever close it? Overwhelmed by Raul's last comment, she' dropped her face into her hands and wept. Pictures from the movies, with criminals shaking and screaming in the electric chair were making her feel sick. Luckily, Brad arrived at that moment.

The hotel owners liked Brad. She knew they wondered how he could have married such a loony. Rose had had enough and went into the house. She poured a small glass of water, carried it into her room and used it to take a Valium. She lay in bed waiting for nothingness while Brad smoothed things over with Raul.

Lying there, she decided that they wouldn't be able to deport her. She would have to get out of bed to be deported and she was going to lie there forever with the covers over her head. She imagined the Princes on either side of her. She needed them. This had to matter to somebody.

Finally she drifted off and sat on the beach with itzamna. Ek chauh was digging a hole in the sand. Beside him was pokey and four other dogs. They were wrapped in wire and they were dead. One wire came away from each dog and converged with the rest before running along the shore to raul's hotel.

"I can't fight this," rose told itzamna. "It's too much."

"Yes, you can." Itzamna was sitting in front of rose with his back to ek chauh, staring straight at her with his sad brown eyes. "There are as many levels of compassion as there are souls on this planet."

"But there's no compassion here," said rose. She turned her head and noticed the wires and started to cry.

"You can do this," said itzamna. He moved over and lay next to her. Rose rolled on her side and continued to weep as she watched Ek chauh roll each dog into the hole, pushing them along the sand with his nose. The wires had disappeared. "We can't let the bad people win."

Some of the staff at the hotel were sympathetic. One of them confessed to Rudi that he'd seen another hotel worker mixing poison into ground beef. Rose didn't need to hear it to know it was true, but it was good to hear it anyway.

After that day, Rose slowly realized that something good actually came out of Pokey's death. There were no poisonings for a long time. She didn't think that the owners had grown a conscience; it was the aftermath they couldn't handle.

Chapter 15
Making Them Pay Attention

News of Pokey's death circulated quickly as most things do on a small island. Rose thought that people were probably surprised. They would assume 'The Dog Lady' should know how to protect her animals, especially her own dogs. Calls of support from friends and people she'd worked with offered some relief, but she wasn't able to return to her normal routines.

The first week after the poisoning Rose didn't leave the house. She surrounded herself with the dogs during the day and at night she went to bed early. Brad left her alone but Rose was aware that there would be a time limit.

As the mind-aching fog slowly lifted, she started to feel moderately functional and decided to talk. Brad suggested that they sit in the courtyard so they went outside and down the stairs.

Rose settled back into one of the deck chairs and closed her eyes. Brad sat upright on one of the cement benches ready to listen. "I'm willing to do the work," she started. "I need space and time without sorrow. I can't handle the brutality and stay focused at the same time. It takes too much energy to keep the heartache of it all under control." Rose waited for Brad to say something. When he didn't, she continued. "It's easier to process a personal act of cruelty, still disgusting, but random; but in this case the poisonings and electrocutions are an attitude and way of life of this community."

Brad stood up and watched some of the pups in the corner. "What should we do about it?" he asked. Rose smiled. Brad didn't participate in most of the rescue work but there was always a "WE" when he spoke of it.

"I'm working on it," she said. "I have an idea. I need to get Jennifer to help me translate." Rose swung her legs over the side of the lounge so she was facing Brad. "I'm thinking of making a poster. Poisoning dogs is illegal but difficult to prove. At least I can make people think about it. It was the princes who suggested it." Rose was grinning at her husband. She knew she was about to share something that would make her look insane.

"What are you talking about?" Brad looked confused.

"Well, I haven't told you about my princes, but maybe it's time I should introduce you."

Brad looked to one side like there was someone there who would agree that Rose had finally gone nuts.

"Oh, don't look like that. They're dogs. I read about them in a legend. Two brothers. Itzamna is the older brother and he's golden brown with white fur around the neck. Ek Chauh is black and they're built like big powerful greyhounds." Rose put her hand out to indicate their height. Now that she'd started this she needed to tell Brad in a way that could help him appreciate them the way she did. "When I'm really overwhelmed or sad or confused they give me comfort. I can see them next to me, they help me work out answers. Sometimes I feel so alone in this. I know it sounds crazy but I need the company."

"I'm always here. Rose, you can always talk to me." Brad sat back down on the bench. He looked hurt.

"I know that, but you don't want to hear all the details. It's just a way of working things through, because more and more, it's all up to me. Other people help, they care, they volunteer, but somehow, this has all been brought to me." Brad was about to say something but Rose held up her hand. "I know, I brought it on myself, I'm not blaming anyone. No one's making me do this. In fact, I'm not sure where all this enthusiasm has come from. I don't know why I care so much, I just do."

Brad's cell phone rang. He looked at it, pressed something and put it back in his pocket, then signaled for Rose to go on. "I've asked Kat how she feels about the rescue work. She says she just doesn't like to see animals suffer, but for me it's more than that." Rose was quiet for a moment. She was trying to come up with an example. "Okay, here's a shocker. I know that you hate it when someone knocks on the door around dinner time or after, but secretly, and again, I can't explain it, there's a part of me that hopes they're bringing me a puppy I can help."

"That's what you're thinking when I'm pissed off about the interruption. Shit, I really don't get it." Brad stood up and moved into the other deck chair. He made a big deal about it like this information just made him too tired.

"Oh, stop being so dramatic. I don't mean I want puppies arriving every day, I'm just telling you how I feel sometimes. See, I really do need the princes. They understand." Brad shook his head and raised his arms in defeat. "Okay, so maybe this wasn't the best time to tell you about them. I know you've been watching me. I'm not going nuts. They're in my head, but I need them. They support me when I'm down and they listen to me when I need to think, and they care as much as I do."

"This is pretty weird," said Brad, making circles with his finger around his right ear.

"Oh no, it isn't. You know exactly what I mean. You're just trying to make it look like I'm crazy. I've seen you muttering away to yourself. Who are you talking to?" Rose sat back in her chair and pulled her knees up to her chest.

"Okay, I get it, but its bit overboard."

"Probably," said Rose. "But look at our life."

"So now I know who you're talking to when you mumble. But if they start sleeping in our bed, that's when I draw the line."

"They already do," said Rose grinning broadly. She wasn't going to let him completely off the hook. He wasn't that straight. Moving to Mexico in the first place wasn't exactly a logical thing to do in most people's eyes.

Jennifer was happy to help with the poster. They worked on it together. In big letters at the top it said, "PARENTS BEWARE." Under that was a skull and crossbones. It was solid black and consequently visible from a distance. Underneath, it said that someone was putting out poison to kill the animals and it was a threat to children who played in the community. Rose had initially written that the poison spread deep into the environment as other birds, iguanas, mice, etc., ate the poisoned carcasses, but Jennifer thought that was too much information for one poster and Rose finally agreed.

Jennifer, Gretchen and Rose plastered the center of town with posters. They put them everywhere, using duct tape so they would be secure. They put three per bench in the square between the church and the government buildings, and taped one and sometimes two on every electrical pole running along the main shopping area. They were careful to post on public properties only so no individual would feel targeted. Anything that was maintained by the government got a poster—street signs, garbage cans, even the playground equipment in the park. No one could go downtown and miss it. Afterwards they sat at an open bar downtown and watched people's reactions.

"Everyone's looking at them," said Rose.

"It looks like they're reading them, too," said Jennifer, noting the amount of time that people spent in front of the posters.

"More people can read now. The island's definitely developing a middle class," said Jennifer, sipping a cold dripping beer.

"It's the new jobs," said Gretchen. "All the new hotels and restaurants.

"We have three people working at the book shop and tons of other new businesses have opened up in the last five years, right?"

"Okay, so what does a 'middle class Isla Mujeres,' look like?" asked Rose.

"It has to do with the walls of their house," said Jennifer. "If the walls are strong enough to hold a hammock that means it's not a hut. At least that's what someone told me."

"And the family would probably own a scooter, right?" said Rose, and then she saw something across the street that made her jump to her feet. "Look at that," she said. "That guy ripped down our poster."

"Sit." Gretchen said, touching Rose's chair. "It's going to happen. Maybe he's taking it home to show people."

"Oh sure," said Rose as she sat back down at the table. She swept her hair up and readjusted the clip on the top of her head. She couldn't stand the feeling of hair on the back of her neck when it was hot, and it bothered her more when she was stressed.

"Did I tell you I saw a family of five on a moto last week? Incredible," said Gretchen, trying to distract Rose.

"How about the ones with that wooden stool in the front and the rest of the family crammed on the seat behind it? All without helmets?" Rose said.

"Believe it or not, helmets are mandatory," said Jennifer.

"Oh yeah," said Rose, "I think they have a long way to go with that one. Have you seen the helmets they use? I saw a guy with a plastic bowl on his head; he'd made holes in it for the chin strap." Normally Rose might have found this amusing but today she was irritated.

A long silence followed her words. The bitterness in Rose's voice had changed the atmosphere. Finally Gretchen turned to her and asked, "How're you feeling?"

"I think I'm still pissed off at the whole island over Pokey." Rose looked uncomfortable and then stood up. "Sorry, I'd better go. You guys watch out for our posters, okay?"

"Stay," said Gretchen, touching her arm. "Finish your drink, anyway." Reluctantly Rose sat back down in her chair.

"By the way, did a family come to see you about some pit bulls?" asked Gretchen.

Rose stopped staring at the posters and turned to Gretchen. "Oh that," she said. "Rudi made me go down to the gate, something about pit bulls. I reminded him that we can't take pit bulls, but he insisted. He said that it was an older couple and I should talk to them."

"I didn't know that you felt that way about pit bulls," said Jennifer.

"Don't get me wrong," said Rose. "I actually think pit bulls are some of the most loving dogs, but the ones I get are so messed up and I'm not a dog trainer. If a poodle gets into a fight with another dog, it's not a big deal, but if a pit bull does, it can be a disaster. I have to protect the dogs I already have." Rose took a sip of her Diet Coke. "Sometimes I think that Rudi believes I can do anything to help any dog, or maybe he just wanted to distract me. I know he's been worried since Pokey died."

"So what happened?" asked Gretchen.

"They were outside the gate, a tall, older guy with really thick glasses and his wife, who was about half his height and twice his width. His wife did the talking. She told us her husband had lost his job and she was having health problems and they couldn't afford to take care of their two pit bulls, Pinky and Terry. Two huge pit bulls named Pinky and Terry. Can you believe it? The whole time she was talking both the husband and wife were struggling with one of the dogs. Each one had a rope around its neck, and it was obvious they'd never been leash trained. Finally Rudi tied the male to a tree so we could talk."

Rose leaned forward in her chair. "Look at that, there are four people looking at the poster."

"They're definitely noticing it. I think it's the skull and crossbones that catches their attention." The group wandered off and Rose continued her story.

"These dogs were huge. Their heads were the size of basketballs, and surprise—neither of them was sterilized. I asked them if they could keep one of the dogs, and they told me they had Pinky's puppy at home, and that was all they could handle. So I asked them who the father was and the woman told me it was Terry. She'd already told me that Pinky and Terry were litter mates and it didn't seem to bother her at all. I'm thinking, great, inbred pit bulls." Rose dropped both of her hands on the table to illustrate her frustration.

"Anyway, Rudi asked the couple about spaying and neutering the dogs. They agreed, so he went inside to get a crate and forced it into the trunk my car. It barely fit."

"So, did you get them spayed and neutered?" asked Gretchen. She had pushed herself away from the table and draped one arm over the back of her chair.

"Not right then," said Rose. "When we put Terry in the crate and the couple started to walk away, he went berserk. I mean barking, and crying, and chewing on the crate. He was going to ruin it, so I yelled at them to come back. The husband let Terry out of the crate and then crouched down and hugged him. I mean, it was sad, these dogs needed to stay with this family. So I offered them food for the dogs…"

"Oh, you didn't. You'll have every dog owner on the island coming to you," Jennifer said. "I'm going to get another beer; do you want anything?"

"Why don't we get some wine?" Gretchen suggested to Rose.

"Sure, why not?"

Jennifer ordered the drinks and then turned back to Rose. "Tell me you didn't offer to buy them food."

"Just wait!" said Rose, holding her hand up. "I told them that there was a group in the US that will help feed animals in dire situations. I said that I can only set it up for two families and they were the second family. Anyway, the wife was so happy she started to cry. So that was it. They were overjoyed. I think it was the right thing to do. The taxi they'd come in had waited, and the wife got in first and called Pinky. Pinky probably weighed as much as the woman did, but the dog jumped in the taxi and crawled up on top of the lady and buried her huge basketball head under the woman's chin. Pinky whimpered while the woman cried. I've never seen anything like it."

"Unbelievable," said Gretchen. "How did they fit the husband and the other dog in?"

"The cab had to come back for the husband and Terry," said Rose, leaning back while the waiter placed glasses of wine in front of her and Gretchen. Rose lifted her glass. "Here's to the pit bull family. They made me feel better."

They clinked their wine glasses with Jennifer's bottle of beer. "I mean, think of it. I didn't take any dogs in. I just had to buy a little more food, and I saw people who truly loved their animals. There are all sorts of different ways to help. We just need to figure it out, and I really needed something positive like that."

The three women sat back, sipped their drinks and shared the good feeling the story imparted.

"What would you do without Rudi?" Gretchen asked, breaking the silence.

"I don't know. He's made so much of this possible. He just has a way with the dogs. He told me that he has an older brother who's retarded." Jennifer winced and started to say something, but Rose interrupted her, "I know, politically incorrect, but those are Rudi's words. Anyway, he said that no one ever talked about it. They didn't send him to school. He was just there, part of the family, the way he was. Rudi said that he had to watch out for him. His name was Giermo. He told me that the hardest part was Giermo was so much bigger than him and when he got frustrated he used to beat up on Rudi and Rudi was never allowed to fight back. I think it taught him a sort of patience, an understanding that most people wouldn't have at his age."

"How old is Rudi?" Jennifer asked.

"He was fifteen when we built the house, so he's eighteen now. Imagine, he hasn't been home since he started," said Rose. "Rudi's has also told me about the farm people in his community and how they see dogs completely differently—not like pets, but they're treated well. He doesn't like what he sees here, how people treat the animals."

Jennifer sat straight up in her chair, "Look," she said, "Someone's taking a picture of our posters."

The next morning Rose passed the square after buying coffee and was disappointed to see that every poster had been taken down in the night. When she got home, Brad was waiting for her in the courtyard.

"You did it," he said the minute she walked in.

"They took down all the posters," said Rose. "Can you believe that?"

"It doesn't matter."

"What do you mean it doesn't matter? I wanted everyone to see them."

"Look at this. It's in the paper, the 'Por Esto'. There's a big picture of the posters on the bench right on the front page." Brad held the paper in front of Rose's face. "You did it," he said. "You made them all see it. Fantastic!" Brad gave Rose a big bear hug; they stayed that way for a while. It all felt good to Rose.

That night she dreamt she was on the beach with the Princes. As usual, Itzamna, was sitting next to her, and Ek Chauh was playing in the waves with Pokey. It was so good to see him. More dogs kept joining them until there were at least twenty.

Itzamna sat up next to Rose. He was taller than all the other dogs, and was obviously watching each one closely. These weren't dogs that Rose knew, but she felt safe. Soon the beach was covered with dogs and she still felt safe. Itzamna told her that they knew she could help.

Chapter 16
The King

Rose knew that her reputation as a crazy dog lady was spreading. The islanders were asking for more help, but really couldn't figure out why she did what she did. Even when she went to the bank, the teller would ask, "Are you 'The Rose,' who takes care of all the dogs?"

Rose always replied, "Yes, do you want one?" But she didn't mean it. She rarely gave her dogs to islanders anymore. She suspected that she'd already saturated all the responsible pet owners. She kept track of her dogs that lived on the island, and was thrilled when the owners came back to her for parasite medicine, shampoo, tick and flea preventions, and vaccinations. It was an added bonus when adopting one of her animals; she would do everything she could to help them take care of their dogs properly. She also insisted that they bring the dog back to her if the owner's situation changed. That way they always had an out if it got to be too much. Once a dog came through Rose's gate it was her dog forever. Even when they had wonderful homes in the US or Canada, they were still her dogs. She wanted pictures and updates for the rest of their lives.

Her adult dog population continued to grow. Often an island family would come to the house and say that their neighbor didn't want their dog anymore. Or sometimes people would admit it was their own dog but they couldn't keep it because someone in the household had suddenly become allergic. One of the most incredible reasons that people gave up their dogs was due to doctor's orders because a wife or daughter was pregnant. At first Rose didn't believe that the doctors actually said this, but she found out that some of them really did. Not that it mattered—if they didn't want their dog, Rose didn't want them to have it. She knew that once a dog was abused, it was never the same again. She'd seen the head ducking and tail between the legs too often.

More of the Islanders and tourists were bringing animals directly to Rose. One tourist showed up in tears, clutching a little black ball of fur wrapped in a towel. The hurt and shock on her face reminded Rose of the way she'd felt when she was tending to that first truly pitiful pup in recovery at the spay and neuter clinic.

"Why don't you tell me where you found the pup, while I give it a bath and a checkup?" suggested Rose, gently touching the towel. The tourist was reluctant to let her little rescue go.

"That would be wonderful. Do you have time?" she said, finally handing over her treasure. "My name is Denise," she announced, following Rose along the driveway and into the courtyard.

"I always have time for puppies." Rose replied, collecting clean towels and shampoo on the way. She had a special washing corner where the sun would shine long into the afternoon. "Poor thing's so skinny," Rose said as the water flattened the pup's fur and revealed a clear definition of her backbone and ribs. "So, tell me how you found her."

Denise sighed. "Well, my husband and I have rented a small apartment halfway down the island. We're trying to learn Spanish and wanted to stay where we would be with locals rather than English-speaking tourists. This morning I was on a walk when I noticed a woman sweeping the sidewalk. She kept sweeping the same area over and over which was what caught my attention." Denise paused, stunned at the size of the tick that Rose extracted from the pup's ear.

"As I got closer, I realized that she was sweeping a puppy off the sidewalk. At first, the puppy thought it was a game and kept returning for another sweep but soon it was obvious that the sweeping was for real. The old woman was giving the little thing a harder whack each time, like unwanted garbage. So I asked her if I could have it. I swear she gave me the strangest look, as if she didn't know what I was talking about. I mean, I know my Spanish is bad but I'm pretty sure that I said it right. After I picked the puppy up, she just kept sweeping like the two of us didn't exist. So I took the pup to the bookstore and they told me to bring her here."

Rose knew she would have to explain the local attitude. "It's very sad." Rose was using the corner of the towel to wipe the blood out to the puppy's ear where the tick had been attached. "The islanders, especially the older islanders, are afraid of dogs. They see them as dirty, tick and flea infested, and unpredictable. But, also you have to remember that these people grew up with packs of wild dogs, and instead of taking the chance that an unknown dog might be friendly, they've simply rejected them all.

You've seen these people walking with large sticks and rocks to defend themselves against the dogs." Denise nodded. "The older dogs will take off when someone nearby just raises their arm. I've even had an old woman throw rocks at my rescue dogs when I was walking a group of five. She probably didn't think that all five dogs could possibly be with me." Rose started massaging the shampoo into the pup's fur. "It has to stay on for at least five minutes to kill all the ticks and fleas," she explained.

"I've noticed how skittish the street dogs are. Self-preservation I guess, right?" asked Denise.

"Yup. Those are the ones that survive. This one probably wouldn't have, if you hadn't found it." Denise seemed pleased to hear this.

"What'll you do with her?" Denise asked, as they watched the puppy sliding around on the wet soapy tiles.

"Well first, what should we call her?" Rose said.

Denise stared at the puppy's face for a minute. "How about Bella?"

"That's great," agreed Rose, not mentioning how many Bellas there were on the island already. It was one of the more popular dog's names. "I'll keep her upstairs tonight, de-worm her and give her some good food. I'm sure she'll feel better in the morning."

Denise stood up and started to pace back and forth across the courtyard. "Do you think," she finally said, "I mean, if I checked and it was okay, that, maybe, we could babysit her for a while, you know, like at our little place, here?"

Yes! Thought Rose. "You'll have to check with the people you're renting from. If it's okay with them, it's okay with me. I always need foster homes." Denise held Bella while Rose rinsed her off and then picked up the towel. While Denise rubbed the pup dry, Rose cleaned up the bathing station. After that they gave Bella some food and sat together on a bench watching her eat.

"I probably should be getting back," said Denise.

Rose stood up and said, "Why don't you find out if you can foster the pup and let me know?"

That was usually how a tourist adopted a dog from the island. Rarely did they foster an animal and not take it home with them, unless they lived in Europe with long quarantine restrictions. Denise came back the next day with her husband and the good news that her landlord had agreed to allow them to have the pup. Rose gave them dog dishes, a leash and collar, some food, and a few puppy toys. They were so happy, and it was a relief for Rose not to have one more puppy. Better yet, she knew more space was about to be freed up. Cally was arriving the next day, and this time she was bringing a group of helpers.

Cally had asked Rose if she could bring some vet tech students to her house. She enjoyed introducing the students to Mexico and teaching them how to work at spay and neuter clinics. Usually Cally went into smaller communities overlooked by the more established animal welfare groups. That was actually where Rose had met her. She and Brad had been visiting friends in a small town outside of Merida and heard that someone was setting up a clinic nearby. Of course, Rose wanted to see what was going on and when they arrived, Cally mentioned she was shorthanded. They'd stayed two extra days so Rose could volunteer through the end of the clinic.

On this trip, Cally and her group had already been working in a small town named San Cosme and were stopping by for two nights at Rose's before their flight back to Houston. The students planned to sleep on inflated mattresses in the courtyard and then help Cally do wellness checks on Rose's dogs and puppies.

There were four students, all women. One of them had produced a foot pump and they were taking turns inflating their mattresses. Cally, forever the teacher, was talking to them about a dog they'd seen on the way to the house. "I think she had a TVT (Transmissible Venereal Tumors)," Cally was explaining. "We didn't see that in San Cosme because it's so isolated, but it's sexually transmitted and when it gets into an area with unaltered dogs, it spreads quickly."

"Is there a cure?" asked one of the students.

"Yes, but it's expensive and the animals have to be crated during treatment. Spaying and neutering's the answer. If they aren't sexually active, they won't get it and if it goes untreated, it keeps growing until it kills the animal."

"I've been watching a beautiful dog with a TVT dying slowly for months," said Rose. "In fact, I was going to ask you to look at him."

"Is he bad?" asked Cally.

"Yeah, he's bad." Rose said.

"Where is he now?" Cally asked over her shoulder as she bent down to help one of her students unhook one mattress from the pump and hook up the next one.

"Have you seen the wooded area, just down the road across from the sandy field?" said Rose, pointing in that direction.

"You mean at the back of the market?" asked one of the students, who had just sat down after taking her turn with the foot pump.

"That's right," said Rose. "Where the little stores are, and the tortilla factory. The student nodded. "Well, the dumpsters out back are a great source of food for the strays. I love it, because lots of the dogs hang around there and I can keep an eye on them. The largest male has been the leader of that pack for years. He's so handsome, or he was." Rose paused for a minute thinking about the dog. "His coat was this beautiful golden tan, and he has a band of long, white fur around his neck and down his chest. I've seen his coloring come through in so many of my puppies, but we could never catch him. He's regal, strong, and handsome, or he was, so I named him King. I used to think that he was a perfect example of survival of the fittest."

By now all the students had finished with the foot pump and were emptying out their back packs.

"Whenever I walked to town and back, and passed behind the market, I'd give every stray I saw a visual checkup, and I'd talk to them. I wanted them to get used to me in case they ever needed help." Rose leaned back on her lounge chair and put her legs up. "About three months ago I noticed that King had an open sore near his testicles. I'm always checking on testicles, seeing who needs to be neutered. Sick, right? Anyway, after that I kept an eye on the sore, hoping he'd been in a fight and that it wasn't a TVT but I knew it was. Over the last few months I've been watching my King disintegrate." Rose took a deep breath and readjusted her hair clip. "I knew there was nothing I could do, even if I could catch him. There was no way I could cage him for weeks of treatment. You just can't keep a feral dog like him in a crate for that long." The students had stopped what they were doing and were listening to Rose.

"God, it's been awful to watch. He's just slowly wasting away. He's getting skinnier by the day and his shiny fur is dull and dry."

"Where is he?" asked Sydney, the oldest student.

"He's around. He's just skin and bones. I don't think he has long to live." Rose got up and headed for the stairs. "Come on," she said. "I've made a lasagna."

The next morning while Rose was poaching some chicken for a sick pup, one of the students knocked on her kitchen door. She appeared agitated.

"They sent me to get you." she said, breathing heavily.

"Who sent you?" Rose asked, wiping her hands on a dish towel. "What's up?"

"A woman named Gretchen caught a big dog on the beach. She said it's King, and she sent me to see what you wanted to do." The student was wiping sweat off of her forehead with her sleeve. "We were just walking by and saw a group of people standing around something on the sand."

"I knew it would be soon, but… today? Tell them to wait. I'll be there as fast as I can." Rose rushed into her bedroom, she needed syringes and the euthanasia drug that Paolo had insisted she keep in case a dog was clearly dying and he was off the island.

A small crowd had gathered around King. The dog was on his side with a rope around his neck. Rose nodded to Gretchen who was sitting by King's head. She knelt in the sand next to Gretchen and removed the rope from his neck. She could see the tumor; it was bigger and looked like cauliflower.

"What should we do?" Gretchen asked.

"Let's not move him." Rose stroked his neck. "But we just can't let him suffer any more."

"I'll do it," said Cally. Rose handed her the solution and the needles.

King didn't flinch when Cally probed for a vein. She found it quickly and drew back on the needle. Blood flooded into the syringe. She looked at Rose. There was no changing her mind once the euthanasia solution was injected.

"Go ahead," said Rose, stroking his head. Cally slowly emptied the syringe and King closed his eyes for the last time. But his heart was still beating. It took one more dose before his kingly heart would give up.

Rose sat with him for a while before she laid his head in the sand and went to her car. She drove to the south point where she could be alone and watch the turquoise waves break into foam on the shore. Then she let herself cry. She hated crying; once she started, all the backed-up pain shoved its way forward, demanding its own bucket of tears. Rose cried for every dog that suffered and every sad story that she kept to herself.

That evening she went to bed early and hoped she wouldn't wake up for twenty-four hours. As she lay there waiting for sleep she gathered her princes around her. With Itzamna on her right, she realized that she'd imagined him to look so much like King. It made perfect sense—he was the older brother, the one who always knew what she should do. And Ek Chauh on the other side, smaller and younger, not as serious. "I'm not strong enough for this," she told Itzamna.

"You're tougher than you used to be. Lean on me," he said, stretching his neck out so she could nestle her head into his white collar. "You are me," he said. "We can do this together."

Chapter 17
Some Comic Relief

Rose struggled for days with the death of King. Happening so soon after losing Pokey, it felt like the losses were piling up. Brad had tried to cheer her up but stopped, discouraged, after a few attempts.

"I'm sorry, Brad," she told him. "I know I'm not much fun these days. I just need a bit of time."

"Why don't you call Kat and take her to lunch? She's always annoying enough to cheer you up," he said.

"All she wants to talk about is Greer. It was probably a good thing that he didn't arrive until the end of that clinic or both of them would have been useless. You should see them together." Rose gave Brad a hug.

"Ah, long distant relationships, coming and going, sex and desire. That's just what you need." Brad patted her on the behind. Rose smacked him on the arm and laughed for the first time in days. "Seriously," he said. "What are you going to do today, Rose? I really think you need to get out."

"I just don't feel like it. Everybody's watching me too closely." Rose shivered like it gave her the jitters.

"Well then—" They were interrupted by the phone ringing. Rose picked it up.

"Hey Rose, its Gretchen."

"I can recognize your voice," said Rose irritably.

"How are you?"

"I'm fine, I'm just fucking fine." Rose rolled her eyes. "I just need everyone to stop asking me that."

There was a pause on the phone. "Okay," said Gretchen. "How about a little dog rescue?" Rose didn't say anything so Gretchen continued. "I'm visiting some friends over by the navy base and there's a dog on the street. I've asked around and it doesn't appear to belong to anybody."

"Ha, that's what they all say. They never belong to anybody."

Gretchen paused again. Rose held the phone away from her ear and took a deep breath.

"My friend's never seen this dog before," said Gretchen. "It just showed up and sleeps on the street all day. It's not very big."

"Is it friendly?" said Rose.

"We haven't approached it. I mean, this dog is dirty."

"Are you still there now?"

"Yeah, I'll be here all morning," said Gretchen.

"Okay, give me half an hour. Keep an eye on the dog and call me if it takes off." Rose put down the phone and looked at Brad. "Okay," she said, "I'm going out." Brad gave her a thumbs-up.

She went to the garage and selected a medium-sized crate and then loaded it with the fire-place gloves that Brad had bought her. He'd assured her that they were so thick no dog could bite through them but

Rose complained that she couldn't bend her fingers, either. After that she loaded a towel, leash and collar, a can of dog food, and some baby wipes into the crate.

It was a short walk. She headed south past the church and the government buildings that walled in two sides of an open square in the middle of downtown. It was the same classic design used in most of the older towns of Mexico. When she crested the hill on the other side of the square she spotted the dog right away. Gretchen and her friend were sitting on the curb watching it sleep. It looked like the dirty end of a mop.

"Is that the dog?" asked Rose, sitting herself on the curb next to them.

"Yup." Gretchen said.

"Have you given it any food or water?"

"Nope, we just called you. We were afraid it might run off if we approached it."

"Okay, Gretchen, how about you circle around the dog with the crate and I'll come up behind it?" Rose caught the amused look on Gretchen's face. Here they were again.

"I think it's good that we've had practice and the dogs are getting smaller, right?" Gretchen chuckled.

"At least the dogs are getting smaller and I brought these stupid gloves. Brad got them for me. He said he liked me better with arms and hands."

"Okay, then you do the grabbing," Gretchen said, and they both stood up.

"Yeah, but you have to make sure to close the door right away," said Rose. As they approached the dog it still didn't move. It didn't even look up when they gathered around it. Gretchen slowly walked around by its head and Rose came up from behind. After putting on her gloves she nodded to Gretchen to open the door and hold the crate in place. When Gretchen was ready, Rose grabbed the pile of dirty fur in the middle and tossed it into the kennel. The poor dog yelped in fear but the whole thing was over in seconds.

"That was perfect," grinned Gretchen. "We're getting better."

Gretchen's friend drove them to the clinic in her golf cart, where Paulo pronounced the dog undernourished and probably suffering from Ehrlichia (bacterial infection caused by tick bites) and an ear infection. It turned out that the dog was easy to handle. He hadn't needed to be grabbed. He sat happily in Gretchen's lap while Paulo put together the medicine the dog needed.

Clipping and bathing him later that day, Gretchen discovered a poodle under all that filthy fur. He was lethargic and scared, but he ate well and endured the usual pills and shots without a fuss.

Gretchen named him Pepe La Peu because of a beige stripe down the middle of his back. She took charge of his care, which was unusual. "I found him," she told Rose defensively when she came through the gate for the third day straight. Pepe stood on his hind legs spinning and dancing with enthusiasm when he saw her, so she picked him up and let him lick her face. Rose thought the whole thing was funny. She'd seen Gretchen with lots of dogs but had never seen her take such a personal interest. And the face licking. Gretchen usually hated that.

Gretchen never missed a day. She would play with Pepe for a while and then knock on Rose's kitchen door begging her to watch something new that Pepe did.

"You think everything that dog does is brilliant," teased Rose, who still couldn't get over Gretchen's enthusiasm.

"No, no, this is really something," she'd say. "This little guy is different."

"Obviously," Rose muttered under her breath. When they got down stairs, Rose was glad to see that Brad was home. He and Rudi were watching Pepe roll Rudi's soccer ball with his front paws while he walked along on his back legs.

"He does the same thing with the wheelbarrow when I use it," Rudi told them. "He gets so excited. He pushes his way between me and the tub and puts his paws up like he's helping to push it."

"And he's got more tricks." Gretchen turned to Rudi, "Get the baby carriage."

"Where'd that come from?" asked Rose, looking at a rusty, old doll pram.

"Rudi says he found it in a pile of garbage and was going to fix it up for a friend's little girl." Pepe raced over when he saw Rudi put the pram on the driveway. He jumped up, put his paws on the horizontal handle bar, and then pushed it to the end of the driveway. He was stuck there until Rudi turned the carriage around so Pepe could push it back the other way.

"He's like a circus dog," said Gretchen proudly. She picked him up and held him tight while he licked her face.

"Maybe you're right," said Brad. "When was the last time the circus came to town?"

"I don't know, let's see. That was a while ago," said Gretchen.

"How long?" Rose said, counting backwards.

"It was four or five months ago," said Rudi grinning. "I went twice."

"Well, if the circus left five months ago, that would've given Pepe time to get as dirty and matted as he was," said Rose. "We've had him here for almost three weeks. The timing's perfect. I mean, I've got to admit this is unusual."

"Well then, where has he been all this time?" Gretchen asked, putting him back on the ground.

"Someone probably took him in," Rose said. "But when he started to get so dirty and matted they didn't want him anymore and threw him in the street. I bet they live close to where we found him."

"Well, they're not getting him back," said Gretchen, "now that he's all cleaned up and so handsome."

The next day Rose asked around, trying to find someone other than Rudi who'd gone to the circus. Rudi admitted that he'd missed most of the show; he was there to see the cowboys. Eventually she found someone who'd confirmed what she already suspected—there'd been a small poodle pushing things around. The dog had worked with one of the clowns, but they couldn't confirm that Pepe had a stripe down his back because he was dressed up like a little girl.

Gretchen took Pepe La Peu home. She couldn't stop herself. Rose sent him with his file, the same as she did with every dog she adopted out, but she changed the history to say, "Ran away from the circus."

Chapter 18
Hurricane Wilma 2005

It was the beginning of October when Brad and Rose returned to the island after a three-week visit with Rose's daughter in Colorado. Before returning to Mexico, Brad traded in their car for a small RV. With the long drive and two dogs, Napoleon and Sol, they'd decided it would be the most relaxing way to travel—no hotels, no dirty gas station bathrooms, and Rose could make their meals along the way. They enjoyed the ride, taking it easy, grateful for the quiet time together. The trip took ten days, and by the time they drove into Cancun, they'd been away for over a month. Rose was so relieved to be back. Gretchen and Pepe La Peu had stayed at the house and Rudi had taken care of the dogs, but the place needed her personal attention.

The first week home was all about nesting, as Brad put it. Rose took her time settling in. She'd missed the smell of their house; it was like cut wood and dry sand mixed together. She'd especially missed the broad exciting ocean view. Their time away made her appreciate their bed with its Guatemalan cover, and the smell of her clothes, scented with the sea air.

And, she was looking forward to getting to know the new dogs and a litter of puppies that had been left in a box by the gate while they were away. In total, she was feeling good, and happy to be home.

Rose's tranquility was disrupted by the weather channel reporting a tropical storm forming in the Atlantic. Initially it was hardly noteworthy, being small and coming so late in the year. But Brad watched the updates and kept Rose informed, more often than she wanted, on its path and size. As the reports persisted, the white, swirling, raindrop-shaped indicator on the map of Mexico started to move north and west in their direction.

Isla Mujeres is just off of the northeast point of the Yucatan Peninsula, where the hurricane season lasts from June until November, though the majority of storms occur between July and October. The last major hurricane to hit their area had been Hurricane Gilbert in September 1988, long before they'd moved to Mexico. They'd experienced a few near misses, but hurricanes were usually drawn northeast by the warm waters of the Gulf of Mexico before causing any damage on Isla Mujeres.

Earlier that summer, the island had a brief visit from Hurricane Emily, which had been damaging but not devastating. Therefore, by Brad and Rose's calculations, the storms were done for the season. Sadly, they were not giving the random patterns of storms due concern.

"Rose, the storm's getting bigger." Brad told her as he pointed at the television that hung on the wall in their kitchen. "Isla's right in the middle of that grey area showing its path."

"Rose, you need to come look at this," was his next warning. Brad had started to talk about leaving and as his concern grew, he rarely strayed from the weather channel. "This storm's getting bigger and it's still coming straight at us." It was the "us" that bothered Rose the most. The weather channel was always showing hurricane predictions, but "us" meant them, their house, and her dogs.

"I've always thought that the people who stayed during hurricanes were out of their minds," Rose told Brad, "but we've got nineteen dogs. I've just got the house the way I like it and Rudi can't take care of everything. How can you even think about leaving? What about our books, my mother's table and—"

"Wait a minute," he said, holding up his hands. "Somehow if we stay… you think we can save these things? Is that what you're really thinking? If the projection doesn't change, we're leaving."

"It's going to change, it always does," said Rose. They'd been on the island for years by now, and it had always changed, veering off to the right at the last minute. Brad just looked at her and shook his head. "Have you talked to Rudi about this?"

"Rudi wants to stay with the dogs. He thinks the room over the garage will be safe. It's high and on the leeward side of the house. The storm will be coming in from the ocean."

"But we can't leave him here alone." Rose said, trying to picture their house in the storm but couldn't come up with an image that warranted leaving. She'd watched them build it. The house was solid cement.

"He'll be okay unless the whole house blows away and that's not going to happen. We can set him up with food. He'll have the bathroom. We'll fill up buckets of water. He's been through hurricanes before, he's sure he can do it." Rose wanted to argue with Brad but she knew it wouldn't do any good.

"Okay, I'll help get the room ready for Rudi," she finally agreed, "but it doesn't mean I'm leaving." Brad ignored the comment.

They stocked the room over the garage where puppy camp had started with canned food, bottled water, granola bars, fruit, and anything that would not perish quickly. Then they dragged in their couch and set it up with extra pillows and blankets. Brad brought up a little refrigerator they'd bought and plugged it in. "When the electricity goes out Rudi can use it like a cooler," he said. "Now we have to do something about the rest of the place."

"I have no idea what to expect," confessed Rose. "I've been trying to picture it, but can only envision the house being carried away, "Wizard of Oz" style, or being left alone. I can't seem to separate any parts that would be damaged more than others. I mean, what about the front of the house, it's all glass. How do we prepare for that?" Rose looked around the house. "It's going to miss us. I just know it."

"We have to go anyway." Brad persisted. "We have to move the RV. At least we can get that to a safe place."

Rose kept mentally willing that grey area that projection the TV kept showing, to move east.

"It hasn't moved," Brad kept reporting.

"It will."

Rose called Jeannie and Addy at the Bed and Breakfast. "What are you going to do?" she asked.

"Ah, crap," Jeannie said, "all the guests have left, we weren't full anyway, but the last couple got out yesterday. Addy and I are putting things away. I have mates in Valladolid, and we're going there later today.

"You're leaving?" Rose was shocked. She thought everyone but Brad would want to stay.

"Absolutely! I was here for the last storm and you don't want to stay if you've got somewhere to go."

"Have you heard from Gretchen and Jennifer?"

"Jennifer's staying," Jeannie said. "I tried to talk some sense into her, but she won't listen. I'm not sure about Gretchen. You're going, right?"

"Brad's insisting. He wants to get the RV away from the coast." Rose paused. "But I don't want to leave the dogs."

"Listen, love, you get off the island." Jeannie said sternly. "The dogs will fend for themselves. They'll find a safe place. You listen to Brad."

"I'm glad Kat's not here, I know she would stay."

"She probably would have," said Jeannie. "She never did have any sense."

Kat had left the island before Rose and Brad returned. She'd gone up to visit Greer, and then extended her stay for a week. Rose was sure that she wouldn't come back now. Not until this was all over.

After mentally cataloguing everything she owned, trying to decide what mattered and what didn't, Rose went to bed. Brad stayed up to watch the reports. She placed Itzamna and Ek Chauh next to her on the bed. Ek Chauh wanted her to stay. He was worried about the puppies. But Itzamna wanted her to go; he said she wouldn't be able to help any animals if she was hurt.

Only when the wind woke Rose in the early morning did she start to get a feel for what could happen. She was sure that the house was shaking. She got out of bed and joined Brad in the kitchen. "Where is it now?" she asked as she started the coffee but was distracted by the winds rattling their windows. "Is this the hurricane yet?" Rose asked.

Brad shook his head. "The storm isn't even here yet. We're not even in the lighter part of the path."

"If it gets worse will the ferry be running?"

"Good question. We better get ready." Said Brad.

Rose poured her coffee and took it into their bedroom. She kept chattering, nonstop, sipping coffee and piling things on their bed. "It's like picking a door: door number one, the windows in the bedroom will be broken and we'll wish we'd put everything in the living room. Door number two: the windows in the living room will be shattered and we'll wish we'd put everything in the kitchen. Door number three will be total devastation, no, door number three, the windows in the kitchen will be carried away in an enormous crashing wave and we'll wish we'd put everything…somewhere else. I'm afraid we'll come back and we'll have done it all wrong. How can we know?"

"We can't know," said Brad as he unfolded a tarp to cover the bed, "and would you quit with the damn door shit!"

The wind had died down, but it was still dark when they drove to the car ferry dock. The dogs wouldn't sit still and were climbing over everything packed in the back of the car. Sol had been increasingly agitated during the last few days and it was rubbing off on Napoleon. Rose wondered if they sensed that she and Brad were upset or if it was some type of dog radar for storms; if animals could predict earthquakes, why not hurricanes?

Brad was concerned that the 6 a.m. ferry would be crowded, so had insisted they leave at four thirty a.m. He'd expected long lines of cars at the dock but was surprised to find the lot empty. Maybe other people knew something he didn't. Scanning the empty parking lot, Rose's first thought was Maybe we can go home. They waited for the sun to rise and when it finally did, it lit up an eerie sky. If something could be pink and green at the same time, that's what it was.

"What've we missed here?" Brad asked. They were still the only car waiting. "Maybe the ferry's been canceled?" Rose had no response.

Promptly at five thirty, a man arrived and opened the ticket booth. When asked, he said he was not sure if the ferry would run and reminded them that whether it crossed or not was up to the Captain of the Port.

When a few other cars arrived, Brad started to settle down, at least about the ferry being the right choice.

Feeling secure enough to stray from the ticket booth, he and Rose walked to the far end of the parking lot, where there was a long row of fishing boats rammed up onto the sandy beach. The port was on the leeward side of the island and a good place for boats to weather a storm. Each vessel was swarming with men shuffling aimlessly from one end of the deck to the other.

"The boats look so strange, all beached like that. Why don't the men go ashore?" Rose asked.

"Those boats are from all over, like Cuba and Haiti, and probably don't have the papers to land on Mexican soil so the crew has to stay on board."

"You should've heard them yelling at people yesterday when I drove Rudi to the store," Rose said. "They were hanging off the sides of the boats, shouting at everyone. People completely ignored them."

Brad and Rose stared at the boats until it began to rain and the wind pushed them in the direction of their car.

"Everything feels a little off, doesn't it?" said Rose. "It's like it smells wrong, or is the wrong color." Brad nodded. Everything was different.

"Why aren't they leaving?" said Brad, looking at his watch. "It's past six o'clock! The guy in there has to know something by now."

"What'd he say?" Rose asked after Brad talked to the man in the booth.

"He said the Captain of the Port was still not sure whether to send the ferry. He's worried that they won't be able to land on the Cancun side and after that they still have to turn around and come back here. They want the ferry on this island with the other boats." Rose's first thought once again was Good, I can go home and take care of my dogs.

A moment later, the man at the ticket counter yelled, "Yup." He was leaning forward out of the booth so everyone could hear him.

"Yes! We're going," Brad said with relief. He quickly bought their ticket and they were the first car to drive aboard the boat, followed by only a handful of other vehicles. Their car was at the very front of the ferry, which was covered in the middle but the front and the back were open. Rose usually loved it when they were the first ones to board. It was a strange sensation sitting in the car and looking ahead at the ocean while moving forward, like they were driving their car over the water.

The old ferry rumbled as it pulled away from the dock and headed west towards the mainland. Sol was panting heavily by the back window, and Napoleon kept jumping from the back seat to Rose's lap and then back to sit next to Sol.

Then, suddenly, the ferry slowed and started to turn around.

"Are we going back to the island?"

"We must be," said Brad, slumping towards the steering wheel. The engines grew louder as the square boat struggled to change direction. It was half the size of a Walmart, and not built for maneuverability. Finally they were staring at the parking lot again. But then the boat started to move away from it.

"I get it," said Brad, with relief in his voice. "It must be easier to land this way."

Riding backwards, they watched the span of water grow between themselves and the island. The farther they got from shore, the more the ferry began to rock. It was being lifted and dropped as the flat-bottomed boat moved over huge mounds of water coming in from the open sea. Helplessly, they watched their Island disappear behind heavy, grey streaks of rain and rising swells.

By the time they reached the trailer park the rain was hard and steady, soaking them completely as they removed the canvas cover off the RV and unloaded their car.

Their original plan had been to drive both vehicles inland, but Brad was concerned that the roads out of Cancun would be inundated, so they left the car behind and headed to Merida.

They drove west in silence, each processing a hundred concerns. "The house is solid cement," Brad finally said. "It'll make it and there isn't anything inside that can't be replaced." Rose wasn't thinking about the house. It was Rudi and the dogs that troubled her the most. It was the wild dogs, and the street dogs, and the dogs with owners who would never let them in the house. It was the image of them wet and terrified.

Chapter 19
Leaving The Dogs Behind

Rudi had told Rose that if the storm got really bad he was going to open the gates and let the dogs fend for themselves. His room wasn't big enough to share with eighteen other creatures.

Two of the new dogs were Doberman Pinchers, a four-year-old male named Thai, and an eight-year-old female named Tia. They'd belonged to an American who'd lived on the island for years and when he moved on he did so alone, simply leaving the animals behind. The neighbors brought them to the house. Thai had a deformed foot, and Tia had a heart condition and they didn't like cats. The day they were brought in they'd chased away Keno, Rose's only cat.

The newest litter of pups were in the garage. They were the last thing she'd checked before they left. The bigger dogs had their ramshackle kennel with a tin roof. It too was on the leeward side of the house, but how much shelter would that provide? They knew they couldn't leave eighteen dogs in the house. If the windows blew out, that wouldn't be safe, so they'd decided to leave them in their kennels with food and water and the doors open. Rose was not happy with the situation but hadn't been able to come up with a better solution.

The RV park in Merida was typical for Mexico but had no resemblance to RV parks in North America. A good Mexican campground was a rugged field with a few electric plugs and water hoses. A bad one was two extension cords behind someone's house. Luckily this park was in the first category and next to a shopping center.

They parked, plugged in, and hooked up the water. It was late afternoon when they arrived so Rose heated something in the microwave and they went to bed before it was dark.

The next morning Rose was woken by a stream of Spanish, too fast for her to understand. Brad was on the couch fiddling with the satellite radio, trying to find the right station.

"Have you heard anything?" she said, pulling her hair back from her face.

"It's hard to tell what's going on," he said, sounding frustrated.

"What does the TV report?" Rose asked, climbing out of bed.

"It's a local station. They keep playing stupid soap operas." Brad gulped his coffee. "I'm trying to get Fox News or CNN through the satellite. It came through earlier. I heard William Longeness reporting from the hotel zone in Cancun. He said the storms hit Cozumel and it's bad. And then I lost the signal."

"What does 'bad' mean?" Rose wondered aloud as she sat down on the couch next to Brad.

"He said that in Cancun there were sustained winds of sixty miles an hour and gusts that got higher than that, lots of rain and flooding."

"So is that the hurricane?" asked Rose, hoping that was as bad as it would get.

"No, I don't think it's even over Cancun yet," said Brad.

Rose went into the bathroom to brush her teeth. She studied her image in the mirror. Her dark blond hair was a mess but she didn't brush it.

She twisted it on top of her head and stuck it there with one of her hair clips. After she brushed her teeth, she rubbed some cream on her arms and leaned out the bathroom door. "It should be passing on soon, right?"

"I've no idea, maybe later today," said Brad, working the dials. "Have some coffee."

Rose pulled a mug from the cupboard and filled it. "How are we going to sit here not knowing? I'm going to go crazy!"

Brad stood up and stretched. He'd been bent over the radio for too long. "Let's walk over to the mall and have something to eat. They might have some TV monitors or at least a newspaper. Why don't you get dressed while I feed the dogs?"

The mall was one department store called Liverpool which had all the usual merchandise, plus a restaurant with a television set in each corner. When they walked in, they were disappointed to see more soap operas on every TV, so Brad bought a newspaper before they sat down. Still, they couldn't find any information about the storm hitting Cancun, only a report on Cozumel which had been heavily damaged, but no details.

That first day was long. Having spent most of her life inland, Rose realized there was so much she didn't know about hurricanes: how long they lasted, what the different categories meant, how much wind it took to blow a house down, and much more. She asked Brad and he didn't know, either.

The next morning they returned to the restaurant, hoping for an update. This time the news was on. The storm was huge and dragging along at six miles an hour.

"They're saying that 6 miles an hour is slower than most," Brad told her.

Rose gave up on the menu and slid closer to Brad. "This is like knowing you're going to be in a car crash but not knowing when or how bad it's going to be," said Rose. Then the lights went out. A few high windows kept the store from going totally black. And the nearest employee politely smiled, picked up her purse and left. Everyone was leaving.

They left the booth and walked in the same direction as the workers. "Ask somebody." Rose nudged Brad.

He stepped directly in a woman's path and said, "Que pasa?"

"The storm," the woman replied with a heavy accent, "Moving inland." She pointed at the ground, "this here." She looked worried and shifted from side to side like she wanted to get past Brad. "I have mother, children," she said. Then she darted around him.

"I guess we should drive south to Isla Aguada. Let's check the satellite news and then decide." They walked outside into the wind and rain. Déjà vu, thought Rose. They were in the same position they'd been in two days earlier, running from the invisible storm, and didn't know anything more than they did then.

The satellite news confirmed the storm's direction. But, it turned once again before reaching Merida.

Rose was fighting the waves, trying to grab Sol. The wind kept rolling him just out of her reach. Itzamna swam by her with a puppy in his mouth while Ek Chauh was swimming behind Tia, the old Doberman Pincher, pushing her towards the shore. Rose tried to scream at Itzamna that she'd seen another puppy, but her voice was useless in the storm. Brad was on the shore pulling other dogs up onto the sea wall and then bells started to ring. Rose woke up, and found herself shoved up against the headboard of the bed. For a second she didn't know where she was, then she saw Brad reaching for his phone.

It was Gretchen. "Are you both okay? I've been trying to reach you for days," she said, forgoing "hello." Rose could hear her talking from the other side of the bed. Brad handed her the phone and went straight to the radio.

"We're okay. We're in Merida in our RV. Where are you?"

"I'm in Mazatlan."

"I thought that you'd stayed on the island."

"Jennifer stayed. I was worried about Pepe La Peu and I have friends here. I was lucky, I got the last flight to Mazatlan. All I had for Pepe was a duffle bag, which I unzipped at one end so he could poke his head out. I was so relieved they let him on the airplane. They made sure I knew it was a rare exception because of the storm."

"Have you heard anything?" said Rose.

"Oh my God," she started, "it's so bad. The island was massacred. Then the hurricane went inland and then came back out and hit the island again from the Cancun side." Rose listened, her heart beating in the back of her throat, and she pulled the covers up under her chin. "Cancun is devastated. There's flooding everywhere. The hotel zone is absolutely destroyed. People have run out of supplies and no one is allowed into the area. It's too dangerous."

"What do you mean "too dangerous"?

"I'm not sure—looting, bad water, glass everywhere…"

"What do you know about Isla?" Rose asked. After all this time of desperately wanting to know about the island, Rose was afraid to hear.

"There's still no communication," said Gretchen. "I heard the island was cut in half but there's no confirmation. We can only assume they got what Cancun got."

"What's she saying?" asked Brad, now fully awake and making coffee.

"They still don't know anything about the island." Rose told him, leaving out the "cut in half" part.

"Listen, I've already started to raise money; you guys have to buy supplies." This was so Gretchen, a person with a plan. "I wanted to go there myself but the airport is closed to non-military personnel, for now, anyway. When are you going back?"

"As soon as we can," Rose answered, suddenly afraid that all her worst fears could be reality.

"Look, I have a thousand dollars already," Gretchen said. "Buy everything you can."

"What kind of stuff?" said Rose.

"Everything," Gretchen said. "Okay, mmm, let's see… medicine, diapers, canned food, juice, wipes, buy lots of wipes. Who knows what the water situation is." Gretchen started talking faster, a bit of panic on the edge of her voice.

"What kind of meds would be needed most?" Rose said, hunting for a piece of paper and a pen. "Antibiotics, maybe eye drops, Neosporin and bandages? What else?"

"I'm not sure. Let me ask around and get back to you on that," Gretchen said. "Look, I've got to go, just start buying things right away. I'll call this afternoon. I'm so relieved to talk to you. It's been torture. Not knowing—" there was a pause on the phone, "it's horrible." Rose was surprised by Gretchen's voice, she'd never heard her this upset.

"I know what you mean," said Rose sympathetically, glancing at Brad.

"Don't worry. Your house could never blow away," Gretchen assured her.

"The house isn't my concern."

"I know. I'll talk to you this afternoon."

Rose hung up the phone, and turned to Brad. "Gretchen wants us to buy everything we can and take it back to the island. She sounds really worried."

He nodded and poured two cups of coffee. "But still, we don't know when we'll be able to go back."

"We have to go back as soon as we can," Rose said firmly.

"Let me see if I can get the news." Brad leaned around the corner and handed her a cup of coffee before turning his full attention to the radio.

Rose put on the same clothes that she'd taken off the night before and took the dogs and her coffee outside.

"The roads are all blocked." Brad told her when she stepped back inside. "The entire central part of the Yucatan peninsula is flooded."

Rose let that sink in for a moment. "How long do you think it'll stay flooded?" she said finally.

Brad looked at her as if he wished he had the answers. "I don't know. It's just one more thing about hurricanes that I've never asked myself. How long does a place stay flooded? Where does the water go if you're already at sea level? What happens when it all gets mixed together?" Brad drank his coffee. "Let's go to the Sam's Club and check out what kind of supplies we can get."

Sam's Club was crammed with people. There was a sign outside saying that there were no more generators but there would be some towards the end of the week.

They started to go thru Gretchen's list until Brad had to go back out to the parking lot to get another shopping cart. Rose told him to meet her at the pharmacy. When it was her turn she explained that they wanted to take a variety of medicines back to Isla Mujeres and asked for suggestions. The pharmacist was very helpful. He piled medicines on the counter, explaining why he thought they were important and when he thought of something else, sent his assistant to get more. After the pharmacy Rose worked her way up and down the aisles, feeling heavier with each step. The air in front of her was getting harder to move through, pushing back on her, making her struggle for oxygen. By the diapers she started to feel light-headed and was grateful for the support of the shopping cart handle. She stalled there, staring at the adorable babies on the boxes, and thought about her puppies. It was the shopping that was getting to her. In order to figure out what they should buy she had to run through the possible situations that would be causing the need. One after another, hopeless pictures were stacking up in her mind's eye.

Brad noticed the change in her and stood very close so she could lean on him. They stayed like that for a while. "What size should we get?" Rose finally asked when she could breathe again.

"Let's start with a general small, medium, and large," said Brad. He knew what was going on in Rose's head and that there was nothing he could say to make it easier.

Their motor home had so much storage space they shopped again the next day. It was a relief to have something to do. Finally, on Thursday the pharmacist told them that one road to the coast might be passable by Friday. It was a southern route where the flooding had been less. Rose was so excited that she couldn't sleep that night. They were going home.

Keno, the dog rescues one cat

Chapter 20
Floods

At 4:30am the next morning, Rose gave Brad a shove. "Brad," she said. "Brad, its 4:30, get up."

"Are you crazy?" he asked, rolling away from her and pulling the covers higher over his shoulder.

"Get up, come on," Rose pulled the covers off of her husband. "We can get organized and be on the road just as it starts to get light."

"I need sleep," he said.

"No, you don't. We've been hanging around for days. Get up." Brad dragged himself out of bed and went straight to the bathroom while Rose made coffee.

They unhooked, made sure their supplies weren't going to roll around, wrote a note to the family at the park, and left while it was still dark. The street lights of Merida led them to the edge of town, where they stopped to walk the dogs and waited for enough light to continue.

Everything looked normal for the next three hours of the trip; soggy but intact. The road led them south past Chichen Itza, one of the biggest ancient ruins in Mexico, then farther south to Tulum. After that they planned to take the coastal highway north along the Riviera Maya.

None of the roads they'd driven on were flooded, but as they approached the coast, signs of the hurricane became unmistakable.

Then everything changed. Twenty miles north of Tulum, the landscape started to fall apart. So many trees were downed that little settlements, ones normally hidden, were visible from the road. When they turned onto the coastal highway, the destruction grew more disturbing with each mile. The trees by the road were simply flat, as if a giant had smoothed them over like one might smooth hair on the top of their head. The tall cement poles that held up the electrical wires were all down. It was hard to believe that their slender forms could block enough wind to force them over, but obviously only one would have to fall to take the rest of them with it. Any road signs that remained upright were twisted like crumpled paper. The gas stations were roofless. Anything that could be knocked down was down, snapped, distorted, warped, and deformed. Brad drove slowly, ready for debris on the road, but they found out later that the army had been clearing it since the day the hurricane moved on.

Cancun itself was more of what they'd already witnessed, but worse. The shopping mall was mangled at one end. The Sears store looked as though some enormous creature had taken a bite off the corner of the building. Along the streets, just like on the highway, the vegetation was bent or flattened, making it possible to see things they never knew existed. Sand, palm branches, smaller bits of debris that were still on the road formed a vague pattern. The streets had been flooded waist high and deeper, but as the water receded, it would have flowed like a river, lining things up and then leaving them to settle with a certain directional consistency.

Mentally transferring these images to the streets of Isla Mujeres was eroding Rose's last bit of hope. Finally, they were minutes from the car ferry, and from there, an hour away from the island. Rose felt herself sinking into her seat, willing the RV to slow down, suddenly afraid of what was waiting for them. Her mouth was so dry that she didn't think she could talk if she tried. Even if she wanted to, what could she say?

After buying a ticket and some bottled water, Brad eased the RV onto the same ferry that they'd ridden less than a week before.

"I feel like we've been gone for months," said Rose. Those were the only words she had. There was one hour of exile left. Mutely, they sat in their van, watching the island grow bigger and both leaned forward, straining to see differences in the familiar sky line. Nothing obvious caught Rose's eye.

The ferry arrived at the dock which didn't seem to have suffered any damage. Brad edged the RV off the ramp, drove to the far end of the landing and exited the parking lot. The road was an obstacle course of sand, branches, and pieces of people's homes. There were many buildings that still had roofs but the windows sparkled with shards of glass, and the curtains were being drawn outside to flap in the open air. The amount of sand on the street increased toward the center of town. It was piled high beside the road, creating enough space for one lane. Brad kept a steady pace, worried about getting mired in the muck. And then he noticed the drooping power lines. They were too low for the RV to pass under.

He tried calling Rudi on his cell phone, not expecting much. Miraculously, Rudi answered almost immediately. After their Hello's Brad said they could talk soon, then told him what he needed.

"The power lines are too low for the RV. Could you meet us at the end of the road, next to the field where they had the circus? And could you bring some sort of pole to lift the wires? And Rudi, put one of the squeegees or something rubber on the end." Brad looked over at Rose. "I don't want you getting electrocuted." Rose didn't say a word. She was relieved that Brad hadn't asked any questions. They would know it all soon enough.

It didn't take long before Rudi skidded around the corner on his old green scooter, slipping in the sand but keeping his feet close to the ground on each side to stay upright. He had a long pole topped with a squeegee tied to the handle bar.

"Hola!" he said with a grin. Rose gave him a huge hug as if they'd been gone forever, and Brad shook his hand and patted him on the shoulder.

"You survived, eh?" said Brad.

"Yes, we made it," he replied in Spanish.

Brad was aware that they were blocking the only road through town, so he wanted to get started. "Okay Rudi, there's a ladder on the back of the van. You'll have to climb up on top and lift up the wires so we can go under them. Be careful; keep the wires on the rubber part of the squeegee."

"It doesn't matter," said Rudi, "there's no electricity."

"Still no electricity?" asked Brad.

"It may be a while," said Rudi.

Brad started the RV. He inched along the road as Rudi lifted the wires at the front of the RV and walked them to the back and then he did the same thing at the next set of wires. Once they were off the main road, the downed lines were less frequent.

All of a sudden Rose realized that the island hadn't been cut in half at all. The low area where this would've happened was just past the ferry dock and she'd have noticed if the ocean had cut a path next to the landing. She hoped this was a sign that other things weren't as bad as they were originally reported.

Maneuvering the RV was slow. The narrow lane had been cleared for small island cars and scooters and so much sand was piled on each side; it resembled a plowed lane after a snow storm. They encountered more drooping wires over the next section which slowed them down again. Rose couldn't stand the wait any longer and got out to walk.

Finding the gate to the house unlocked and slightly ajar gave Rose a jolt. The door was never left open. The dogs would get out. Rose's knees were threatening to go limp as she slipped through the opening and found no dogs in the driveway. She willed herself to look left toward the kennel. The door was closed, but crowded with noses and paws. She, held her breath and counted: one, two, three…fifteen. Maybe the other three were in the courtyard, she thought, but even fifteen was an enormous relief. At that moment six fluff balls waddled out of the garage. Rose was so overjoyed to see them she momentarily forgot about the three missing dogs. Still weak in the knees, she gave in and sat on the driveway, letting the puppies tumble all over her. Relieved, apprehensive, exhausted, she lay flat on her back, lifting each pup over her head and examining their magnificent little faces. There was no hurry now. She would see the rest soon enough.

Still lying on her back, she started to look around. She could see that the trees had lost branches and the palapa roof over their front door was gone. Turning her head to the right she saw the remains of it pushed to the side of the driveway. The smaller trees and potted plants were missing, probably in someone else's driveway.

Rudi came through the gate and rushed to her side with a look of concern. "I'm okay," Rose assured him, realizing how it must've looked. "I just had to lie down with the puppies. I desperately needed some puppy loving." He grinned, understanding, and left her there to pull the gate open for the RV, then warned her that she was going to get run over.

"I don't see any broken windows, Rudi," Rose said after he helped her settle the pups back in the garage.

"The broken ones are all in the front," he told her.

"How many?" she asked, making a face like she was preparing for a slap.

"Lots."

Rose didn't feel up to seeing that side of the house yet, and there was still the question of the missing dogs. "Rudi, I only counted fifteen dogs in the kennel?"

"I know." The look on his face told her that this wasn't going to be good.

"Who's gone? Are they really gone?" He nodded. She tried to remember who she'd seen.

"Tia died a few days ago," Rudi said sadly. "We aren't sure if it was her heart or if she ate something. The beaches are covered with rotting fish and worse. And Estrella died. She was so weak I put her with the pups." Rose nodded. Estrella had been sick before they left. "I checked the garage when the storm let up a bit, and found her. I took her outside and then went back upstairs."

"Who else, Rudi?" Rose was sure he was saving the worst news for last.

"Truma. I opened the front gate when I found Estrella, and some of the dogs left, some stayed. After everything was over they all came back except Truma. She just never came back." Truma was four months old and white with big black spots. One of them circled her left eye. A school girl had found her in the street and brought her in a month before the hurricane. Truma was a spunky thing and Rose hoped that she'd charmed someone into taking her in during the storm. It was better than thinking of it in any other way.

"Have you looked for her?" Rose said.

"Not a lot. It's hard to get around and I thought she might come back on her own."

"Maybe she still will," Rose said hopefully. "I guess we'll have to wait."

Finally Rose could no longer put off assessing the damage to the house. They walked inside the front door and stood in front of the empty swimming pool. "It took two days to get the sand and palapa branches out of there," Rudi said as they stared down at the dirty tiles.

"What's all that?" Rose asked, pointing to the white streaks on the windows and walls.

"It covers the whole house." Rudi told her. "It's what the storm did, plastering everything with salt, sand and probably bits of trees and palapa."

"Is it hard to get off?"

"Nah, we can get rid of it. I've just been cleaning up the glass and clearing the pool and the driveway first."

"No, no, I'm sure you've done a lot, I was just curious." Rose wasn't trying to criticize this man who'd stayed when they'd left. She turned towards the stairs. "Oh, Rudi, what's it like upstairs?"

Rudi looked down at his feet. "Your bedroom's the worst. The glass doors in the front are broken. One of them swung in and broke the corner windows and then I guess when all the wind came through it blew out the doors between your room and the living room. Your mattress was soaked but I put it outside a few days ago and it's slowly drying."

Rose started thinking of all of the things that she'd piled on the bed. Would it just be gone? I guess it was door number one, she thought, remembering the morning before they left. "We'd better go upstairs," she said.

The kitchen wasn't too bad but the living room was littered with glass. All the sliding doors on the ocean side were broken and from there Rose could see the smashed doors to her bedroom. One of them was simply gone, its frame twisted and suspended from the ceiling. The other door must have swung open and hit the wall with such force that it split in half from top to bottom. It was dangling by its lower hinge. Stepping carefully Rose went into her bedroom. She could see shards of the corner windows hanging dangerously from the top and jutting up from the bottom. The walls, which had been painted brick red, were covered with an uneven coating of the same white residue as the courtyard.

Rose was surprised to find her tile mirror still hanging on the wall. It was lopsided, suspended on its wire support, and it must have swung back and forth in the wind because there was a groove in the cement wall beneath it. Amazing, she thought. The wind was strong enough to rip doors and windows out of their frames but somehow a tiny wire kept this mirror on the wall.

They continued to survey the rest of the bedroom. Every wooden surface was pitted and weathered like the bow of an old boat, and every cupboard door was waterlogged and sandblasted and hung sadly warped on twisted hinges. Nothing closed, or if it had been closed, it didn't open.

"We're so lucky that no windows went out at the back of the house," Rudi said. "It would have created a draft through the building and sucked everything right out." He showed her the window in the kitchen where the cement had crumbled all around it. It was obvious it wouldn't have stayed in place much longer.

After the tour Rose felt overwhelmed but relieved. Of course, there was no electricity and no running water but the RV had a generator and a fully working kitchen and they were lucky to have it. As for the house, it could be repaired. Not knowing had been worse than seeing the actual destruction.

Brad had pushed the warped gates shut after parking the RV so Rose could finally open the kennels. It was a joy to touch all her babes. Nicole was the first to come bounding out, such a beauty, black with a white chest and feet. Although it was taboo for the dogs to jump up, this day was a free for all. Rose couldn't wait to touch each one of them.

Luna was all over her. They'd called her that after the moon but it turned out to be more appropriate as in "loony," which is exactly what she was. Someone had brought her into a spay and neuter clinic and never picked her up.

Silvia looked like a blond, Greyhound with a Lab head. Gorgeous and regal, she held herself high, and maintained a lean, muscular shape no matter how much they fed her. She'd come in with an odd litter found on the beach. All the males had long tails while the three females only had short stumps. Silvia was the only one left from that litter and she loved Rose. Whenever she saw her she would spin in circles and leap for joy. Unfortunately, she was a fence jumper and no matter how hard they'd tried to keep her inside the gate she would get out and find Rose.

Yoga classes were the hardest. They were held in a three-walled building just two steps up from the sand. Rose would position herself by the entrance in case Silvia decided to come in. Some days during the class when Rose had her eyes closed she'd hear the teacher say her name in a quiet but slightly annoyed voice. When she looked up it was inevitably Silvia, who had stealthily crawled up the two steps and sat as close to her as possible without touching. Instead of being embarrassed Rose felt proud. You couldn't miss her as "the dog lady".

Perrafaira was there, sitting a bit aside from the rest of the dogs. She was also a fence jumper, but even more independent. And, she was one of the ugliest dogs Rose had ever seen. She was barrel chested with long skinny legs. The fur on her body was reddish brown while the fur on her head and legs was black. And to really add character she had a white Mohawk. It amazed Rose that whenever they were in town everyone knew Perrafaira and she would wag a greeting to all that came near. She'd been given to Rose by the cat lady on the island who was worried about her because she chased motos. Her name was originally Perrafea which means ugly dog but Rose had changed it to Perrafaira, a misspelled version of the English word fair. Rose wasn't going to call her ugly dog.

When Rose settled herself back down on the driveway, Butler was the first one to nudge his way onto her lap. Paulo had brought him to the house after someone had dumped him at the clinic. On the drive to Rose's house Butler was so frightened that he'd wedged himself under the driver's seat of Paulo's car. They had to pry him loose. He looked like a small black schnauzer and fortunately he responded well to their love and attention.

Each of her dogs had a story and every one of them loved Rose. She spent the hour, while Rudi took Brad on a house tour, carefully checking every animal from head to toe. She felt relieved; it was finally over. They'd really only lost one dog, both Estrella and Tia were already sick, and she was still hopeful that Truma would come home.

Finally, satisfied that her dogs were okay, she climbed into the RV, exhausted but jittery, relieved but worried, overwhelmed but planning and ready for action—but not in any hurry.

Chapter 21
Relief workers

That first night at home, Rose made Rudi and Brad a hot meal before they all went to bed with the sun. They'd planned to check out the rest of the island the next day.

When explaining Isla Mujeres to those who had never been there, Rose likened it to a small boat with someone heavy sitting in the stern and to one side. The bow was the tall cliffs at the south end, and the high side of the boat was the rocky Caribbean coastline, while the Cancun side quickly dropped to sea level, ending at the northern point's sandy beach. So the western side and northern end of the island had the worst flooding. The baseball field, which was closer to the north point, had become a lake and the roads leading away from it were completely submerged. Rose watched people collecting personal belongings from their homes by boat. They had to climb in through second story windows.

Gretchen called the first morning. She was desperately trying to get a flight into Cancun but with little success, so she wanted information. "Imagine," Rose told her, "If you filled your neighborhood with water high enough to reach the second story windows. That's what I'm seeing and wherever the water has receded there's debris, everything from mattresses to rooftops, bird cages to wrecked cars." Rose was back in their RV after a quick tour of the island on Rudi's moto. "Someone said that Mundaca Park has been destroyed, but I haven't been there to see it." Rose promised to call Gretchen back when she knew more and then left with Brad to check on their friends.

When they arrived at Jeannie's, they were shocked at how exhausted both Jeannie and Addy looked. Rose hugged them and once again felt guilty about leaving. She'd been feeling that way all day, everywhere they went.

"Three days," moaned Jeannie, "three days in the back room stretched out on two of the lounge chairs we'd brought in from the balcony."

"No lights, no phone, no radio, and no information. It was really hard," said Addy, "and the storm went on forever." She pulled her hair back with both her hands trying to form a pony tail, but she had nothing to tie it with, so it was back hanging limply around her face as soon as she put her arms down. "It was so loud; the noise is still ringing in my ears."

"Why the lounge chairs?" Brad asked.

"We'd hauled all the stuffed furniture upstairs because we knew there'd be flooding," said Jeannie. "But we were warned to stay downstairs. Just too much stuff flying around. I mean it worked, we're okay and the inn's okay, but all a bit of a push. I'll tell you that." Jeannie kept looking around like she still couldn't believe the mess. "Some broken windows. A door crashed right through a window upstairs and landed on the couch. After that everything got soaked. It's slowly drying. There's some broken dishes and lamps, but I see how lucky we are when we walk around town. What a mess!"

"I thought you were leaving," said Rose. She started to pick things up, wanting to help, but couldn't find a dry or clean place to put things, so she gave up.

"We were leaving," said Jeannie. "But we didn't get out in time. The ocean got rough really fast and they cancelled the people ferry earlier than a lot of us expected. We just came back to the Inn and tried to make the storage room livable." Jeannie was rubbing her left arm above the elbow. Rose had noticed the bruises on both her arms the moment they'd arrived. "How did Rudi fare at your place?" Rose told them about the dogs and the damage to their house and then gave them boxes of sterile wipes and some canned food.

"Oh, and I've got granola bars for you, Addy," said Rose. "I know how much you love them." When they left Addy was chewing on a granola bar, looking wide-eyed and shaken.

Next they visited Jennifer, who'd stayed in a cement one-story home with three of her friends. They'd decided ahead of time that out of all their homes, it was the strongest. The three of them were sitting on the little covered porch at the front. Jennifer had moved the chairs back outside. "The hardest part was keeping the water out." Jennifer said. She laughed awkwardly and rubbed her red-rimmed eyes. "We sandbagged the doorway but with the force of the water and the wind, it came in anyway. Ultimately we were safe and soggy. I worried about the book store, though. At least we'd moved all the books."

Jennifer sat down as if talking about it made her tired. "We boxed them all and put them upstairs at Jeannie's. Some of them got wet but most of them were far enough back, away from the broken window. Did you see that door that came flying through?" Rose and Brad both nodded.

Everyone they talked to had their own awful version of the storm. The stories ran from rough to terrifying. The worst was Jack and Henna, who were new to the island and had just finished building their house. The storm caught them when the hurricane came smashing over the island the second time after threatening Merida. It came in so fast that they literally had to run for cover. They'd grabbed their cat and stowed away in a windowless store room, waiting and listening as the winds ripped their new home to shreds. Every one of their windows was broken, the frames tortured into odd shapes. Most of their belongings were sucked out and carried off.

What Rose noticed the most was how traumatized people looked. They seemed almost zombie-like, shuffling slowly from A to B, looking worn out and fretful.

One couple had gone to check on the rest of their family during a lull in the storm, maybe when the eye passed over. Unfortunately they stayed too long and had to tie themselves together with heavy ropes just to keep from blowing away as they struggled to get back to their house and dogs.

Another woman, Marta, had taken the last people ferry to Cancun before the storm hit. "It was difficult," she explained to Rose, "but I eventually found a hotel room. Soon after the storm got really bad the wall on the other side of the hotel was completely ripped away. The guests from those rooms came over to ours. They saw the wall start to crumble and shake and got away in time. When the storm let up I went down to the street to a pay phone. I had to wade through waist deep water to get there and stupid me, of course, the phone didn't work. You can't imagine what I saw," she closed her eyes, obviously seeing it all over again. "There were at least a hundred people crammed into the building next door. They were actually dumping buckets of refuse out the window. Into the water I was wading through," she said.

"I ran back to my room and stayed there. When the storm was over someone told me that some buses were taking people to Merida, and oh my God," she shuddered, "I had to go back into that water to get to the terminal. I waited there for hours. Finally I got a bus, a local bus, one of those old rickety things. It was slow but kept moving. When we reached the flooded roads, I thought we were stuck. But the driver and other passengers opened up every window like they'd done it before, including the front wind shield that folded down. Then they all sat back down and the driver charged into the water. The other people knew what was coming. I had no idea. Instead of pushing through the water, the water ran right through the bus. With less resistance we made it to the other side before the engine seized up."

"Oh my god," said Rose trying to imagine the water going straight through the bus. She put her hand on Marta's back but Marta didn't seem to notice and talked on.

"We made it to Merida. I'll never forget it. Since then I've bought every antibiotic I can get my hands on. Ugh, all that filthy water! I mean all of my parts were immersed in that water."

After listening to Marta's story, Rose was relieved to see some happy faces when she took the supplies to the Red Cross. She felt guilty as everyone cheered when she arrived. It was important to her that they knew the supplies were paid for by money Gretchen had raised.

"You know Gretchen who has the bookstore?" she asked one volunteer, as he piled three bags of Huggies into his friend's arms.

"Si!" He answered with a big grin, "We all know Gretchen." He was speaking Spanish and Rose was speaking Spanglish which is somewhere between bad Spanish and bad English.

"Well, Gretchen raised the money for all of these things. She was in Mazatlan during the storm." Rose repeated this to everyone who showed up to unload. They were so excited to get the supplies. Relief in larger doses had not arrived.

After stacking the provisions on tables inside the building, they coaxed Rose indoors to take pictures. Everyone was standing behind the piles of supplies. The man they picked to take the pictures was doing so with someone else's camera and didn't understand where the view finder was, plus Rose suspected he'd been drinking. He kept taking pictures of their legs or just their heads. After each picture the volunteers would pass the camera around and roar with laughter. It was a warm moment full of relief and gratitude, not just for the supplies but for survival and community.

As days passed, they got used to the sight of destroyed buildings, just like one might get used to looking at an old neglected warehouse or a dilapidated barn in the countryside. It becomes part of the scenery.

Rose found some out-of-the-way spots to put food out for the dogs. The street dogs were everywhere, pawing through the garbage for something to eat. Owned dogs seemed to be staying very close to their homes, as if they were afraid the storm could return. What Rose worried about, even more than the food was fresh water. Normally street dogs got their water from pools and fountains, and puddles after the rain, but everything was mixed together. Any standing water would be salty and dirty. Rose used the water filter they kept for emergencies in the RV, and left pails of water at different intervals. She and Rudi checked and refilled them as often as they could. They rode around on Rudi's old scooter with paint buckets sloshing water on both sides.

Rose called Gretchen to report on things and to tell her how much the islanders appreciated the supplies.

"I'm coming to Isla," she Gretchen. "I'm coming with a relief group from HSI (The Humane Society International). They're concerned about the animals on the island. You even know some of them."

"That's fantastic! Who's coming?"

"Norma Mandel, the vet from our first clinic, and Chris something, he's the Central American rep for HSI, plus Cory, she does disaster work now…maybe Cally. There might be others. I'm not sure."

"I haven't seen Cory since she trapped dogs for us and it'll be great to see Norma again," said Rose. "When are you coming? Where are you all staying?"

"We're coming tomorrow. Regular people still can't fly into Cancun, you have to be part of a rescue delegation."

"Really," said Rose. She had no idea what was going on in Cancun.

"If you don't mind," said Gretchen, "I was hoping the relief group could stay with you."

"Of course they can. But I don't have enough beds and there's still no electricity." Rose paused, starting to reconsider her offer. "The whole front of the house is open, most of the windows were broken."

"Don't worry. They've got inflatable mats. These guys are used to rough conditions and come prepared."

"Okay, that'll work. What time?" Rose asked.

"We arrive together at one. I've had to fly to the States to fly back into Mexico. I'm leaving Pepe with friends."

Rose told Gretchen more about the damage to the island. She suggested a few supplies that people needed the most and then they said good bye. She found Rudi in the driveway and asked him to sweep both the living room upstairs and the courtyard downstairs so the group could sleep in either place depending on the weather. Luckily, Rose had stocked the RV with meals like spaghetti and frozen lasagnas so she could feed large groups of people if needed. No stores would be open on the island for a while.

Rose was waiting on the dock when they arrived on the four o'clock ferry. There were four women and two men, each with a huge backpack with things like Leatherman tools and water bottles hanging off on clips and belts and loops. Their shoes were the big sturdy kind people might wear trekking and their clothes were a practical tan or green.

They looked the part, except for Gretchen, who was not officially in the group. She wore a colorful bandana holding back her wavy brown hair, a pink t-shirt and cut-off jeans. Cally fit in perfectly because 'ready for anything,' was the way she dressed all the time. Norma introduced Chris and Paul, then Rose led the group on the short walk to her house and showed them where to put their gear.

They piled everything in the courtyard and wanted to get right to work. The first place on their check list was the zoo. The island zoo was in Mundaca Park, where there'd been extensive damage. Originally, the park had been a large estate owned by an old pirate. At least, he tried to pass himself off as a pirate, but he'd really made all his money in the slave trade. Now it was a park and someone had added a horrible little zoo with a cage full of monkeys, a huge boa constrictor, another cage with a couple of kudamundes, (which look like a monkey/raccoon mix) and then a beautiful, sad jaguar. There may have been other animals, but Rose wouldn't know. She never went there.

Somehow the Humane Society had heard that the jaguar was in trouble. His cage was in the woodier part of the park and the soil had been so saturated by the storm that his enclosure was sinking and completely surrounded by water. When they arrived, the poor thing was obviously agitated. He was pacing from side to side in his tiny, tilted jail. The park workers were struggling in the mud, attempting to build a bridge across the new moat. One of them had been caring for the jaguar for years and was frantic about the large cat's dangerous situation.

Rose's group was not there to help. As the first wave of disaster relief, their instructions were to observe and report back. Hearing voices behind her, Rose turned and saw Paulo coming towards her with a group of people she didn't know. Paulo said they had a plan, and the part that Rose liked the most was the jaguar would be relocated to a reserve for large cats.

After assessing that situation, they walked to the other end of the park where a rustic enclosure had been built to house the unfortunate island dogs that were picked up by the ecologia's brutal dog-catchers. The area was low and plagued by mosquitoes, and Rose had trouble finding it before she realized that it'd been completely washed away. She was thrilled.

After that, Norma, the vet, wanted to drive through the small colonias to check the damage and talk to people, and she was worried about strays. If the family home had been destroyed, the family would most likely have moved in with relatives on the island or the mainland, where the people would be welcome, but their dogs probably would not. They were simply left behind. Initially the dogs would stay by their homes where the neighbors knew them. But as they spread out and scrounged for food they would be labeled "street dogs," and that would bring trouble. Rose and Rudi had been expanding their food and water drops, but they could never cover the entire island.

That night, Rose made everyone a huge lasagna dinner, and after eating, they took turns using the foot pump to inflate their beds. Gretchen stayed until everyone was settled in, she wanted to ask the group for help.

"Would you guys mind going with us to Rancho Viejo?" she asked Norma. "Paulo told me that his group from Cancun had vaccines from Mexico City for the dogs. "

"Where's Rancho Viejo?" asked Cory.

"It's on the mainland next to Cancun but it's actually part of Isla Mujeres," said Gretchen. "It's a nasty area located between Cancun and the Cancun City Dump. It smells so bad that the land's cheap. Nobody would live there if they didn't have to. The people are poor and mostly relocated families looking for work."

"Oh, it's awful," added Rose, "the garbage trucks roar back and forth along the streets even though it's residential. The roads are full of holes and tight curves and bits of garbage that fly out the back of those trucks as they bump and turn."

"And the homes that I've seen there were definitely not hurricane-proof," said Gretchen. "If families have had to move out I'm sure they'd leave their animals behind."

"Let's go," said Norma. "That's what we're here for, to see where help is the most needed." Cory nodded. "What time do we leave?" she said.

They left early in the morning, traveling in two large, black, government vans supplied by the vets working with Paulo. Rose and Gretchen followed behind in a borrowed jeep.

They needed a place that was central enough for people to easily bring in their dogs. Finally, they found a good spot on a corner with enough room for people to line up with their animals. As soon as they stopped and opened the backs of the vans, locals crowded around to see what was up. Word travelled fast.

The lead vet stood on the bumper of the van to explain. "We've got vaccinations, some medicines and lots of dog food. It's all free, but you don't get anything unless we vaccinate your dog first. We'll be here all afternoon so please spread the word."

The earliest arrivals were all puppies. They were easy to carry and the children proudly displayed them as Rose and Gretchen made a big fuss over how cute they were. Rose loved to talk to the children and never failed to ask them if they'd hugged their puppy that day. Then larger dogs started to arrive or more precisely they were being dragged by a rope tightly fastened around their necks.

The line grew quickly. At times it got out of control; most of these animals had never been on a leash before, or around so many people or other dogs. They were grumpy after being yanked along and subjected to such unfamiliar territory, and they were all big, mostly they were kept for protection.

"The houses are frail, easily broken into," Gretchen explained to the rescue group. "Some don't even have doors—forget about a lock—so the dogs are it. They're chained up all of their lives by the front of the house, where they are expected to be the doorbell and security."

One of the Mexican veterinarians insisted on writing out the owner's names in order to account for the vaccines he'd been entrusted with. This kept slowing things down. Rose, Gretchen, and Cally had to wait as the line trudged slowly up to the red plastic Coca Cola table that was the main desk. Eventually, their job was to keep people separate enough to avoid dog fights. As they fill sacs with dog food they also had to watch out for the children who kept returning after trading dogs with their friends, trying to get an extra bag. This really bothered Cally, but Rose didn't care. She was always happy to give people more dog food.

It was a long day but a big success. Gretchen and Rose decided to return the next week. Food and drinkable water was scarce and they were sure that there had to be many more hungry dogs.

Chapter 22
Rancho Viejo

After the relief group left, Gretchen and Rose returned to Rancho Viejo. This time they went with Addy in Jeannie's small Honda. It was packed with as much dog food as the wheels could support, plus bags of donated leashes and collars.

After crossing to the mainland, Addy had to pay close attention while driving the overloaded car along the badly damaged roads. Most of the time they had the streets to themselves. The hurricane had destroyed many of the local cars or rendered them too dilapidated to maneuver around the widening pot holes that were filled with murky water, making it impossible to know how deep they were.

This time they decided to drive straight to the dump at the end of the road, and then work their way back. They kept going as long as they could, until Addy started to feel sick from the stench.

"I'm sorry, I can't go any farther," she said, pulling the car to the side of the road. "I'll throw up for sure."

"Don't worry about it. That was probably the last house back there," said Gretchen. "No one could live with this smell."

"Sounds good to me," said Rose. They backtracked to what looked like a small junkyard. The buildings in the middle were literally fenced in with rubbish. There was everything from car parts to ratty couches to a huge plaster doll holding a hamburger and children were climbing all over the stuff like some sort of pop-art playground.

"Here come the dogs." Rose pointed.

"How many?" asked Addy, turning the car off.

"I see three, and here come the kids." The kids surrounded the car, and the women got out. Rose visually checked the dogs first, and then told the children how handsome their pets were. After that, she pulled a bag of collars from under the car seat and let them pick one per dog. The little girls picked out bright orange and pink collars and the boys picked black ones with florescent silver stripes.

"You can adjust the size like this," Rose started to demonstrate. She reached for the smallest brown dog to check the fit, but it backed away. The kids laughed and grabbed him, and held him tightly while Rose carefully wrapped the collar around his neck. After that, she helped the girls with their collars. Meanwhile, Gretchen and Addy opened the trunk and filled two plastic bags with dog food.

"Would you like some food for your dogs?" Gretchen asked the children in Spanish. No answer. "What do your dogs eat?" They shrugged. So Gretchen offered some choices. "Tortillas?"

"Si, Si," the tallest boy answered.

"Chicken bones?"

"Si, Si."

"And when was the last time you hugged your dogs?" Rose asked, like she always did. The kids were stumped by that one. Rose wasn't sure if it was her bad Spanish or the question that had rendered them speechless, so she walked over to Gretchen and hugged her. "Like this," she said.

The children all laughed. Gretchen pushed her away which made the children laugh even more. By then two women had come up behind the children. They appeared to be the mothers of all six.

"We don't want the children hugging the dogs." One of the mothers said, "They're covered with ticks and fleas." Rose saw her opportunity. She pulled out the tick and flea meds the relief workers had left her and asked if she could demonstrate where to put the drops on the dogs. The dogs backed away again as she approached, so the tallest boy held them one by one as Rose spread the solution under the fur between their shoulder blades.

"Gracias," she said to the boy who helped her, and then she turned to the rest. "Okay now, don't touch that spot for two days. After two days it's okay, you can check for ticks and fleas." Rose knew they would check. The smallest boy held up his arms like he was showing off his muscles and said, "Pulgas muertas," (dead fleas).

Gretchen handed out coloring books with pictures of children feeding, bathing, and walking their dogs and little packs of crayons that a restaurant had donated. When the kids sat down with their coloring books, the rescue group moved on.

They visited more families along the road and then turned right, following a sign that said "Town Square." Below it was an arrow constructed of sticks nailed to the wooden pole, which held up the electrical wires that were of no use at the present time.

The settlements were farther apart after they turned and most of them were abandoned, so Addy continued to drive while Gretchen and Rose watched for strays.

"Wait," Gretchen said loudly, making Addy jump in her seat. "I think I see something over there, maybe a dog. Let's pull over."

"Okay," agreed Addy. Rose was the first out of the car. She walked up an overgrown dirt road towards a jumble of wrecked buildings. There were old, cracked buckets and rusty metal tubs everywhere, literally junk stacked up on junk. Gretchen's dog had disappeared, so Rose spread food on the ground in case he was too shy to come out while they were there. It was obvious that the place had been deserted.

"No dogs are going to come out while we're here," said Gretchen.

"You're probably right," Rose agreed, and then something caught her eye. "But, someone's coming." Gretchen followed Rose's gaze to the duck that was waddling towards them out from behind one of the dilapidated structures. There were others behind it.

"Look at this," Addy said, waving Gretchen and Rose over so they could see behind the piles of debris. Behind the ducks came a goose, a turkey, and then more birds. Gretchen's elusive dog must have been worried that the birds would get all the food because he crept out from under a bush and approached one pile of it while the birds headed for another. By then, chickens and roosters had appeared, as well as pigeons, more geese, more turkeys, and some other birds they couldn't identify.

Gretchen was facing the road. "Wow," she said and pointed down the way. "Wait til you see this." Turning up the driveway was a row of what they decided must have been guinea hens, ten of them in a perfect line heading straight for the food.

"I'm going to get another bag," said Gretchen, who'd already poured the last of a fifty-pound bag out in six different piles to prevent food fights. She dragged the second bag out of the car while Addy ladled water out of a rusty barrel into anything that would hold it. Rose took pictures as she sat on a stump watching in amazement, until the crackle of a branch caught her attention, turning towards the sound she saw a little black nose sniffing the air. Something under the bush knew there was food, but was afraid to go past Rose to get it.

"Come here, little guy," she said, and reached her hand towards what looked like a skinny yellow Lab puppy. The puppy backed away barking, so Rose stood up and waded through the birds to get a handful of food. She stepped back towards her stump and held it out in the pup's direction. The hungry little pup moved closer, drawn by the smell, and then backed up again, barking nervously.

"Hey, Gretchen, help me out here," Rose called. Gretchen looked up and understood the situation immediately. She circled around behind him while Rose kept his attention. When she got within two feet she tossed the extra shirt she had over his head, and Rose grabbed him. Like most puppies, he gave in right away. They wrapped him up properly, letting his head stick out but keeping his front paws in until they could assess his mood. There was no need to worry. Rose soon had to scoop up more of the dry kibble. He'd devoured the first bit, without chewing, right out of her hand.

Since the hurricane they'd already rescued a female puppy. Rose had found her hiding under a wrecked car and named her Wilma so they decided to call this guy William. He was a mess. The usual, thought Rose. His tummy was covered with scabs, mange had attacked his feet and ears, which he'd scratched or chewed raw. His eyes were goopy, and he was flea infested and filthy dirty.

"I've counted seven chickens," said Addy as she joined them to check out the puppy.

"How many ducks do you think there are?" asked Rose.

"There has to be at least twenty and then as many geese. It's hard to believe that someone would just abandon all these birds," said Gretchen.

"You know," Addy said, "I'm not sure anyone ever lived here. Those buildings don't look like they've been lived in for a long time, anyway."

"Who can tell these days?" said Rose.

The three women sat on a log next to the road and watched the huge assortment of birds demolish the last of the dog food. Two larger dogs had appeared but they stuck to their own mound and the birds kept to theirs. There were no fights or trouble of any kind. Even the strutting turkey was just showing off. He didn't attempt to dominate or push anyone around.

"Did you take pictures?" Gretchen asked. Rose was usually the one with the camera.

"Tons!" Rose said. "No one's going to believe this. Let's spread a few more piles and check out the end of the road."

"Can we put it out on the way back in case we need it further along?" said Addy. "The sign said 'dead end.'"

"Good thinking," Gretchen said.

The little car endured the rough terrain with more agility without the two fifty-pound bags of dog food.

"Shouldn't a town square be in the middle of town?" said Addy, as the road abruptly ended at a hill. It literally came to the hill and stopped, like the road was there first and then someone had dropped a hill on it. Deciding that they must have passed the turn, Addy backed up until Rose spotted a sandy lane they'd understandably missed. They turned left and drove along the sand until it ended. Once again, there was a sign that said, 'Town Square.' "This is too weird," said Addy. She put the car in park and they all stepped out.

"Do do do. Do do do," said Rose in the tune of the Twilight Zone TV show. "Do not adjust your television…"

"Stop that," said Gretchen, "This is giving me the creeps."

Rose surveyed their surroundings. "This is just an old gathering place," she said. They were standing next to a clearing about an acre in size, bordered by rustic buildings. Straight ahead was a small church with a screened-in porch built onto its right wall. Then, past a narrow strip of sand was an old house with three old trucks in front of it. Only one of them had all four wheels. Completing the picture was a larger structure with just three walls and a roof. The interior was lined with benches, more precisely planks on logs.

Gretchen called out, "Bueno?" Eventually a young man came out of the house with a look that said "What?"

"Is this the town square?" Gretchen said in Spanish.

"Si," he replied flatly.

"For what town?" Gretchen asked.

"These parts," he answered, making his lack of interest in any conversation obvious.

"Does that include all of Rancho Viejo?" Gretchen said.

"No," he answered and then started to poke under the hood of one of the trucks. When he banged on something, a flurry of dogs vacated the shade underneath.

Rose leaned towards Gretchen and whispered, "They didn't even bark at us. How weird is that?"

"Really weird and really bad," said Gretchen quietly. She was watching the sad collection of dogs relocate in other shaded areas.

The bigger ones were bone thin and moved away from the truck with their tails between their legs. The younger ones were just as skinny but friendlier, not yet tainted enough to resist a cooing dog lover. They came closer but only one tiny, black, emaciated creature let Rose touch him. He was bald between his eyes, which gave him a quizzical look, like furrowed brows. He was a splotchy, scabby, smaller, black version of William, who was sleeping in the car. Rose picked him up without any coaxing.

"Is this your puppy?" she asked the man under the hood of the truck. He ignored her so she turned to Gretchen.

"Is this your puppy?" Gretchen asked again in Spanish. He lifted his head and looked at them like they'd asked him about aliens. Then he shrugged his shoulders.

"Can I have this one?" Rose asked. She held the black pup up for him to view.

"Whatever," he answered as if it was a dumb question. Then he went back to work, conversation over, so they ignored him back and spread food around for the other dogs. The bigger dogs were shy at first, but once the bravest one approached the rest joined in. Rose picked up a handful for her pup and he gobbled it up, so she scooped up a second handful.

"We'd better head back," suggested Addy, adding that she was worried about William. They'd left him in the car with the windows rolled up so he couldn't escape. Addy had parked in the shade but the afternoon heat could still be substantial. Rose bent down for a last look under the truck. She spotted one more dog, a pup. He was a tragic sight, one of the worst she'd seen. She remembered Paulo saying that when a dog or puppy gets that bad, that skinny, that hairless, it was almost impossible to bring them back to full health.

Gretchen and Addy were anxious to go. Both of them were standing next to the car looking impatient. "We have to get back to the dock in time for the six-thirty car ferry," said Addy. "If we miss it, what will we do?" She was right and Rose had two pups already. Hugging the little black one closer to her heart she joined the others in the car. She put the black pup next to William gathering her shirt around the two of them while trying to convince herself that she couldn't save them all. But the image of the skinny hairless puppy stayed with her.

Once they were back on the road William and the black pup cuddled closer like littermates. There was much to be done before the two would be adoptable, but Rose couldn't think of anything she'd rather do.

"I think we should call him Hero," Addy suggested. Rose noticed tears on her cheek when she turned around to look at Hero.

"That was awful," started Rose, but then stopped. Let it go, she told herself. For Addy's sake and for her own she let it drop.

She reached for Gretchen, touching her on the shoulder, and gave her a look that said, 'no discussion,' but as usual Gretchen already knew. Gretchen and Rose were different ages, and at different stages of their lives, but when they were working with the animals they were always on the same page.

Back on the island Gretchen helped Rose bathe and pick the fleas and ticks off of their new babes and then she left to meet her friends. Rose was tired and felt good about what they'd done but couldn't stop thinking about that last pup. To give up on him while he was still alive had seemed reasonable that afternoon, but by nightfall, she couldn't believe she'd done it.

Jennifer was part of the group going to Rancho Viejo the next day, they knew that it would take two trips to cover an area that size. She had to pick the dog food up at Rose's house in the morning, and when she arrived Rose was waiting. She told her about the pup under the truck and warned her it was unlikely that he'd make it through the night. Checking on him would need a detour from the planned route, but Jennifer agreed to check anyway. If he or she was there and still alive, no matter what, Rose wanted her to bring him home, even if it was to die where he would be cared for.

Gretchen arrived shortly after the others left and helped Rose set up a portable pen for the Rancho Viejo pups. She understood that it was important to keep them isolated long enough to get a feel for their health. And she knew that Rose would watch them closely for any signs of illness.

"I'm sure they're just tired," said Gretchen, seeing the concern on Roses face.

"They've barely come out of that crate," said Rose. "I guess it's a nice cave for them to hide in, but I can't even vaccinate them until they're better. It's a risk." Rose sat down, "it's always a risk bringing in new animals. And if they catch something here at the house, I feel like it's my fault."

"Where else would they go?" asked Gretchen. Rose knew there was no other place.

She spent the rest of the day sorting through what was left by the hurricane, trying to decide what was worth keeping. Many of her books had been ruined. Pictures were broken, furniture was destroyed, curtains were ripped and stained but she was hesitant to throw out too much, because replacements and repairs were going to take a long time. Every building within a hundred miles had been damaged or destroyed and there weren't enough supplies or laborers to get anything done soon.

In the afternoon Rudi helped Rose feed the dogs and give meds to the ones that needed them. New arrivals got de-wormer, the old ones got glucosamine, and they all got vitamins, then Rose went into the RV to cook dinner.

She found Brad taking a break, soaking up the air conditioning. Being a big man, six foot two inches tall and not what you might call lean, the heat and humidity was hard on him. Flopping down on the couch beside him, Rose was reminded how lucky they were. The inside of the RV was heaven while everything else was a mess.

"What did you do today?" she asked Brad.

Brad ran his fingers through his hair and came away with a piece of palapa. "We finished cleaning and boarding up Jeannie's bed and breakfast. Everyone needs windows and we can't count on new glass for weeks, maybe even months. I also walked over and had a closer look at the restaurant. It's totaled. The roof has collapsed and all the equipment inside is wrecked."

"What are we going to do?" Rose asked, rubbing his thigh.

"I'm not going to think about the restaurant right now. It's not like we're going to have customers lined up any time soon." Brad put his hand on Rose's, "I hate that restaurant. Seeing it ruined didn't bother me at all." He put his head on the back of the couch and closed his eyes. "I'd love to just walk away."

"Can you?"

"We signed a lease, we'd still have to pay rent. Let's just hope that the insurance pays up."

Rose could hear the worry in his voice. "Well, we're so lucky to have this." She circled her arms to include their small haven.

"No kidding, I couldn't handle any of this without knowing that I could return to the air conditioning." He sat forward and pulled himself up. "Hey, have you seen the cactus?"

"What cactus, our cactus?"

"Our cactus," he said, mimicking Rose's voice. "I don't know how it happened. It's all speared with glass. It looks like something in a horror movie."

"You mean like some of the round flat parts," said Rose.

"Yeah, but I mean all the round flat parts, all over them."

"Show me," said Rose. Brad got up and opened the door for Rose and made a sweep of his arm. When they stepped out of the RV they were both smiling. We're a good team, thought Rose. She hooked her arm through his and they walked around to the sea side where the cactuses lined the inside of the walls, mainly to discourage fence jumpers, both dogs going out and people coming in, and it worked well. All the plants were skewered with jagged shards as if they had been thrown at the plants sideways.

"Who's here?" Brad asked, after hearing voices. They headed for the courtyard and saw Jennifer in the driveway. She had a huge grin and a bundle of towels in her arms and in the center was the pup. He looked weak but he was still alive. Rose couldn't hold back her tears. She'd left him there. How could she have done that? Who could look at that and walk away? She took him from Jennifer and hugged him with enormous relief and then hugged Jennifer with him in the middle.

Jennifer had named him Rancho and over the next week he slept on a pile of towels in the guest room next to the courtyard. He barely moved.

Rose suspected that Addy felt guilty for pushing Rose to leave that day because she arrived every afternoon and tended to him for at least two hours. She patiently rubbed medicine into his wounds and cream on his mangy skin. Slowly, he grew patches of hair and added fat to his bones. After he got his first vaccination Addy took him home. Jeannie said it was okay.

Rose spent time with Itzamna and Ek Chauh that night. She was questioning them, questioning herself. "There is no such thing as hopeless," Itzamna told her more than once. "It's either over or we aren't finished yet. Nothing's easy."

The birds being fed in Rancho Viejo

Rancho rescured from Rancho Viejo after Hurrican Wilma.
Then Rancho after a long recovery and ready for a loving home

William and Hero from Rancho Viejo in the back of the car

Wilma found at the dump after the hurricane

Chapter 23
Palomo

A few days after their trip to Rancho Viejo, Gretchen called Rose. "Vivian's trying to get hold of you. Is there something wrong with your phone?" she asked.

"Not that I know of. I'm talking to you, aren't I?" said Rose.

"Well, you should call her."

Gretchen gave Rose her number and hung up. Vivian was a vivacious redhead in her late twenties who lived in Canada but had a boyfriend in Cancun whom she visited whenever she could. It had been two years since Vivian had come to the house and adopted a pair of puppies. The pups weren't for her, but she wanted to help and knew that someone in her family would want them.

As predicted, the pups never even made it to Viv's apartment. Her aunt fell in love with them the minute Viv stepped out of the airport in Vancouver. After that, Rose got pictures of them running along the stony beaches of Vancouver Island. It doesn't get any better than this, she'd thought each time an update arrived. These were the happy endings that kept her going.

Vivian had kept in touch, so it wasn't a surprise, considering the hurricane that she'd tried to phone. She was at her boyfriend's house in Cancun when Rose called. Rose told her about the damage on Isla Mujeres and Vivian told her about what it was like in Cancun.

"How is it at Juan's house?" Rose asked. She had heard that the situation in Cancun was worse because of the larger population and looting.

"We're okay. The house needs work and Juan's mother's a nervous wreck. I think she's glad that I'm here."

"I'm sure she is. It's great that you could come down to help."

"I'm glad to be here," she told Rose, then paused. "I'm actually calling to see if you can help me with something?

"What's up?" Rose asked, but she knew what was coming.

"I've seen this dog in the street with a horrible wound on his back. I don't know if it's from the hurricane or not, but it looks infected. I don't even know if I'll be able to catch the dog but if I do, do you have room?"

So many new dogs had come to the house, she knew Brad would have a fit. He's right, of course, she thought, there had to be a limit.

"Sure," she said. She always said yes. "If the dog's bad I'll take him straight to Paulo for treatment. But you know if it's really bad we might have to put him down."

"I know, I know, I understand. It's just that it's one the worst things I've seen. I'll call you if I catch it." They hung up. Rose didn't say a word to Brad. No use causing trouble if it wasn't going to happen, she thought. The problem at the moment wasn't necessarily the number of dogs, it was the number of new dogs all at once and the fact that they were adults. They'd taken them in after the hurricane assuming their families would be back to claim them. So far the dogs were all friendly and getting along, but one aggressive dog could sway the pack.

Rose forgot all about Viv's call until she called again. "Remember the dog I told you about?" she asked after the usual hellos. "Well, that dog actually has owners. Can you believe it? I talked to them, and get this, the dog wasn't hurt in the hurricane. They told me that the dog was being aggressive so they'd tied it up and that's what caused the injury. You should see it." Vivian paused. "The cut's really deep and goes around his entire body behind his front legs. I mean, I can't imagine what they tied him with. It must have been a wire or something like that, and really tight." Rose had no response. She'd heard it before. "Anyway, they offered to sell the dog to me. Of course I said no, so they said I could have it."

"Is it male or female?" Rose crossed her fingers, hoping the dog was female.

"Male."

"How big is he?" Let him be a small dog, she said to herself.

"He's pretty big. Can you take him?"

Rose sighed. "Look," she said, "I don't know if I can keep him here or not. Males are so much harder to integrate with the other dogs. Don't you have a vet that you've been using in Cancun?"

"Yeah, but she's out of town. I tried her first. I knew you'd have tons of dogs."

Rose sighed again. "Okay. Bring him over and we'll take him to Paulo and see what he thinks of the injury. When are you coming?" It was eleven in the morning. Rose had planned to go to the clinic that afternoon. Hattie, one of her new dogs, wouldn't put weight on her front left paw and Rose couldn't see anything obvious.

"Can I bring him over now? I can catch the next car ferry. Juan can drop me off at Punta Sam." Rose knew the passenger ferry would be faster but they didn't take dogs. The car ferry would take anything. One time on the ferry, Rose and Brad had sat in their car with hay chewing camels staring down at them over the back of a truck, all the way to Cancun. The worst was the time they got stuck behind a truck full of smelly pigs.

"Does he have a name?" Rose asked.

"Palomo."

Rose looked around as if trying to find a reason not to go. "Okay. I'll pick you up at the dock and we can go straight to the clinic. I haven't told Brad about this yet. Poor guy!"

There was a pause on the end of the line. "Sorry," Vivian said.

"Don't worry about it." Rose said, feeling the rush of energy that always came when a dog arrived. She laughed as she hung up the phone. Brad knew she couldn't say no.

Hattie cowered on the floor behind the driver's seat as Rose drove to the docks. Her car was small, so she hoped Palomo was friendly. The only space for him would be by Vivian's legs.

She pulled her little, ancient Honda Del Sol into the ferry parking lot where they'd waited so long on the morning before the hurricane. It was hard to believe it had only been six weeks since then. The boat had arrived and cars were driving up and over the steep ramp, one after another. Passengers without cars usually rode on the top deck and exited along a walkway at the side of the ramp.

Vivian was one of the last people off. She had a rope around Palomo's neck. His head was low and he was nervously looking from side to side. As they approached the car Rose was surprised. She'd seen so many wounded animals and had smugly assumed that Viv was exaggerating or just hadn't seen many injuries. Not the case. This poor dog had a gaping infected wound, two inches wide running from one shoulder to the other.

Palomo's white fur made it stand out from a distance. She marveled that he was walking at all.

"Vivian, I thought you were exaggerating," she said when they approached the car. "God!"

"I know," said Vivian, kneeling beside Palomo and stroking his head. That's why he caught my attention. I can't believe he's still alive but he walks around like there's almost nothing wrong."

"How friendly is he?" Rose asked as she stepped away from her car and moved closer to the dog. She put her hand out for him to sniff but he kept his head down. "Do you think he'll be okay on the floor in front of your seat?"

"I think so." Vivian said. Rose knelt closer to Polomo and put her hand out, then gave him a minute to get used to her. "I mean first a car, then a boat, and now a car again. I'm sure this is all new to him." Vivian stroked his head. "He seems comfortable with me. He snuggled up to me on the ferry and I could see how nervous he was. Let's give it a try."

Rose walked around the car. "There's a little dog behind my seat but she isn't coming out for anything, so that shouldn't cause a problem." Rose sat behind the steering wheel, reached over and pushed the passenger door open and then waited while Vivian coaxed Palomo inside. He was so big, he barely fit in front of the seat, which was already as far back as it would go. Once he was settled Vivian straddled him and slowly lowered herself down, closing the door beside her. With Vivian's legs surrounding him Palomo visibly relaxed and rested his head in her lap.

Rose knew that Paulo wasn't at the clinic, but he'd arranged to have a young vet named Angel take his place for a few weeks. Angel was shy and fairly inexperienced so when they arrived he was equally shocked by the wound and surprised that they weren't bringing him in to be euthanized.

"I really want to give him a chance, or at least try," Rose told Angel as he knelt down on the floor to examine Palomo. It was obvious that the wound needed to be cleaned and stitched, but Angel wanted to wait four or five hours before doing the surgery since Viv couldn't tell him if the dog had eaten that day. Vivian gently coaxed Palomo into a large kennel while Rose went back out to the car for Hattie.

"This is Hattie," she explained when she returned. "She won't put weight on her front paw and I can't see anything wrong. Could you have a look?" Angel agreed to check her out, and put her in a smaller cage.

Rose took Viv to the house to see her new gang of dogs. Afterwards Vivian insisted on walking back to the ferry dock instead of being driven, so Rose stayed to help Rudi walk the dogs before she returned to Paulo's clinic. This was a new clinic location, and as usual it was simply a converted house. The last one had been bigger and brighter, but the neighbors had complained. And they were right, it was noisier. He had more dogs staying overnight since the hurricane.

This new location was in a poorer section of the island. The people on one side had to abandon their badly damaged house and the family on the other side assured him that they had no problem with the dogs. But this house was small. It had two rooms and a closet with a toilet. The first room was filled with different-sized kennels. The second room had an examining table in the middle and boxes of supplies piled against the walls. The best feature of this new location was a large fenced-in yard.

By the time Rose returned, late in the afternoon, Angel was working on Palomo. He'd neatly cut away the infected skin, making the wound look better but larger.

"I pulled a piece of glass out of your other dog's foot," he told Rose while he continued to work on Palomo. "Her paw should be fine."

"Can she walk?" Rose asked.

"I think maybe you should keep her inside for a few days. It would stay cleaner that way."

"No problem," she said. "What do you think of this guy?" Palomo was laid out flat on his stomach with an IV running into his front right leg. The bag of fluids was hanging from a hook in the ceiling and it dripped slowly into the narrow plastic tubing. Every once in a while Rose could see Angel's lips move as he counted the drips and rolled the little wheel attached to the line up and down. The wheel was covered with blood, a definite breach in sterile technique, but as there was no assistant to supervise the flow or get instruments for Angel, it was the best he could do.

"You know, you should ask for help." Rose said, indicating the IV line. "I could be here when you're doing a surgery like this, or Rudi could assist you."

Angel dipped his head and Rose was afraid that she'd embarrassed him. But she'd seen enough surgery to know how important it was to keep things germ free. "Next time maybe," she said and Angel nodded.

He continued to work while Rose watched. "I haven't cleaned up his chest yet," he said. "I hope we have enough sutures to close him properly. I'll try to use as little as possible." Angel wiped his forehead with the back of his sleeve. "After that he may be okay if the infection hasn't already spread. I think, when I'm finished, he should stay here in a kennel. It'll be quieter for him," Angel paused, "if that's okay." Angel never told Rose what to do. He would only suggest a course of action and then wait for her to decide. He was too young and inexperienced to insist on anything. He had yet to trust his own judgment, but so far, he seemed to be a good surgeon. She watched as he stretched some line out of the reel in a plastic box that was duct taped to the side of his table. He threaded a curved needle. "The good news," he said, "is that I can use the non-absorbable suture since he'll be here until we remove the stitches." Angel lifted the skin on one side of the wound with a large pair of tweezers and pierced the tissue, then he did the same thing on the other side before making a knot which he reinforced three times.

"Okay," Rose said, looking around the clinic to see what he needed. "I'll bring out a stack of clean towels for him and some food."

"That would be good. We really need towels but we shouldn't feed him until tomorrow."

"Okay. Then tomorrow I'll bring him some chicken and rice. That's always easy on their tummies." As Angel continued to close the wound, Rose stared at the dog's face and wondered what he'd been through. She turned away, determined not to get attached, which of course, never worked even though Angel had warned her that there was a big chance the infection was internal and Palomo wouldn't make it.

Hattie whined and wagged when Rose approached her kennel. It's actually remarkable that all the dogs don't have glass in their paws, thought Rose. The hurricane had spared so few windows. She lifted Hattie up, gave her a big hug, and then sat her on a chair while she cleaned the kennel. More times than not the vets didn't clean the kennels right away, so she always did it if she had the time. At this point cleaning up dog poop, urine, or blood was nothing to her.

Rose took Hattie home and kept her in the house. The electricity had been restored a few days before, so they'd moved out of the camper. Brad and Rudi had finally found enough wood to board up all the broken windows but it made the rooms dark. Yet after the small camper Rose enjoyed the extra space. Still everything was a challenge. Fresh food, clean water, clean clothes, clean anything, and new windows were a long ways off. Brad missed his air conditioning the most.

"Your damn rescue dogs," Brad said, when Rose told him that Hattie was staying inside, "they always pee on the floor."

"I know, I'm sorry, it's just that they get nervous," said Rose, feeling tired. The situation was wearing on both of them. Many of the other ex-pats had left. They'd boarded up their homes and gone back to the US or Canada where they could wait until building materials were available. But Rose couldn't leave, and she didn't want to. The situation reminded her of the house construction except now they also had 40 dogs to worry about.

"That's not it," said Brad. "The dogs pee because they aren't house trained." Rose knew it was true and inevitably it was Brad who stepped in it. Whenever she brought a dog inside she'd get up in the mornings before him to clean everything she could find, including the occasional tick climbing up the walls.

The next day Rose prepared some chicken and rice for Palomo. While she waited for it to boil she called Gretchen. "Wait until you see the dog I got yesterday." She told her.

"I'll come over later," offered Gretchen.

"No, he's at the clinic. I'm on my way to take him some food right now. Want me to pick you up?"

"Can you wait twenty minutes until Anna gets here? I'm the only one at the bookstore," said Gretchen.

A half an hour later Rose swung by the bookstore. Kat was there, too. She'd been back on the island for two weeks. There hadn't been a chance for them to talk, but Rose had the impression that the extra time together because of the storm hadn't been a good thing for Kat's relationship with Greer.

Gretchen was grateful because Kat had brought Pepe back to Cancun with her. It had taken a lot of planning. Kat took an extra flight to pick Pepe up and Gretchen met them at the airport. Kat was so happy to be back she hadn't been her usual antagonistic self but Rose knew it wouldn't last. She was who she was.

Anna arrived and took charge of the book store so the three of them piled into the Honda and drove to the clinic. Unfortunately, Palomo had developed a fever, so he wasn't interested in the food. Gretchen helped Rose clean cages and swept the clinic while Kat sat with Palomo.

"I can't believe he's been walking around for who knows how long with that enormous wound. Then, the minute he gets attention for it he gets a fever?" Rose said. Angel just shrugged. He couldn't explain it.

"Maybe he was about to get one," Kat suggested. She was sitting on the floor in front of Palomo's kennel. He was awake and staring at her with glassy eyes.

"All we can do is wait," said Angel. "I have him on antibiotics. I gave him an injection after surgery. It took over sixty stitches to close that wound. He was out for a long time and that's never good. I would like to have had him on fluids longer but that was my last bag."

"I hope that didn't use up all of your sutures," said Rose.

"Just the non-absorbable," said Angel. He took the two steps to the boxes against the wall and checked his supply. "There's not much left of any kind, too many wounded animals."

"Okay," said Gretchen. "We'll just have to get more supplies,"

"Hey, you've got connections, right?" asked Kat. Gretchen nodded. Rose knew this meant she was already working on a plan.

"I should've thought about all the stitches. They're so expensive." Rose said, feeling guilty. But what difference would it have made, she asked herself, realizing she would have done it anyway. "I'll come back tomorrow," she told Angel as they left.

"You guys want to have lunch?" she asked her friends as they walked to the car.

"I have to work," said Gretchen. "Anna could only stay for a few hours."

"I can't afford it," said Kat.

"Come on Kat, keep me company. I'll pay," offered Rose. "I want to hear about you and Greer." Rose wasn't ready to go home—too many dogs, too many things that didn't work.

Rose got an earful at lunch, but ultimately it sounded like the relationship would survive. She couldn't believe the inane things that had caused trouble, the petty things that mattered to Kat. It made her feel very married.

When Rose got home an old friend of Cally's was waiting for her, and she had a dog with her. This is getting ridiculous, thought Rose.

"I tried to call but the phones are still such a mess," Lisa said apologetically. "How is everything?" Rose made a point of telling her how many dogs she had, and then Lisa explained the situation in her part of Cancun. To Rose, all the stories were the same—everything destroyed and no materials for repairs and dogs, always dogs with nowhere else to go.

Rose felt a spike of anxiety. Was every person she'd ever met in Mexico going to bring her a dog? Was there nowhere else? She felt the heavy weight of responsibility. Other people could walk away, but she couldn't. Why can't I say NO?

She motioned Lisa to join her on the bench by the front door. The dog followed. A black and white, medium-sized dog with longer fur than most street dogs. "I've been watching her for a while," Lisa explained. "She lives in the street near my place and everyone feeds her. I thought she'd be okay, but there's so much rotten stuff around and so many more strays since the hurricane, it's just not safe anymore."

"What's her name?" Rose asked, waiting for Lisa to ask her if the dog could stay.

"Pancha, and she's so sweet." Rose stared at Pancha. She does have a sweet face, she thought, but what's with her body? Her torso narrowed towards her tail and her hind legs were farther apart at her paws than at her hips.

"Can you get her to walk around for me?" Rose asked Lisa.

"Sure," Lisa stood up and walked in a circle and the dog followed.

"Is there something wrong with her back legs?" Rose said after Lisa sat back down.

"She's been like that since I first saw her," said Lisa. "Sometimes she seems stiff when she gets up, but she walks okay. I had her vaccinated and spayed about a month before the hurricane."

Lisa was always saving dogs, but she couldn't keep them at her house. She rented and already had four which was the limit according to her landlady. They talked some more and then finally Lisa asked. "Can she stay? I've got to get back to Cancun. Everything is such a mess."

"Yes," said Rose. Of course, yes, she thought.

Lisa handed Rose seventy dollars before she left. "I know it's not much, but the hurricane has cost me a lot of money."

"Don't worry. This will be a big help," Rose said, and she meant it.

Pancha was not pleased to see Lisa disappear through the gate, and Rose knew exactly what the dog would do next. She'd press herself against the gate while the other dogs checked her out. After a while she would start growling at them and they'd leave her alone. Rose would feed her there at the door, and it would be two or three days before she'd start to join in. They all did it. The puppies joined the other pups immediately, but the older dogs had learned to be wary. If they'd been on the street fending for themselves, other dogs were competition, not companions, at least until they spent some time together in a safe environment.

Brad arrived home in the early evening. "Where'd that come from?" he asked Rose, lifting his chin in Pancha's direction.

After Lisa left, Rose cleaned the kennels next to the driveway where she could watch Pancha. With those back legs, the dog probably wasn't a fence jumper but Rose wanted to make sure. "Lisa brought her. Isn't she adorable?" Brad just looked at his wife and shook his head.

"You think every dog is adorable," he said.

"Well, they are." Rose struggled out of the kennel. Making an exit without letting any of the dogs out was always an effort. She put her arm through Brad's and they walked towards the house. She was relieved that he made no more references to the extra dog.

"Hey, there was a big thing on the news. President Fox came to Cancun and promised all sorts of assistance. He's sending electricians from other parts of Mexico to get this area back on line properly." The electricity hadn't been dependable since the storm. There'd been brown-outs, and black-outs, and a house at the south point that had burned down from an electrical fire.

"You just want your cable TV," Rose teased.

"Damn right," he said. Once inside, he'd gone straight to the fridge for a diet Coke. "It'd be nice to get back to normal, if only just a little."

After dinner, Rose carried her camera outside and took pictures of Pancha, who hated the flash. She kept turning her head to one side and then looking back at Rose as if to say, "What the hell was that?" The picture was for the files she kept on every dog that came to her house. She recorded everything that happened to them including meds and vaccines. It was the only way to keep track.

Pancha adjusted to the pack in just twenty-four hours even though it was obvious she liked people better. Within a few days she'd started sitting beside Rose, gradually leaning into her and then setting her head into Rose's lap. She didn't even care that the puppies climbed all over her legs. She had a person and that made things okay.

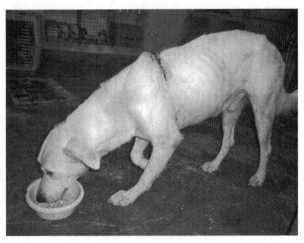

Palomo as his stitches are finally healing

Chapter 24
Help And Supplies

Pancha wasn't an energetic dog. She preferred to sit on a pile of towels and watch the rest of the pack play, although within a week she became the undisputed queen of the females. Rose spent extra time with her for the first few days, keeping her close while she and Rudi worked on the kennels. They were in constant need of repair, hurricane or not.

"Rudi," Rose said when they finished weaving wire through the holes in the first kennel, "don't feed anyone that rice and chicken that's in the fridge. It's for Palomo, the new dog at the clinic."

"Are you sure?" said Rudi. "I saw Palomo this morning when I talked to Angel at the clinic. He told me to tell you that Palomo still has a fever."

Rose sighed. "That can't be good," she said. Her attempts not to worry about the dog were failing miserably. "Did you deworm Pancha?"

"Yah, and I've given everyone their meds." Rudi paused and then asked, "Can I take some food for the dogs on my friend's street?"

"Of course, take all the food you need," Rose said. "We should have extra since we stopped the food drops."

Rudi smiled. He'd developed strong ties to the local community and Rose suspected that he would be helping the animals even if he wasn't working with her. He'd mentioned more than once that he had friends who wanted to help.

Rose was counting bags of dog food when she answered Kat's call. "Hey, I'm at the clinic," she said.

"What are you doing there?" asked Rose, peering into the plastic bin of kibble.

"I was just going by and thought I'd check on Palomo." Rose knew that Kat had also stopped because she thought Angel was cute. "He looks miserable. Angel says his fever's up. What should we do?"

This had started to happen regularly. People assumed that Rose knew more than she did and it made her nervous. Islanders had begun bringing their pets to her front gate for medical treatment. Either the vet's clinic was closed or they didn't like him or they were afraid of the cost. If the treatment was simple there was no problem, but it was up to Rose to be forthright about her limitations. She made sure to tell the dog owners that she wasn't a vet and started each recommendation with, "if it were my dog, this is what I would do."

"We'll just have to wait," said Rose. "Like Angel says. If the fever persists he will change the antibiotics."

The next day Palomo's fever hit one hundred and five so Angel started him on a different antibiotic. This was his third day of fever and Rose was getting anxious. She wanted to stay at the clinic with him but there was too much to do at home and she knew it wouldn't help. On her way to the car the phone rang.

"Bueno, hello," she answered her phone.

"Hello, is this Rose?"

"Yes, who's this?"

"Hi, it's Geena," a woman said. "I emailed you."

"Oh yes, hi Geena, are you here?" Geena was a vet who had a clinic in New York City. She'd been emailing Rose for months about a trip to the island. That was before the hurricane. Since then she wrote again and said that she wanted to come and help the animals. Rose's first thought was Palomo.

"My husband Thomas and I arrived yesterday. What a mess," said Geena.

"I know and I'm so glad that you still came, we could really use your help."

"I'm here to help," Geena said.

"Are you available today?" Rose asked.

"I'm available every day. What do you need?"

"There's a dog at the clinic that I would like you to look at. We've stitched a huge wound he had around his torso and he's had a fever for three days. I'm really worried."

"Okay, how can I get there? We're at Pedro Del Sol."

"How about I pick you up in half an hour?"

"One more thing," Geena said. "There's a dog. A large brown female by our cabin. She looks like an Irish setter with shorter hair. It's her stomach, it's bloated and hard. I don't think its puppies, maybe a tumor."

An hour later Rose helped Geena drag the reluctant brown dog into the clinic. She was shy, but fortunately not aggressive and she permitted Geena and Angel to poke at her. Geena didn't seem fazed at all to be working on the floor in such a primitive clinic. Quickly she and Angel agreed that they'd have to open the dog up to know for sure. While they worked things out Rose checked on Palomo. He was moving around a bit more than the day before and as she rubbed his ears and his head felt cooler.

"I'm going home to cook chicken for Palomo," she told the two vets. They were still crouched over the dog and too involved to acknowledge her. It took Rose an hour to buy the chicken, poach it and return to the clinic. By then it was all over. The brown dog had been pregnant, but she was carrying too many puppies, none of which survived and one of them was stuck in the birth canal.

"That dog would've died a horrible death," Geena told her as she washed up. "We spayed her while we were in there." Rose was grateful for the care and sorry about the puppies, but the real truth was that they didn't need more puppies. I wonder if I should be sad, she thought. Because I'm not.

Rose turned to Palomo. "How can I do this?" she asked Itzamna. "How do I care and stay sane at the same time? Rose imagined Itzamna in the clinic with Palomo when she wasn't there. The image eased her concern. She could see him lying in front of the kennel, resting his head on the rise at the bottom of the door frame. She had Ek Chauh at home with the older dogs, watching over them, assuring them that living in a crowded kennel was temporary, that things would get better. She wanted her princes to say the things that she couldn't, to fill in the gaps. She needed them in her mind, assuring her, helping her to keep her priorities straight. There was no manual, not for a rescue in Mexico in your back yard.

There were four new dogs in the clinic. Angel was out of room and out of kennels. In desperation to help them all he had tied one of his new patients to the leg of his examining table. There was never enough of anything. Rose had an ongoing mission to secure supplies. Where ever she went it was on her mind.

During a visit with her daughter in Colorado, Rose called the local animal shelter to ask for spare kennels. It was a pleasant surprise to hear that they were anxious to free up space in their crowded storage rooms. When Rose and her daughter turned into the parking lot of the shelter, someone had already stacked the kennels outside. It took an hour in the fading Colorado light to jig saw pack the crates into the car as Rose refused to leave even one behind.

The really hard part began the day that Rose returned to Mexico. They arrived at the airport at four in the morning and after unloading a suitcase and the two incredibly heavy stacks of crates Rose kissed her daughter goodbye.

She was flying United Airlines but there were only American Airline skycaps working at that early hour. They were not permitted to help passengers traveling on other airlines, so the skycaps stood there and watched as she struggled to load her suitcase and one stack of crates on a cart. When she arrived at the counter inside the terminal, she was relieved to find there was no line. Still breathing heavily, Rose handed her ticket to the attendant who grunted a few questions and then looked behind her.

"What are you going to do with those?" he asked signaling towards the kennels.

"Oh, that's only half of them. The others are outside," Rose informed him proudly, still so pleased to have so many.

"Well you'll have to bring in every piece of your luggage before I can check you in."

"Okay," Rose agreed. "Can I leave these here while I get the others?"

"You can't leave your luggage unattended," he told her.

Rose looked around the airport. There were no other people except airport employees anywhere near them. She leaned into the high counter and said, "But I'm leaving them with you. Isn't that okay?"

"Not until they're checked in. Until then, you can't leave them there," he said officiously.

"Okay. Let's check these in and then I'll go and get the others." Rose pointed towards the doors.

"You can't check in until you have all your luggage and you'll have to pay a fee for extra bags," he said, raising his chin arrogantly. Rose was trying hard not to laugh. It was so early and he was so grouchy.

"What do you think I should do?" she asked, dropping her large tote bag on the ground.

"I can't tell you what to do," he said.

Rose was getting irritated. Of all the problems she thought she would have getting the kennels back to Mexico, this wasn't one of them. "If you watch my bags, isn't that okay? I mean you work here?"

"I can't do that," he said, arranging some papers on the desk as if the conversation was over.

"But there's no one else here. I can be very quick."

"You seem to be missing the point," he said, speaking slowly as if Rose couldn't understand the language. "It's airport policy that you cannot leave your bags unattended."

Rose decided her best hope was the American Airlines skycaps. She'd seen one of them looking guilty as they'd all watched her struggle. Annoyed at the silly situation she grabbed her tickets and passport off of the counter with a great frustrated sweep before she pulled the cart away from the desk. The cart was so heavy that she had difficulty turning it around. She moaned loudly as she struggled to get herself in the right direction and then she noticed the luggage x-ray machines next to the counter and her heart sank. There was no way that her stacks of kennels were going to fit through those machines.

Once outside, Rose paid for another cart and loaded up the second stack and then she proceeded to push one cart forward, and then go back for the other and push it a short ways, keeping them both close enough so as not to seem "unattended." At last one of the skycaps took pity on her and helped her inside. "Thank you very much," she said loudly.

Finally she was back at the counter, still the only one there.

"You can't just send those things stacked like that," the same unhappy ticket man said to her.

"Look," she said, "I run an animal rescue in Mexico. Do you have a dog?" she hoped he did.

"No, I'm allergic." Great, she thought, and then tried something else.

"I thought you seemed stuffed up. I just had a cold myself."

He looked up at her and said, "I've had this thing for weeks. I just can't get rid of it." Now we're getting somewhere, thought Rose.

"That would drive me crazy. I felt like my head was going to explode," she added sympathetically.

"Yes, I've had a constant headache," he said, then sniffled.

"I'm so sorry," she said. "It must make it really hard to get up this early to go to work and deal with customers when you feel that bad." He eyed her suspiciously.

"Yeah, it's tough," he said with a bit of that officiousness back in his voice. "Can I see your ticket?" He smiled weakly. "What are you going to do with those crates?"

"I brought a roll of duct tape to tape them together. I was waiting to see the best way to send them before I did it." The ticket agent told her that they could travel the way she had them stacked so she taped the crates together. They were awkward and very heavy, making it hard to get under and around them but finally she had them securely connected.

"I will have to charge you for an extra bag," he said.

"I knew you would," Rose said. She handed the man her credit card. "Can I use this?"

"Yes, that's fine." As she finally left the check-in counter, she turned towards the x-ray machine with a feeling of dread. Rose was sure the men who ran it had been watching the entire fiasco and weren't looking forward to dealing with "the difficult crate lady," either. They huffed and puffed while making a big show of moving the kennels into position, but then, to Rose's great relief, went over them with a hand scanner.

Finally it was done and Rose headed for security. She handed the security guard her ticket. He looked at it and then back to her and said, "I'm afraid you can't wear open toed shoes on the plane," and pointed to her flip flops.

Rose was not ready for another battle and was about to say something not very nice when he started to laugh. Her check-in debacle had been witnessed by everyone at that quiet time of the morning. Rose laughed too, and a little more than she meant to.

It had cost one hundred dollars to transport twenty crates, and when she realized that they hadn't charged her an overweight fee, she felt like she'd deserved that break. Doing the math, the crates had only cost five dollars each.

Watching the poor sick pup tied to the examining table for lack of kennels, Rose was wishing she still had some of those crates. But they were all gone, used for one thing or another.

Rose moved through the small clinic, checking out the four new dogs. She was thinking that every waking minute of every day her family, her home, all of it was now wrapped up in dog rescue. Would it ever be enough? She knew what Itzamna would say. And that's why she needed him.

Chapter 25
New Connections

Geena's brown stray dog recovered well. She was up and whining the day after her surgery, showing her contempt for confinement by clawing and chewing at her crate. Even the biggest crate in the clinic was too small for her, and after a day her whining Angel finally tied her up in the yard next to the clinic where she was much happier.

Palomo was better as well. Angel had changed some of his medication, following Geena's advice. His fever was down and the stitches on his back were showing no signs of infection. However, the stitches on his chest looked puffy and red. The problem was that he was lying on them all day so they weren't getting a chance to dry out and heal. When Rose helped Palomo outside to empty his bladder, just those few steps wore him out and he huffed his way back to the kennel.

As they continued to discuss Palomo, Geena walked into the clinic. She'd come to check on her patient. "I'm feeling lucky," she said. "With so few taxis around I managed to flag one down and I'm so glad to find you here." Geena turned to Rose, "There's another dog that hangs around the bungalows. You should see his leg." Geena made a zigzag motion with her hand. "I've named him Pedro. He's been keeping us company on the beach and sleeps outside our door. Do you have a thermometer?" she asked Angel. Angel picked up a thermometer that was sitting on his table and wiped it with a piece of cotton he pulled from a jar of rubbing alcohol. Geena headed outside to check the brown dog's temperature. She was already talking when she walked back through the door. "I don't think that he was born that way. Pedro, I mean. Unfortunately, it looks like his leg's been broken more than once and healed badly on its own."

Kat arrived while Geena was talking. "Hey Rose," she said, "I've been looking for you." The short shorts were back. She'd dyed her hair from brown to blond and she was looking good. Rose introduced Geena and Kat. The contrast in their appearance was incredible. Geena dressed like Cally, for comfort and concenience, while Kat's long slender body, now topped with blond hair, and in her short shorts stood out like a movie star's.

Kat spotted Palomo. "How is he today?"

"He's better but still has a low fever," said Rose. "We're worried about the stitches on his chest—he's always laying on them so they aren't healing as well as the ones on the top."

"Why don't you make him a hammock?" said Kat. Everyone in the room looked pleased. The idea was so brilliant.

"What a fantastic idea," said Rose. "I bet Jeannie could make one. She's always sewing something. Would you mind talking to her about it? It would have to be a fine mesh and low to the ground like a cot."

"Not a problem," said Kat, obviously pleased with herself. "I planned to see her later anyway. I was going to see if she could hire me to do a bit of cleaning."

"What about Addy?"

"She's going to waitress at Olivia's for a while, just for a change." Kat sat on the floor and stroked Palomo's head. "Jeannie thinks it will be good for Addy to spend more time dealing with people. The condo rental business is ridiculously slow since the hurricane and I thought it'd be nice to do a little cleaning. I've got good music and a headset and I won't have to talk to anyone."

Kat turned to Angel and asked him about Paloma, so Rose left with Geena to check on Pedro with the zigzag leg. It was easy to spot Pedro at Geena's bungalow. His front leg took an odd turn midway down and then another turn at what might be considered the dog's ankle. Apparently he was still using the leg but it looked like it should collapse under his weight. Geena's husband, Thomas, was in a hammock between two palm trees and Pedro was enjoying the shade beneath him. Geena talked away about possible corrective surgeries and other veterinarians she knew who were specialists. It was clear that she already pictured him in New York City, with transportation a mere detail to be worked out.

After seeing Pedro, Rose drove Geena to her house to look at a few of the dogs with problems. Pancha was next to them the minute they came through the gate so Rose walked up the driveway and called Pancha to follow. Geena stayed behind to observe her movements.

"Something's all wrong with that back end. Do you know anything about her?" she asked.

"Not a thing. She was found on the streets of Cancun," Rose explained.

"She seems to get around fine. I'd leave it alone unless she's in pain. What happened to that pup's ear?" Geena was pointing at a one eared dog.

"Oh, that's Una, she's new," said Rose. "One of the boys who lives at the dump heard some whining and followed the sound. Someone had put Una in a box and left her there. Animals are abandoned at the dump all the time. The next day the boy found this puppy in the same area, and the two of them looked so much alike that we called this one Dos. Sometimes we just run out of names."

Geena picked up Una and sat down in the bench by the front door. Una was thrilled with the attention, but had little patience for the prodding of her ear, which was simply a bump. The skin around it was loose, as if the ear had flopped over and attached itself to her head. Una squirmed until she freed herself and ran off. "It looks like she was born that way," said Geena. "It would be okay if the ear flap had been completely sealed but its open a bit at the bottom." She crossed the driveway and grabbed Una again and turned her so Rose could see what she was talking about. "We'll have to remove the earflap or it'll collect dirt inside and cause trouble. What else have you got for me?"

Rose took Geena around to the seaside of the house. It was a nice big space for the dogs to play. The first dog to greet them was Pinky who had horrible skin problems and then Stretch arrived with the huge lump on the top of his head.

"What do you know about Pinky?" said Geena.

"The vet found her on the road to Merida. I think he saw her as a challenge. She was skin and bones, had heartworms and very little fur." Rose knelt beside Pinky. "I think she might be a black Lab but it's hard to tell right now." Pinky was in heaven as Rose stroked her back. Most people avoided touching her, including Rudi.

"This looks like demodex mange. It's hereditary or stress induced but not contagious. I'd give her weekly injections of ivermectin and put her on antibiotics for a long time, and as her health improves, hopefully her skin will too." Now they turned their attention to Stretch. "Was he out during the hurricane?" Geena asked while moving the bump around on his head.

"They were all out at some time except for the puppies."

"This is definitely an inflammation of some kind. It isn't attached to the skin or the bone. Keep an eye on him but it'll probably go away on its own."

As they went from dog to dog and Geena gave advice for the different ailments, Rose wished she could keep her at the house for ever. Eventually she pulled a pad and pencil out of her bag to write down all the instructions. When they got to the eighth dog, they looked at each other and started to laugh. The dogs were all such a mess and so desperate for attention. After a while it was so not funny, that it somehow was very funny. The rescue was full and the dogs were bumped and bruised like everything else in the wake of the hurricane.

When Geena and Thomas left for New York they took Pedro with them. "He's right beside me," said Geena when she called to say they'd arrived safely. "He's just as happy as he could be."

"Tomorrow I'll x-ray his leg and we can decide what to do from there."

"What a lucky boy," Rose said, and hung up the phone feeling lucky as well. She told Brad all about it when he got home that afternoon.

"Too bad Geena can't take all of the dogs. How many are there right now?" Brad asked, as he looked out the kitchen window. Rudi was herding the dogs to the side of the house where they would spend the night in their kennels.

"You know I never count. It changes every day—one out, two in, or whatever."

"That's the problem right there," said Brad. He turned to look at Rose. "One out and two in." Rose hated these conversations. They made her tired. She sat on one of the stools in the kitchen and rubbed her eyes. The only way she survived the stress of too many dogs was to accept that each dilemma didn't have to be resolved right away. She simply had to wait and it worked out. It had to.

"You know we'll work it out," she said, jumping off the stool and walking towards him. "We always do." She hugged her husband.

"Yeah, but I'm not sure that we've ever had this many," he said, hugging her back.

"I know," conceded Rose. And she knew Brad knew that even though she didn't have the answers, she was planning, working on solutions, and alert to all possibilities.

"Sorry," he said, "I know you're working on it." He settled his chin on the top of her head. "You amaze me. You always find the answers."

We'll be okay, thought Rose. When people asked her about the dogs and what she was going to do with all of them, she loved to tell them this old story: A little boy saw a huge ocean wave wash thousands of starfish up on the beach. He raced over to help them by picking them up and throwing them back into the sea. Meanwhile an old man came by and asked, "How are you going to save all of those starfish?" The boy replied, "One starfish at a time."

They were her dogs. There was the big picture and the little picture, and she worked them both, one dog at a time. And when things were too overwhelming she summoned Itzamna and Ek Chauh. They had joined her or she had joined them. They were her strength and her comfort and she was their arms and their voice.

Rehoming dogs was Rose's biggest challenge. This part of the rescue was evolving slowly. Cally was still taking dogs to Houston and Rose was happy to hear that Geena wanted to treat and find homes for her dogs with health issues.

Some of the dogs that came in after the hurricane were eventually picked up by their families when they returned to the island. But most of them were going to be with Rose until she found a better place for them.

The hurricane, their hurricane, had made the front page of Time Magazine as the 'Storm of the Century'. It was a big deal, a genuine cataclysmic event, and to deal with its aftermath, she simply resolved that everyone had to stretch themselves and push harder. Her Grandmother's favorite saying was, "if you don't push yourself, how will you ever know how much you can do."

The smaller breed dogs were easier to place both locally and with other rescue groups but since the storm she'd taken in a larger percentage of big dogs and Palomo was soon to be one of them. It took a month for him to heal but with his recovery came other problems, he was difficult. He was used to the streets and picked fights; he bullied the other males and often jumped the fence. Pancha was the same. She bullied the females and reacted poorly to strangers.

Rudi was the one who handled them the best. Palomo knew Rudi was the boss and Pancha just loved to sit with Rudi in the evenings after everyone was fed.

Chapter 26
Addy

More and more often, Rose's days started with a phone call asking for help. In the spring before the hurricane she'd hired someone to set up a website for the rescue. The timing was perfect; it included a Pay Pal account for cash donations and a list of supplies that people could bring down if they wanted to help, but it also made her more visible and cemented her as the 'one to call' when a dog was in trouble.

Gretchen and Kat were coming to the house more often. Kat especially. "How is my Palomo?" was always her first question after she came through the door. The idea of it amused Rose and Gretchen. Kat had gone to the clinic to snag herself a cute veterinarian and instead she was snagged by a big white dog.

"He's feeling his oats and causing trouble." Rose told her.

"Wow, that's great, just my kind of guy," said Kat. Rose was pleased that Kat had taken an interest in Palomo, with her at the house more often Rose felt like she'd found a partner. Kat was happy cleaning rooms for a change and she had great stories to tell about the guests at Jeannie's bed and breakfast. The job switch made her seek out company instead of hiding from people in her free time.

"Listen," Kat said when they'd finished the kennels and were sitting by the front door. "I was having coffee at the Mango café this morning when I saw this dog grazed by a taxi. I mean it was inches from being squashed. The poor little thing crawled under a parked car so I went out to see if it was okay. Get this," said Kat, reaching forward with her arms to illustrate, "I'm down on my hands and knees and guess what, I can see two of them."

"What did you do?"

"I coaxed them out one by one and handed them to some tourists who were at the restaurant and wanted to help."

"Did you ask around? They must have an owner," said Rose.

"I asked everyone and no one knows a thing. I guess these dogs fell from the skies," Kat added sarcastically. "Anyway, one of the tourists that helped is staying in a rental house and took them home. I didn't want to bring them over until I talked to you. I mean, look at this place." Kat spread out both her arms. "You've got a zoo here."

Rose leaned forward on the bench and put her elbows on her knees. She cupped her face in her hands and said, "Okay, bring them over. Are they big or small?"

"Small."

"Male or female?"

"One male, one female."

"That's a relief," said Rose. "I don't know if we could take another large male dog."

Kat returned with the two little dogs that afternoon and then stayed to help Rose bathe them. They'd let Palomo in the courtyard while they worked and he surprised them both by being gentle and sweet with the smaller dogs. Kat went on and on about it and then took Palomo for a walk before she left.

Rose called the new dogs Ruby and Taylor. They looked like a schnauzer-terrier mix. Ruby was black and Taylor was blond but their color was the only difference between them. They had obviously been well cared for and were probably litter mates; when one jumped, the other jumped, when one ran, the other ran, when one turned, the other turned. Rose called them "The Fish" because they moved in sync like a school of fish.

They were such a delight and so happy together that Rose was hoping to adopt them out together, but it didn't happen that way. Ruby was adopted within a week by an American man living on the island. It was such a good home and a good match that Rose knew it was the right thing to do.

The following day a young couple, Mark and May, brought medical supplies to the house. They'd emailed Rose after seeing the website, so she was expecting them. Every morning from that day on Mark and May came to volunteer, and when they left to go back home they took Taylor with them. The timing was perfect. Taylor had been depressed since Ruby was adopted and had happily curled up in May's lap every chance she got. May just couldn't resist her, and Mark predicted that his mother would adopt Taylor on sight.

May called Rose after they left, "Mark's mother phones me every day with a new Ruby story," she told Rose. "You'd think that Ruby glowed in the dark."

"That's such great news," said Rose, feeling a rush of happiness. One more starfish back in the ocean, she thought. "Tell her I want pictures."

"Hey, by the way," May said. "Mark and I have been talking about this since we left the island. We want to start a rescue for animals here in Minneapolis."

"Just like that, out of the blue?" Rose asked.

May laughed, "Well," she said, "I've been looking for something different and Mark is doing well enough at work now. If we're careful we should be able to pull it off." And then May started to ask questions, but unfortunately Rose had very few answers. She confessed that the creation of her rescue had been a complete accident. And the rules and regulations in Mexico had absolutely no resemblance to a similar situation in the US.

When Kat arrived Rose told her about the new rescue. It meant so much to Rose to have someone to share the news with who really cared, even though it wasn't an official partnership. Kat invited herself to lunch and asked if she could bring Palomo upstairs with them.

"Of course," said Rose as she climbed the stairs to the kitchen. "Brad's not here."

"Great, I'll tell you all about Greer," said Kat. Palomo bounded up the stairs and reached the kitchen door before Rose. She let him in first.

"Does that mean things are getting serious?" Rose pulled lettuce and cheese out of the fridge, holding them high out of Palomo's reach and taking them to the counter.

"Never!" Kat grinned broadly. She sat on the floor where Palomo immediately crawled into her lap. "I've never seen a fifty-pound lap dog before, have you?" she said.

"That dog adores you," said Rose, slicing the bread.

The phone rang. It was Jeannie Tull. "Is Kat there?" she asked after saying hello.

"Are you here?" Rose asked Kat, muffling the phone on her shirt.

"Who is it?" Kat was repositioning her legs under Palomo's heavy weight.

"Your boss."

"Tell her to come over for lunch."

Rose put one hand on her hip. "I think I've made you feel too much at home," she said.

"Rose, you make everyone feel at home."

"Yes, Kat is here." Rose said into the phone. "Why don't you join us for lunch? I'm just throwing something together."

"Is Addy there, too?" asked Jeannie.

"No, why?"

"I'll be right over." Jeannie's B&B was downtown, only a five-minute walk to Rose's house.

"What's up with Addy?" Rose asked Kat. "Have you ever asked Jeannie if they're related or something?"

"Enough! Off!" Kat shoved Palomo off of her lap. "Nope, she's never said anything and I've never asked, but I want to." Kat stood up and went to the sink to wash her hands.

"Here. Start chopping this stuff for the salad." Kat made a face and pulled out the chopping board. She knew where everything was.

When Jeannie arrived they sat down to eat at the kitchen island. Both Kat and Rose wanted to know why Jeannie took care of Addy the way she did. But Jeannie didn't mention why she was looking for Addy so Rose decided they'd have to wait until she was ready to talk about it. "So did I tell you about my newest dogs?" asked Rose. "We call them Paula and Sammy and they're both crazy."

"Where did they come from?" Kat asked with her mouth full of food.

"Paula was tied to our front gate and Sammy was brought to the house by her owners. They told me that she'd always been crazy. Both dogs are hyper, play too rough with the other dogs, and overwhelm anyone who comes near them. They bark at everything, eat the wire fencing, gnaw and scratch at the wooden doors, drag anyone walking them down the street, nip at the puppies, and want all the food. They're a nightmare." Rose looked at Kat. "They make Palomo looks good.

Kat scowled, "Get Rudi to work with them," she suggested.

"Oh, that's the other thing. I haven't told you. Rudi has picked a horrible time to become a pain in the ass. He's discovered women and he's bringing them home. Can you believe that?" She picked up the salad bowl. "More salad?" she asked.

"I'll have more unless you want it, Kat?" said Jeannie, reaching for the bowl.

"Help yourself," said Kat.

"Finish it," said Rose.

"I'm terrified he'll get married and move out or something like that." Rose carried her plate to the sink. "I've got that website now, and with the adoption page to update and blogs that Brad keeps pushing me to write I just don't have enough hours in the day. I can't lose Rudi."

"I don't know how you do it," said Jeannie sympathetically. "But the website is key. You need it to raise more money. It's like you're paying to work your ass off."

"I know, but things will get better." Rose didn't want to talk about the money issues. She got up, grabbed a sponge and started to wipe the counter around the sink. "What's up with Addy?" she asked, to change the subject. And then she decided it was time to know. "Why are you looking for her?"

"I just worry about her," said Jeannie, lifting her arms so Rose could wipe the island counter. "I don't know how she can live through each day being as sensitive as she is. She got really upset this morning when she found a dead mouse in the trap I'd put out. I forgot to move it before she saw it. She just seems so lost sometimes."

"God, it sounds like you're adopting her," said Kat. She'd cleared her plate and sat back down on the floor, feeding Palomo leftovers, asking him to sit before each bite.

"I guess I sort of am." Jeannie said. "I wish she had just one quarter of your toughness, Kat. She'd be way better off."

"Hey, I paid a high price to be this tough," said Kat defensively.

"I meant it as a compliment Kat, tough is good," said Jeannie, handing her more bread crust for Palomo.

"Yeah, I wish I could be tougher with the dogs," said Rose. "It would make my life easier. But don't give Kat too much encouragement, Jeannie. You know, Kat, you could hold your tongue occasionally." They all laughed. Kat enjoyed the trouble she caused.

"Well, I just worry about Addy," said Jeannie. "I've never told you this, but she's actually my niece."

"Finally," said Kat. "We've all been wondering who she was and why you took such good care of her."

"Well, I'm telling you now. Way back, it's seems like a life time ago, my sister got pregnant, and rather than facing our mother, she ran away to the US. Then a few years ago she got sick. It's a long story and I've kept it quiet because someone might be looking for Addy." Jeannie hesitated, like she was deciding how much to tell. "It's not as mysterious as it sounds. Addy's stepfather was abusive. I think that's why Addy is the way she is.

She saw him hurt her mum and could never do anything to help her."

"I can't imagine how rough that would be for a little girl," said Rose.

"It happens," said Kat.

Jeannie looked like she had more to say. "Go on," said Rose.

"Well, my sister had breast cancer. She'd had all the treatments, but it came back. Poor thing never really had much of a life." Jeannie paused, stuck on a memory.

"How is she now?" Rose asked.

"She died, and when she knew she was dying she arranged for Addy to come here for a visit and then she asked me if Addy could stay. Of course, I said yes but I don't talk about it because the step father could be looking for her. He'd legally adopted Addy and I'm sure he thinks that my sister tricked him. He was like that, never wanted anyone to get one over on him."

Rose got up and poured Jeannie a glass of water. "The good news," Jeannie continued, "is he doesn't even know my last name or where in Mexico we are. I changed my name when I came here, fresh start, what the hell, you know."

"Wow." Kat said. "You're full of surprises today. She's lucky to have you."

"Wow back," said Jeannie. "I think that's the nicest thing you've ever said to me."

"Well, I have had a head ache all day." Said Kat displaying a broad grin.

"Bugger, I'll remember you said it." Said Jeannie. Kat bowed.

"Keep going," said Rose.

"Well, I've just been worried about Addy lately. The hurricane was really hard on her. I think it made her feel vulnerable, like her life before." She paused, took a sip of water and the started again.

"Also, I'm feeling better about it, like her step father won't find her or maybe he isn't looking. There's no legal trail to my name. I was a big fan of Jethro Tull. My mother always said I was thick as a brick, meaning my body, not my head. You know, this was England around the time of Twiggy, so a brick compared to a twig meant really big as in 'me.' Never cared for my mother much, but I liked the song, so I picked Tull. With a "T" I still had the same initials."

"Oh my god you are full of surprises and what a story," said Rose. She slid off her stool and walked to the windows. "That would be horrible for a little girl, no wonder she's so emotional." It made Rose want to find Addy and just hug her for a while.

"Yeah, I worry."

'You know," said Rose, "there's always an answer, not necessarily right away, but it'll come. Addy has you, and she's safe now. It just takes a while. I mean, I'm sorry to compare this to the dogs but even my worst dogs get better after time with us, feeling safe and loved."

"Really, Rose," said Kat, "that's your advice. We should put Addy in a kennel until she feels better." Kat mimicked the motion of shutting and locking a door. Both Jeannie and Rose were caught off guard by Kat's statement, and couldn't help laughing.

"Kat, you're off the head," said Jeannie, using one of her favorite expressions.

"Palomo doesn't think so," Kat said, and as if answering her, the dog licked her face.

The fish were found under a car after being abandoned

Chapter 27
Rose

Rose was proud to have earned the reputation as someone who had no other agenda than helping the dogs. But she'd heard of poseurs, even in the rescue business. One woman who lived in Kansas started a website for her animal rescue; she called it BARK (Better Animal Rescue of Kansas). In the beginning she did some good work, funding spay and neuter clinics, raising money for Mexican rescues and collecting supplies for them. But as time passed it became clear that her true passion was scuba diving. As she raised more and more money through her well-maintained website she used less of it for animal rescue and more of it for scuba diving trips in Mexico, during which she would distribute just enough supplies to cover her tracks.

Then there was the woman in Cancun who opened a rescue and used the money she raised to build her house. She took in dogs, of course, but they often went hungry as she added more rooms to her home. Most of these people started with good intentions, but animal rescue is hard work. After a while they probably felt that in some way they'd earned the right to spend the money they raised—on themselves.

Brad and Rose had been using their own money for years. They had fundraisers on the island but the islanders were poor, so it fell on the foreigners to support the dogs, and there were lots of worthy causes competing for donations. After many years the financial situation was getting serious and Rose had seen too many good rescues go broke.

Rose had tried everything she could think of to raise money.

"How about skin creams?" Jennifer suggested at one of the volunteer meetings. Jennifer had a good eye for business. Brad fondly called her the hippy capitalist.

"Sounds great, let's try it," Rose said. Soon after, she spent hours researching the perfect cream, and Gretchen designed labels for the bottles. Rose called the cream Ocean Potions and sold it in the local stores. People loved the scent, and sales were small and constant but not enough to make a real difference with the costs of the rescue. One year she set up a running race on the island. She called it the K9K but it was so much work that making it a yearly event was out of the question. She had donation posters and cans in Jeannie Tull's bed and breakfast and the book store, and that helped. Rose's main problem was that she couldn't depend on a certain amount of income that would help her plan for the future.

She finally gave in. The first person she thought of was Jennifer so she set up a meeting.

They met at the restaurant downtown and sat in the back so they wouldn't be disturbed. After they ordered, Rose confided in Jennifer that she was overwhelmed. She couldn't run the rescue, take care of the dogs, keep up on the website and raise enough money all at the same time.

"I'm not surprised," said Jennifer. "Your rescue is growing; most nonprofits have a person to raise funds, a media person and in your case, let's say, an adoption coordinator. You're doing all of it. I think it's time for you to decide the direction you want to take."

"Oh please, not all that mission statement stuff. You know I'm no good with that."

"It's not all about a mission statement. At this point there are two questions: do you want to grow and do you want to work with other people on a steady basis? I can help, but you're the one who needs to decide where the rescue is going. And to fundraise you'll need to give people a clearer picture of what you do."

A waiter arrived with their drinks. "Diet Coke?" he asked.

"Here," said Rose, reaching for the glass.

"Did you really want two waters?" the waiter asked Jennifer. She nodded.

"I do need to change things," said Rose, removing the straw from her glass and taking a drink. "And I really appreciate that you know about this stuff. I just got into this to save puppies and it's turned into something much bigger than that."

"Rose, you passed the simple puppy thing a long time ago." Jennifer took a packet out of her purse and stirred its contents into one of her waters.

"Energy drink?" asked Rose.

"Something like that," said Jennifer, and then drank half of the glass at once.

"Maybe that's all I need," said Rose. Jennifer didn't laugh. "Okay, I give in," said Rose. "So I assign people, probably all you guys, specific jobs, and then hash out the details of each area. The first thing is the money. I need some for the dogs at the rescue and some for spay and neuter, which is really, our long-term solution, right."

"That's good," Jennifer said. "We know that the spay and neuter part is the sustainable answer." She picked up her napkin and wiped her knife and then did the same with her fork. "That's what it's all about. That's what people want to hear."

"That's just it," said Rose, wondering if she should be cleaning her cutlery too. "I think that things are moving forward. We have more people coming to the house to volunteer, more people bringing us supplies, and more rescues wanting to find homes for our dogs. I feel like we've made people pay attention and now it's time to do more. But money is the main problem."

Rose wanted to keep the conversation focused on the money because it had occurred to her that nobody else really understood how much she and Brad were spending. She'd never done a budget. They had just been filling in the gaps between the costs and the donations.

"Yeah, money is always a problem. I don't know how much you spend on the rescue. It's just a given that all community outreach will cost more than anyone ever expects."

Rose nodded in agreement and took a sip of her Coke. "I feel like one of those political cartoons," she said. "The wind is blowing me sideways while I'm clutching onto a dog's leg, wanting to keep doing what I'm familiar with. Just out of reach is a spay and neuter clinic with 'the solution' stamped across it." Rose ran the cool glass across her forehead. The waiter arrived with chips in a basket and salsa in a clay bowl.

"Picante!" He warned them before leaving.

"I don't even speak Spanish yet," she said.

"But look what you've accomplished already," said Jennifer, grinning before dipping her first chip. "You were dumb as a board when you started."

"Ha, thanks a lot." Rose sat back and thoughtfully fingered her glass. "You know, I was a pain in the ass when I was a kid. And I was a teenager just at the end of the hippy years, which made me a 'hippy wannabe.' The idea was to create a new path, not follow an old one. So here I am, a leader by obsession, but not by skill." Rose dipped a chip and popped it in her mouth. "Wow, that's hot," she said, reaching for her drink.

"I mean, I often feel out of place," she said, fanning her mouth, "caught between young and old. Look at you, you still believe you have time to change the world."

"Yeah, and so can you," said Jennifer.

Rose shook her head, "Hell, I've got friends who are thinking about retirement. They have grandchildren."

"You've still got tons of time. What are you talking about?" Jennifer said. She leaned back so the waiter could put her empanadas on the table.

"More salsa?" he asked.

"Si, por favor," answered Jennifer. He returned with the salsa and Rose's salad and asked if they needed anything else.

"Agua, por favor," asked Rose. She pointed to the salsa. "Wow, that salsa's hot." She turned back to Jennifer, "I know I have lots of time, but I wonder if I have the energy."

"My friend Nell," continued Rose, "Has a rescue in Akumal. She wants Brad and I to help her with some spay and neuter clinics down south. There's still small towns that are devastated by the hurricane and need help. I could start there, gain experience, I just don't know if I want to."

"You're just overworked," said Jennifer sympathetically. "And I think you should go to Aukumal, do the clinics, and learn all you can." Jennifer poured the last of the salsa onto her lunch. "You want any, before I use it all up?" Rose shook her head—her mouth was still burning. "What does Brad say?"

"He might want to come. Now that he's sold the lease to the restaurant he'd like to see other parts of Mexico. "

"So he's not going to rebuild the restaurant. For sure?"

Rose turned her head slowly from side to side, grinning, savoring the information. "Nope, he hated the restaurant. Not that he minded the work; he just hated the way things are done here. He's way too nice to be the sort of shit head that it takes to run a business down here."

"I know what he means. That's why Gretchen and I only have a few employees at the book store." Jennifer paused while she ate her last empanada. "You know, you have all sorts of people who want to help. Now you just need to learn to delegate," said Jennifer.

Rose slumped over her food. "It wears me out just to think about it. It's just easier to do things myself than try to explain them to other people."

"Go with your friend Nell. The more you know the better. If you want people to donate you have to have experience, and a history that shows how much you can get done. You'll have to start writing things down, keeping track of things: re-homing for example, or how many spays and neuters you've paid for, how many animals you vaccinate, all of that. With that information we can work on the other stuff."

"I know you're right. I'll start putting together the paperwork," Rose said. "And I'll ask Brad, see if he wants to work with Nell." Rose waved the waiter over and ordered a glass of wine. "I'd like to be nice and relaxed for that conversation. Do you want one?" she asked Jennifer.

"Why not?" she said, smiling. "I'm not working this afternoon."

"Thank so much, I feel a lot better. I knew you'd be able to help."

"Community development. It's what I do," said Jennifer with exaggerated inflection. "It's all about thinking ahead and putting people in the right places."

When the wine arrived, they toasted to the future.

That night, Rose was chopping vegetables for a stir-fry while Brad sat at the kitchen island going over numbers from the restaurant for the tenth time. They'd been talking about whether or not to go to the clinic.

"Nell really wants us to come," said Rose. "The clinics are in Majahual and Xcalak. She has a team of vets and techs coming from the States but wants local volunteers to handle check-in and recovery. You loved Majahual, remember?

"Wasn't that area hit hard by Wilma?" asked Brad. He pushed his papers across the counter and threw his pencil on top. It made Rose happy that the stress of the restaurant was almost over.

Rose nodded. "And they got Hurricane Dean as well."

"When is it, the clinic?"

"In two weeks," Rose told him.

"When does Nell need to know if we can come?"

"I don't know," said Rose, "probably as soon as possible." She dropped everything she'd chopped into the wok and stirred it with two wooden spoons.

"Let's see if Kat can stay at the house." Rose sprinkled some soy sauce onto the mixture. Can you grab some plates?"

"Okay, but go easy on the soy this time. Last time you made this I was thirsty all night," he said, holding his throat to illustrate his point. Rose ignored him.

"If Kat can stay, let's go."

Rose was surprised. She turned the heat off under the wok and moved closer so she could lean against her husband. She stayed there for a while feeling lucky. "Kat loves staying here, especially now that she's so crazy about Palomo."

Chapter 28
Xcalak And Majahual

Two weeks later Brad and Rose packed up their car and drove south. A local family, who supported Nell's work with the animals, had offered their incredible house as a central location to organize volunteers and supplies before driving to the clinic sites.

Akumal's coastline was unique. Instead of miles of straight sandy beaches, the shore line was like the scalloped edge of an old lace curtain. The beach circled inward between coral outcroppings averaging a mile or two apart. In some of these coves the ocean pushed farther inland creating irregular canals filled with sand, coral, and tropical fish. Nell's borrowed house sat next to one of these canals. The compound had an old-Spanish feel to it with a large fountain in front of the main door, circled by flowers and a brick driveway. It was a pleasant place to start.

This particular lagoon had been deemed a national park so there was a path off of the main road where people could come in and swim. What distinguished this lagoon was the large pieces of coral, flattened on top like mushrooms, scattered a few feet apart but close to shore. Around the base of each mushroom tropical fish picked away like bees in a flower bed. Rose was totally charmed.

After all of the volunteers arrived they packed up an enormous amount of supplies and headed south. Xcalak was their first stop, situated near the Mexican border, just a stone's throw from Belize. Xcalak was a beach community, but not a tourist destination because the sand at the water's edge was filled with sea grass. It made the water look dirty and less inviting to swimmers.

They were met by a gregarious English woman name Gwen, who had asked Nell to come.

"I just can't believe you're here," she told Rose excitedly. "I've prayed for something like this to happen. You know, there isn't a vet or even a doctor for miles. These poor animals get sick; we can't do a thing, and the puppies and kittens, oh those poor puppies and kittens. We have jaguars you know." Gwen went on and on, eventually speaking to no one in particular as she wandered around, weaving in and out of the volunteers while they unloaded supplies into the government building that Gwen had borrowed for the clinic.

"I've lined everything up, some of you are staying a ways away, it just couldn't be helped, but it'll be fine, I just know it'll be fine."

Nell interrupted Gwen every few minutes with a question: Where was the water? Will we have electricity by tomorrow? Will our supplies be safe overnight? Gwen had it all arranged. The building hadn't been used for years so she'd made a special arrangement to turn the utilities on. The group could meet and eat in a low structure next door that was presently being used by the older local women to teach the young mothers how to make items out of shells. The room smelled like an old fishing dock, and there were shells and bits of coral stacked in every corner.

"Don't worry about the smell," Gwen assured them, "we'll get some fans in here and keep the windows open. One of the women will bring your meals and you can heat coffee and tea here on this little stove."

Nell had asked Brad and Rose to stay close in case there were surprises she wasn't prepared for. "I can't eat in here," she whispered to Rose gesturing towards the piles of shells. "It smells disgusting."

"Let me talk to Gwen. Maybe we can arrange something else," said Rose. Nell went back to the government building and Rose found Gwen in a small screened-in porch attached to the shell room. "Oh, this is nice, Gwen," she said. "Can we eat in here?"

"Well," Gwen said, "I was concerned about everyone getting wet if it rained. That's why I suggested you eat inside."

"But this is so much fresher," Rose said, waving her arms around to emphasize the air flow. If it rains we can move against the back wall."

"That would be fine," agreed Gwen, but she looked a bit put out by having part of her plans changed so soon. Relieved, Rose had the tables and chairs moved out to the porch.

In the meantime, Brad was helping place the equipment inside the government building. They had four folding operating tables. Outside they'd placed a long wooden plank over stacks of cinderblocks, creating a rustic table as a check-in desk. The vestibule was the right size for prepping the cats and dogs for surgery, and recovery materials were being put in a small room at the back. It had a door, making it easy to take the animals outside to their waiting owners. It was a good set up. Nell was pleased. She told them it was Paradise compared to some of the locations she'd had to work in.

The town's main buildings were set back from the ocean, and behind them the houses were simple square boxes on stilts. If the family was fortunate enough to own a car, scooter, or bike, they were parked underneath. Property lines were defined by loosely-laid rock walls, and all the roads were sand.

Nell had put Brad and Rose up in a house ten miles from town. She knew this wouldn't bother them as much as the volunteers from the US or Canada, who would prefer to stay together as a group. It turned out to be someone's guest house, decked out with tigers. The bed spread, the towels, mugs, plates, pictures on the wall, rugs, salt and pepper shakers, place mats, napkins—everything was smeared with orange and black tigers. It was more like an invasion than a theme. They settled in and went to bed, too tired to let the tigers overwhelm them.

First days of clinics are usually slow but that wasn't the case in Xcalak. Chatty Gwen had people lined up the first morning. The volunteer doing check-in was a stocky woman with a stocky personality. No one got past her without filling out every bit of information. No cat or dog entered the government building without a numbered tag and all their information on three different forms that were neatly tucked into a large ziplock bag— blues for males and pinks for females. This bag would follow the animal every step of the way. No one moved a patient without their ziplock bag. If someone forgot it, everyone in the room would know. "I need a bag here," a volunteer would announce. "Where are the papers for number thirty-two?" At this point everyone except the doctors would stop what they were doing until that ziplock bag was found.

Any cat or dog that was too skinny or weak would have to be checked by a vet before being approved for surgery. The first unhealthy applicants were two puppies brought in by an old woman. They were in a sack balanced on her enormous breasts which filled the entire space from her chin to her waist. The two little heads were staring straight forward, probably wondering where they were going. She said she'd found them the week before and she knew they were in sad shape. Whether it was true or not, at least she understood that their condition was not acceptable.

"Are they male or female?" the vet asked after he'd been called outside to check on their health.

"Both female," the stocky check-in lady replied, pointing to their pink forms like he should have known.

The vet poked at them, lifted their skin, and checked their gums. "We can't operate on them like this. Let's put them on fluids with vitamins and feed them four or five small meals a day. Maybe by the end of the clinic they'll be well enough for surgery." Rose had been watching the vet and immediately took charge of hooking the pups up on IV fluids. She left the check in lady to explain the situation to the owner.

Gwen had informed Nelly that the Mexican army was scheduled to bring in their dogs the second day. Before the army arrived, all the volunteers made bets on what kind of dogs they'd bring. Most bets were on pit bulls, Doberman pinchers and Rottweilers. Rose thought maybe Labs, like the ones on Isla Mujeres used as drug sniffing dogs. But everyone was wrong. The army brought cocker spaniels: ten soldiers in camouflage, ten dogs. They stayed all day, checking the dogs in and then waiting for them to come out the back of the building, sleepy and spayed or neutered.

The week passed quickly. Every day the old woman came to check on her puppies. Gwen finally explained the situation to Rose. "The old women's husband just died. He was an alcoholic and had disappeared for a couple of weeks. I guess he did it all the time, but this time he didn't come back. Someone found him. He'd been in an old shack in the jungle and the two puppies were with him."

Gwen led Rose away from the check in table like she was telling her a secret. "The old woman lives on the edge of town and has been carrying the pups around ever since. When I saw her with them, I told her about the clinic. The pups are actually looking better. I've been giving her dog food."

Rose checked on the pups the minute Gwen finished her story. They were together in a crate on top of a red plastic Coca-Cola table. Two bags of fluid were hanging from a hammock hook on the wall and two thin plastic lines disappeared into the crate. Rose bent down to see the puppies, they were pressed to the back of the cage, sleeping. She was worried, there was only one day left before they moved on. The final day would be divided into surgery in the morning, packing in the afternoon and driving north to Majahual that night.

Rose barely slept that night. They packed up early and said goodbye to the tigers. She'd originally considered taking the pups home if they weren't healthy enough for the procedure, but after hearing "the dead husband story" she wasn't even going to offer.

The vets usually arrived later than the rest of the volunteers; there were many things to do each morning before the surgeries started. Rose checked the puppies first and saw that the bags of fluid were almost empty. She disconnected the tubes and gently carried the pups outside. When she put them on the ground they stayed huddled together, so she sat on the sand with them in her lap. Eventually one walked off for a squat and then the other, but they came right back. After some cuddle time Rose put them back in their crate.

Mornings were always busy; changing the solution that sterilized the instruments, refilling the gauze tubs with alcohol, checking that each table had scalpel blades and sutures and the right size sterile gloves. It was all the details that needed to be tended to before the real work started.

Finally the vets arrived. "George," she said, "Could you please check the pups before you get started. They seem better."

"I checked them last night," said George, "let's have a look." Rose brought one of them over to George's surgery table. If one was good, they both were good.

George prodded at her eyes and gums, pulled her skin, stood her up to check her balance and poked at a few of her scabs and finally pronounced her fit for surgery. They were put first on the list. After their surgeries the puppies were in recovery for a long time. They weren't that energetic to begin with and the vet tech who was doing their recovery wanted them both wide awake before she would sign off on them to go home.

The old woman was waiting with her sack when Rose took them out the back door. She tried to give Gwen some money to buy food for the old lady, but Gwen turned her down and promised to check on the puppies daily until they were fully recovered. Gwen was confident that they would be well cared for. The old woman had said they were her family now, that her husband had left them for her.

The army bringing in their Cocker Spaniel mix dogs to be spay in Xcalak

The devastation in Majahual

Chapter 29
The Rabbits

The town of Majahual, at least the part closest to the water, had been completely demolished by the hurricane. The highway into Majahual simply ended at a mountain of sand. Nell, who was driving the lead car, found a makeshift road that meandered along the inland side of the first row of surviving buildings. This new thoroughfare met up with the old road only briefly before winding back into the jungle. On that small section of road was a two-story white hotel. It was the only building left standing that close to the water. It had been damaged but was restored enough for the group to stay in.

From the balcony of their second-floor room Brad and Rose could see cars and boats stranded in the mangroves a quarter mile back from the shore line. Literally tons of debris was scattered over a huge expanse of thick, dead foliage. The salt water had killed everything. Months had passed since hurricane Dean had hit the town, but it looked more like it had only been a few weeks.

Del, the owner of the hotel, explained that he'd just finished construction when the storm hit, so the building was strong enough to withstand the blast. He said that the town's major repairs were being done farther back—away from the water where there had been heavy damage but anything closer to the water was literally gone.

That's where the clinic was set up, farther back in a row of cement houses that had been donated for the week. The next day the group of volunteers went to work again, falling into the same routine except for the addition of a new band of locals. One young couple was there solely to catch and bring in the dozens of homeless dogs abandoned by families who were forced to relocate after the storm.

A large group of Canadians lived in Majahual for six months of the year and they all wanted to help. They were an energetic boost offering fresh support. Brad had been working in transport, which meant that he carried the sleeping dogs from station to station or helped move crates; essentially he was there for the heavy lifting.

Brad and Rose worked at the Majahual clinic until everything was running smoothly, and then they left. They had so many dogs at the house, and Rose knew that Kat had little patience for the barking.

The drive back to the island was long but peaceful. "I'm glad we're going back early," said Rose, "it's a long time for Kat to be at the house."

"She's probably going nuts by now. She hates the barking as much as I do." Brad didn't turn to look at her while he was driving. They were passing through 'The Mayan Riviera." And he hated this section of road. It had a reputation for speeding, reckless drivers. Rose had sensed a difference in his demeanor the minute they'd passed Tulum.

"You guys should just ignore the barking, let it become white noise. I barely hear it," said Rose.

Brad shook his head. "It amazes me that it doesn't bother you."

"It could bother me if I let it. You concentrate on it. I've seen you do it." Rose reached over and rubbed the back of Brad's neck. "Even when they're not barking, you're waiting for it."

Rose's cell phone rang, it was Gretchen calling from the book store. She set the phone on speaker so Jennifer could join their discussion.

"How were the clinics?" asked Gretchen.

Rose described Majahual. "I've never seen anything like it." Then she told them about Xcalak.

"Next time we're coming too," said Gretchen.

"You should," said Rose, "which reminds me, I was going to call you. I want to get everyone together. I think we should do something like this on the island. We haven't had a big clinic in a long time."

"Let's ask everyone what they think, see who wants to help," suggested Jennifer.

"How about the day after tomorrow? Can you call everyone? I'll have to catch up on things at the house."

Brad and Rose got to the island later than expected. Kat was happy to be relieved of her duties and left right away. The next morning Rose was giving all of her dogs a visual checkup when Rudi waved at her from the driveway.

"There's someone here to see you. It's that old lady who owns the little hotel downtown."

"What's she want?" asked Rose.

"I have no idea, but she's got some men with her and they won't come inside the gate."

It's never good when they won't come in, thought Rose. She wished Brad was home but he'd gone to buy food. "Can you come out with me, Rudi?" she said.

"Si," he replied. They passed through the gate and closed it behind them to keep any stray dogs inside. Waiting outside was a short Mexican woman in a traditional dress of white cotton, bordered by colorful embroidery, top and bottom. She was carrying a large stick. As soon as the gate was closed the woman poked her stick at the bag one of the men was holding and then pointed at Rose's feet. Rose stepped back as he approached, so he ended up dumping the contents a foot in front of her. Two large brown rabbits with bloody noses tumbled out.

Rose watched them for signs of breathing. They weren't. Then the woman started screaming. Rose listened for a while, trying to pick out words that she knew, frustrated she finally turned to Rudi for help.

"She says that your dogs killed her rabbits," Rudi explained. "Her grandchildren are crying, they were their pets." The woman continued to scream while Rudi translated. One of the men circled around beside the screaming woman so he could see Rose's face. It gave her the creeps. "Her name is Lupita," Rudi continued, "and she lives at her hotel. She says your dogs killed the rabbits."

"What dogs? Did she see it?" Rose asked Rudi, trying to stay calm.

"The rabbits were found dead. She says your dogs from the beach did it."

"How does she know they were my dogs?"

Rudi had to raise his voice, which he never did, to be heard over the screeching stream that Lupita was spewing. "She says that the dogs are yours, all the dogs, you keep them alive."

"She thinks I'm responsible for everything a dog does on this island?" This is crazy, thought Rose. "Rudi, take out your phone," she said. "Have you got the one Brad gave you?"

"Si."

"Do you remember how to use the one part?" Rudi pulled out the phone and poked at the front of it. Then he held it like he was about to make a call, making sure it was pointed in the right direction.

Lupita must have decided that she was being ignored because she moved closer to Rose and grabbed her arm. The men moved in with her. Rose tried to step back. She was almost against the door when she saw Peach, one of her older dogs, coming around the corner towards the house. Peach was a fence jumper.

"Rudi, we'd better get Peach inside," she said. Rudi handed the phone to Rose and reached out to grab Peach's collar, but the dog moved away. Rose had forgotten that Peach didn't like men. At that moment Lupita raised her stick and hit Peach across her back as hard as she could, using both her hands. Caught totally by surprise, Peach howled when the stick struck her and then took off towards the woods, yelping and spinning spastically.

Rose's heart and mind erupted simultaneously, making her feel sick to her stomach. Her first impulse was to lunge at Lupita. Rudi saw her lean in and grabbed her arm but she spun out of his grip. The old woman was glaring at her defiantly. "What the fuck is the matter with you?" yelled Rose. "There's something wrong with your fucking brain, you fucking idiot—"

"Rose." Rudi grabbed her arm again and was pulling her back. "Rose," he said again.

"Oh my god," Rose said, panicking, "she might have broken Peach's back." Rose looked from Rudi to Lupita. "Oh my god, what the fuck is the matter with you? You repulsive witch!" Rose stepped forward and would have tripped over one of the dead rabbits if Rudi hadn't gripped her arm tightly.

"What's going on here?" yelled a voice in English. Lupita's grandson was hurrying down the road towards them.

"Your fucking grandmother just hit one of my dogs. Is she fucking crazy? Rudi, go find Peach. Oh my god, she might've broken her back." Rudi didn't move. Rose realized that he wasn't going to leave her there alone.

Lupita was screaming at her grandson now, and repeating the story about the rabbits. Rose hoped that he'd talk some sense into her but she was disappointed.

"Get off our land," he demanded, turning to face Rose.

"What?" she said.

"This is our island. You don't belong here. Get off of our island."

Rose wasn't prepared for this. "We own this land," she said. "What are you talking about?"

"Of course we own this land," said Brad, sounding slightly out of breath. He had rounded the corner running, obviously he'd heard the yelling. He dropped his bags and stood next to Rose. Normally Rose would've been relieved to see Brad, but she was so mad, there wasn't room for anything else.

"Get out of here!" Rose shrieked at Lupita, ignoring her grandson's command. "Get out of here! If my dog dies, I'm going to throw her body at your stupid fucking hotel. Get out!" Rose had started to move forward again but Brad stepped in front of her and was gently pushing her back.

"Rose," he said, trying to make eye contact.

"She thinks I'm responsible for everything any dog does on this island. She's a fucking lunatic."

"You disgusting bitch," Rose leaned around Brad to yell, as he continued to push her towards their front gate. "I'm not going inside," she said. "I've got to find Peach." She raised her arms to dislodge Brad's hands and then she ran towards the woods. "You fucking bastards!" she yelled as she passed Lupita and her thugs.

She had to climb a rock wall and squeeze through a wire fence to get into the section of jungle Peach had disappeared into. As she jumped down, her pants caught on something and she hit the ground hard. As Rose lay there trying to breath she watched a small green lizard run across the piles of dead branches and disappear into a hole. Then she closed her eyes. The fall had knocked the air out of her, leaving her no choice but to wait until she could refill her lungs. "Peach," she said, when she finally sat up. "Peach, come here. Peach!" She said it louder. Nothing. Her feet were sore from running along the sand and gravel road. She knew that she couldn't possibly go further into the jungle. She'd left her shoes in the house.

Instead, she climbed back over the fence and walked down the road in the opposite direction, away from her home. She went as far as the market and then sat on the steps in the shade. She'd been yelled at before, threatened, even spat at, but this felt different, more treacherous. They'd just returned from two communities where she'd met so many Mexicans who had been happy about getting help for their dogs and cats. Like the woman with the puppies in the bag. And there'd been the army, with cocker spaniels, for god sakes! Is this what these islanders would still be doing if no one was watching? If I don't let them kill the dogs does that make the dogs mine? Rose was so engrossed in her thoughts that she didn't see Brad coming.

He sat on the step beside her. "They're gone," he said, "and I made them take the rabbits." They sat there for a while in silence with people stepping around them to get in and out of the market.

"God, she was crazy," Brad said finally. "After you left she started yelling at me. She called me every Spanish swear word I've ever heard. Rudi got it all on the phone. Good thinking, by the way. I'm glad I showed him how to use the video."

Rose turned to face him. "I wanted people to see the craziness and told Rudi to get his phone out. He got my message right away and pretended he was listening to a call while he aimed it right at that bitch." Rose smiled, "I don't know how much of it he managed to get but he must have something."

Brad reached into his shirt pocket. "You're not going to believe what's on there," he said. "Rudi and I already watched some of it." He clicked on the video and fast forwarded past the part where Lupita hit Peach so Rose didn't have to see that again. "This is awesome," he said, handing her the phone. On the screen Lupita was standing in front of Brad. She was at least a foot shorter and standing so close she had to crane her head back to scream up at him.

"I didn't think old Mexican women talked like that," said Rose.

On the video, Brad was looking down at Lupita like he was watching an alien. Rose started to laugh and held the phone out so Brad could see. "Look at your face," she said. He started to laugh, too.

She and Brad sat there, blocking the stairs to the market, staring at their phone and laughing. Now the locals have more proof that we're crazy, Rose thought.

Suddenly Brad looked serious. "You're bleeding," he said, and reached out to touch Rose's face.

"Oh," Rose put her fingers on the side of her face, remembering her fall. "I'm glad," she said. "We can call it assault."

The next day was the clinic meeting, but Rose's plans for the clinic's location had changed. Instead of holding the clinic on Isla, they would work on the mainland in Rancho Viejo. After what had happened the day before, she decided that she needed a break from the island.

Chapter 30
The Plan

"Where's the wine?" Jeannie asked the minute she entered the courtyard of Rose's house. "I brought chips and salsa. I can't wait to get off my feet."

Rose had a couple of bottles of white wine in a cooler along with other sodas and bottled water. There were glasses, napkins and pretzels on the folding table she'd set up, and everyone was comfortably helping themselves. "I'm sure glad we like the same wines," said Kat, pouring a glass.

"You'd like any wine that was free," said Gretchen.

"I don't see you holding off," retorted Kat.

"The way I feel today, there isn't enough wine in the world," Rose told them. She wasn't feeling up to one of the Kat/Gretchen skirmishes even though she knew it was between friends.

They'd all heard the 'Lupita story,' so she told them about Peach. "It took a while," she said, "But Rudi finally found Peach late yesterday afternoon. Poor thing was scared and hurting but she could walk. I moved her inside with a crate full of blankets to help her feel secure."

Rose and Brad hadn't slept at all that night, and Peach's injury wasn't the only reason. Rudi had pulled Rose back as the old lady yelled because a foreigner can be put in jail for striking a national. And Rose had wanted to flatten Lupita.

"Staying busy and focused is your best cure," offered Jeannie. "I think a clinic is just what we need." Everyone nodded in agreement and Rose savored the warmth of their support.

Rose had already started the planning. "I talked to Cally in Houston this morning."

"Uh oh, we're in trouble now," Kat said, grinning. "Getting two crazy dog ladies together."

"You got that right," added Jeannie. "It usually means a lot of work."

"Okay, yeah, yeah," laughed Rose. "You should all thank me for helping you do your part for the planet." She sat back in her teak lounge chair and took a long sip of her wine. "I think we should do the clinic in Rancho Viejo. Addy, you and Gretchen were there. Jennifer, you saw the poverty and all the sad dogs. They don't have vets or doctors. It was like that in Xcalak. The people were so relieved to have help. There was so much to do. We could've stayed a lot longer."

"What kind of timing are we talking about here?" Jeannie asked.

"Well, we thought the middle of next month. I know it's not a lot of time to get organized, but—"

"Bookings are down since the hurricane anyway," interrupted Jeannie, "if you want to put some people up at my place you can."

"I was counting on that," Rose said, smiling affectionately at Jeannie. "I knew you'd offer."

"I'm in," said Addy with nervous enthusiasm. "Now that I work at night I have all day to help."

"That's great, Addy," Rose said, leaning forward. " But there's going to be some sad stuff, hard to look at. Can you handle it?"

"I already went there with you once, didn't I?" Addy said, folding her arms across her chest. Rose nodded.

"So, is everyone in?" Rose asked. "Kat, you haven't said much."

"Oh, I'm in," she said, sipping her wine. "You know I'm in, I'm always in."

"So far, we've got two vets confirmed and two vet techs that want to come," Rose said. "Cally already talked to them and she has one more vet that's been bugging her about working in Mexico."

"Are all these vets male?" asked Kat hopefully.

"So far, they're all men, and unmarried. All for you, Kat." Everyone laughed. "Actually," Rose said, "I think one of them is coming with a girlfriend who's a vet tech, so you get the other two unless Greer can come."

"I'll ask him," Kat said waving the idea off with her hand. "Are the other two vets cute?" Gretchen groaned and rolled her eyes. Everyone else just laughed.

Rose sat back again and sipped her wine, knowing this was just the start of some serious planning. The rabbit incident had shaken her deeply. She'd returned to the island energized and hopeful. One incident, she thought, and she was worn out. It had made her feel unwelcome and vulnerable.

"The first thing I need to do is find a location," she said. "Cally is making the list of drugs for the surgery and I'm making a list of other supplies. We have to find a place for all of the 'out-of-towners' to stay and of course we've got to feed them." Rose stood up and grabbed a wine bottle. "Who needs more wine?" She went around and topped off each glass except for Addy, who still had to work. Addy didn't usually drink anyway because it made her cry.

"I'm thinking that each of us will have a specific job, and then we can meet once a week to talk about it. Does that work?" Rose asked. Everyone nodded. "Jeannie," she said, and they all turned to her, "How about you handle all of the accommodations, since you know most of the people with rooms to rent."

"I'll check around, see what I can find," Jeannie agreed.

"Great! Addy, I thought you might head up the food. Breakfast should come with their rooms, but we need to have drinks, snacks, and lunches at the clinic. What do you think?"

"Well," Addy said, looking at Jeannie, "I don't know that I could get all the food organized. Does it include dinners?"

"No, no, I don't mean that you'd have to do the whole thing," Rose said quickly. "I just want you to be in charge, keep track of things, ask around, and do some shopping, maybe. We'll all be helping each other."

"Okay, just as long as we're all in on it. Sure, I can keep track." Addy smiled weakly. Her limp hair had been pulled back into a pony tail, probably a requirement at the restaurant where she was working. It looks better, thought Rose, remembering how Addy had looked after the hurricane.

"That's great."

Rose could see Kat rolling her eyes but ignored her. "As far as dinners go, we haven't decided yet. Sometimes everyone needs a break from each other. We could maybe talk to the local restaurants about giving the volunteers a discount. That way, if we give people a choice they can decide who they want to go with, and where. We have a lot to figure out. You guys can help with suggestions, problem solving, everything. Yes?" Everyone nodded.

Rose turned to Kat. "You and Gretchen have had the most experience with dogs and rescue so could you help with animal handling and clinic flow. Where to set up what, stuff like that?"

"I'll talk to my boss," Kat said, smiling at Jeannie, "See if I can get some time off."

"Not bloody likely," Jeannie said with a grin.

"Kat and I can split it, see who's better at what," said Gretchen. "What do you think, Kat?"

"Sounds perfect," agreed Kat. "That way we won't kill each other."

"Exactly," said Gretchen, smiling. She went to the table, grabbed the pretzels and walked around offering them to everyone.

"I'll talk to Jennifer," said Rose, taking a handful of pretzels out of the bowl. "She'll be great at coordinating local volunteers. How about we meet every Wednesday at this time? Does that work for everyone? Free wine and food?" She raised the empty bottle she'd put on the floor next to her chair.

"Works for me," said Jeannie. Kat stopped in front of her with the pretzels and Jeannie took a handful, dropping them in her lap. "But during the clinic, do I have to be there? With all the guts, blood—ugh, bloody hell— testicles and ovaries?"

"You big baby," said Kat.

She'd finished her rounds with the snack bowl and gone back to her bench.

"I'm big yes, but a baby, no way," she said. "My mother wanted me to be a nurse. All English working-class girls are supposed to be nurses or nannies. But I can't stand smelly babies or blood."

"That's not true," Rose said. "I've seen you get all gooey over lots of babies."

"Yeah, and they go right back to their mums when they get stinky, ugh." Jeannie said with a shudder.

"Well, you don't have to see any blood; you don't even have to go to the clinic at all," Rose said.

Jeannie laughed, "Perfect. I'll pick up the pieces when you all get back to the island. Is Brad in on this?"

Rose sat forward and spoke softly like she was sharing a secret. "He's fully in, you should've seen him when we went south to do the clinics. He was totally into it." Rose's face changed. "After the incident yesterday I think he's especially glad that we're working off-island."

After another few minutes of chatting, everyone left. Rose stayed in the courtyard, writing out all the information from the meeting in her notebook, hoping she wasn't in over her head. When Brad came home, he joined her there, fishing a Diet Coke out of the cooler.

"So did you get the ladies on board?" he said, sitting on the second lounge chair.

"Yup. Addy's nervous about doing the food, and Jeannie doesn't want to see any blood, but other than that they each agreed to the jobs we talked about. I think Kat and Gretchen are going to split their tasks rather than work together. I think it's a good idea. They know each other well."

"I guess it's on, then," he said, putting his feet up and leaning back into the cushions.

Rose rubbed her eyes and put her note pad and pencil down on the tiles beside her chair. "I hope I haven't jumped in over my head."

"You're always in over your head," Brad said. "And you always manage. Think of how little you knew when you brought those first puppies home."

"I know, but what do I know about surgery?" Said Rose stretching her arms over her head and yawning.

"You're not doing surgery. You're just making it possible for someone else to do surgery, and this is the only way to stop taking in dogs."

Rose stood up. "Oh, I get it, this is for you." She sat on Brad's lap and put her arms around his neck. "This is your master plan to get rid of the dogs."

"Hell, yeah," he said, pulling her closer. "No more puppy shit to step in on the way to my music room."

"You don't have to clean it up." Rose pushed herself up away from him, feigning anger.

"Yeah, but I know it's there," Brad plugged his nose, "or it has been there, or it's gonna be there." He raised his shoulders indicating helpless defeat.

Rose went back to her chair, picked up her note pad and smacked him on the shoulder with it, then headed upstairs. Brad followed. She'd clean the courtyard up after dinner.

Chapter 31
The Clinic Begins

By the group's third meeting at the Mango Café, everything was falling into place. Everyone showed up on time but Rose.

"Where do you think she is?" asked Jennifer. "I'm working this afternoon and don't have much time." They couldn't start without Rose.

"She probably had a dog emergency," said Kat. She pushed her chair back from the table and stretched out her long legs.

"Well, she could at least call," said Jennifer. "I have to get back to the book store."

"Jen, I'll tell you everything we talk about, if you have to go," said Jeannie.

"Let's order. I know what she likes."

After they ordered, Jeannie tried to call Rose but the line was busy. "She must be on the phone," she said, and helped herself to the chips and salsa the waiter had left behind.

"Well, she can walk and talk, can't she?" said Jennifer.

There was a stir by the door, and suddenly, there was Rose. "Yes!" she said, dancing into the room with her arms over her head. "Karla's going to live," she sang. "Karla's going to live!"

"Who the hell is Karla?" asked Kat, "And where have you been?"

"Oh, come on Kat, you remember Karla," said Rose, settling into the only empty chair at the table. "That little blind, grey pup the school girl brought to the house. I didn't think she was going to make it through that first night. Remember? I called you."

"Karla, right, but what has that to do with you being late?" asked Kat.

"We ordered for you. The salad you usually get. Okay?" said Jeannie. "And thanks for making the meeting earlier today, I have an afternoon check-in."

"No problem," Rose said. She reached for the only full water glass left on the table. "Maybe we should change our meeting time to lunch again like what we used to do."

"So what's the story? Who is Karla?" Jennifer asked. "I want to hear it but I've got to get back to the store so speed it up."

Rose put down her water glass. "It's not a long story and it has a great ending," she said. "Do you mind?" she asked everyone, looking around the table. "I know this is supposed to be a clinic meeting."

"Its fine," said Jennifer. "I'm the only one that has to go early and Jeannie has offered tell me whatever I miss when you discuss the clinic."

"I remember now," said Kat. "You had Karla upstairs for a while. Right?"

"Right! The poor little thing was blind and could barely move. I'm sure someone dumped her by the side of the road. That's where she was found," Rose said, her smile disappearing. "When are people going to learn that we want to help, they don't have to dump their animals if they get sick? That's why they do it you know, they're afraid of the cost." Rose turned and hung her bag on the back of her chair. "Anyway, the dog was covered with ticks so I treated her with Doxycycline and she recovered quickly and got her eyesight back, luckily it was just a side effect of having Ehrlichia, which is what she had. We kept her upstairs because she was so small and weak. But after a while Rudi noticed she was getting fat, so we thought she might be pregnant. I took her to Paulo to get her spayed. He called me that day in the middle of surgery. I bet he didn't even change his gloves. He's so bad that way. I buy them for him, but—"

"What was it? You're killing me here," Kat interrupted.

"Sorry. She wasn't pregnant, she had a tumor. Paulo said he couldn't remove it, and asked if I wanted him to put her down. I asked him if she was in pain and he didn't think so, not yet. So I told him to sew her up and she could stay with us until she was in pain and then we'd put her down. Brad wasn't thrilled but he knew it was only temporary." Two waiters arrived with their lunches. After the plates of food and salsas were all in the right places, everyone started to eat.

"Then what do you mean that she's going to live? Did Paulo decide to remove the tumor?" asked Jeannie.

Rose shook her head. "He'd never removed a tumor before. People here would never pay to have a tumor removed. So, she went to New York. You remember Geena?"

"The vet who helped with my Palomo?" Kat asked.

Rose nodded. "She had a friend visiting the island and told me to send a dog back to New York with him. She wanted me to send someone who needed help. So instantly I thought of Karla. So she went to New York and Geena operated on her. But it didn't go well. She had to remove most of her intestines. The tumor was all wrapped—"

"Enough," said Jeannie, putting down her fork. "I mean, we're eating here."

"Sorry," said Rose. "Anyway, Geena wasn't sure that Karla would make it. She took her to this incredible animal hospital she works with in the city and said everyone in the entire place was rooting for Karla after they learned her history. Geena called me every day with an update. Some days were good, some not so good. It was torture. I didn't even want to talk about it until I knew either way." Rose paused and drank some water.

"I can't believe the emotional ups and downs you go through," said Gretchen sympathetically. "I don't know how you do it."

"Well, it's easier with some dogs," said Rose, wiping her mouth. "But Karla had been upstairs with us for a while. Anyway, that's why I was late. Geena took Karla home from the hospital last night and she's ninety percent sure that she's going to make it. We thought of her as dying for all that time she was with us at the house. But now, to think of her as 'living' is just too fantastic." Suddenly, Rose's throat was tight. She gently lay her fork down beside her plate, hoping that no one would notice her glistening eyes.

"So, what happens now?" said Jeannie, reaching across the table and putting her hand over Rose's.

"Well," she said slowly, "it's all good news from here. Geena works with some rescue groups in New York and they've offered to find her a home."

"That's such a happy ending," said Addy, smiling through tears of her own.

"Yeah, it's pretty incredible," Rose said. "From unconscious by the side of the road in Mexico to a loving home in New York City." Rose continued to eat and then started to wave her fork around. "Wait," she said, trying to swallow quickly. "I haven't told you the most incredible part of the story. I mean you're not going to believe this, no one would."

"What, what?" asked Kat, as she leaned back to let the waiter fill her water glass.

"Well, it's standard procedure to send a piece of the tumor to the lab to check if it's cancerous or not. Geena got the results back the day she brought Karla home. Oh my god, get this, it wasn't a tumor at all. It was a piece of gauze." Rose looked around the table, enjoying everyone's surprise."

"How could that be?" asked Gretchen. She had a chip half way to her mouth and held it there.

"Paulo told me that she'd already been spayed," said Rose. "So who ever spayed her must have left a piece of gauze inside her. It was so wrapped up in her intestines they couldn't tell what it was and just assumed it was a tumor. It makes sense. Whenever I help Paulo with surgery he makes me count—four gauze in, four gauze out. Wow, now I really understand why."

"Oh my god, that's awful," said Jennifer. "Are you sure that the vets coming to the clinic are good?" Rose smiled at her worried face, appreciating that her first thought was the safety of the animals they would be operating on.

"Cally has checked them out," she assured her. "But it does show you how many things can go wrong."

Jennifer checked her watch and jumped up, grabbed her bag off the back of her chair and turned to Gretchen, "Can you pay my share? I have to go." She waved over her shoulder as she headed towards the door. "See you guys later." She'd obviously stayed longer than she meant to, wanting to hear the end of the story.

They all watched her leave. "Poor Jennifer," Gretchen said. "She's so smart, so thorough. She doesn't trust anyone else to do things as well as she does, and most of the time she's right. After that story, we'll probably find her in the operating room counting gauze." Everyone laughed.

"It's actually a good reminder," said Rose, "to hear this sort of thing can happen, just so many things to watch out for. We'll have to stay sharp but we can do this."

After their plates were cleared away they had a short meeting. There wasn't that much left to cover. Their plans were coming together well. Jeannie had booked rooms for all of the people coming in from out of town. Rose and Addy had made arrangements with three restaurants whose owners had agreed to offer dinners at a thirty percent discount to the volunteers on Rose's list. As always, money was tight, so Rose was relieved when two American families on the island donated the funds needed to buy lunches, snacks, and drinks.

Cally had been collecting supplies in Houston, but the anesthesia, pain meds, anti-inflammatories and antibiotics would have to be bought in Mexico. To pay for them, Rose posted on her website and Facebook page asking for cash donations.

"I'm hoping that with all the supplies you're bringing we can average our costs at fifteen dollars an animal," Rose told Cally during one of their many planning phone calls. "If we do fifty cats and dogs each day, which means we need to raise three thousand seven hundred and fifty dollars just for the drugs."

"Do you think we can get that much?" asked Cally.

"I don't know," said Rose. "I hope so. I talked to Brad. We'll make up the difference if the donations don't come in."

"You can't keep doing that, Rose," said Cally. "I mean, you already pay for almost everything."

"I know, but we can pay for it this time. What else are we going to do? Nothing? All we can do is hope that the donations will start coming someday, before we go broke that is."

"I don't want to be around when that happens," said Cally.

"I'm not going to think about it," Rose said. "Something will come up. I just know it will." Rose hated to discuss the money; assigning words to her worries just made them louder.

"Listen," she continued, "I was hoping to have the clinic at a government building or the school but I couldn't find any available government buildings and the school will be in session.

"I've been thinking about that too," Cally said. "I've got a great idea. I picked up some tents we can use."

"What do you mean you picked up some tents?" said Rose. "What for?" Cally was incredible at finding the strangest things cheaply. Rose imagined that she spent her days on internet sites like craigslist or cruising garage sales. She found things like dog crates for two dollars, and one time she bought a thousand syringes with needles for ten dollars. Whenever a vet clinic went out of business or someone cleaned their garage or a company reorganized their warehouse, Cally was there getting things for next to nothing.

"It was a garage sale," said Cally. "Some old Cub Scout leader had these incredible tents. They're lightweight and zip together into different rooms or they can be separate, I just couldn't pass it up. I thought I'd sell them, make a profit, but hey, let's use them."

"You're incredible," said Rose. "How will we get them down here?"

"Easy, I'm bringing down some big crates. We'll put the tents in them. I've already arranged with the airline to fly our bulky stuff. They haven't given me a limit," Cally said, "But I won't push it."

Two days after their meeting Rose and Gretchen went to the school in Rancho Viejo to search for a place nearby where they could set up the tents. They got back to the island late. Brad met them at the ferry where they said goodbye to Gretchen, then Brad and Rose strolled home along the sidewalk next to the beach. The stretch of sand by the ferry dock was for the fishermen, and was covered with long open boats pulled up for the night or for repairs. Fishing nets were strung between the palm trees and fishermen were drinking beer and cleaning the day's catch.

"We went to the school first," Rose told Brad. "I figured it was centrally located and that would make it easier to explain to people where we were having the clinic. We talked to the woman who lives next door, and she said we could set the tents up in front of her place. It's sparse, but the road is wide and the school parking lot is across the street. The woman said we could use her water, which is just a hose, and we can plug into her electric line. She thought that part was really funny because she pointed up to the electric post and told me that she was pirating her electricity anyway. I guess everyone over there does it."

"You're kidding," Brad said, shaking his head.

"I know! It's not perfect but I don't see what else we can do." They stopped and watched the fishermen running mending spools in and out of the mesh that hung between the trees.

"We can use the RV," said Brad. "If it's full of gas we can run the generator. People can use the bathroom and take breaks and eat inside." Rose had hoped Brad would make this offer.

"Thanks sweetie, that'll make a huge difference. This place makes the locations in Majahual and Xcalac look luxurious." They walked on in silence for a while. "This is going to be rustic," Rose said. "It's making me nervous."

"It'll be okay." Brad put his arm around her shoulders and pulled her against his side. "We can call Nell if we can't figure stuff out."

They took their time walking home, stopping to watch the sunset, and trying to enjoy the evening.

Karla Before - she was so skinny we had to put a jacket on her.

Karla After - in her new home!

Chapter 32
Meeting the Group

On the Saturday before the clinic, Brad volunteered to pick up the vets at the Cancun airport. The first to arrive would be Dr. Harold Savoy, the only veterinarian who had insisted on having his airfare paid for. Margaret, his travel companion, was also his older sister and surgical assistant. As he waited in the arrival area, Brad held up a clipboard with their names on it. He was surrounded by twenty other sign-holding van companies waiting for the automatic doors to open and liberate their passengers.

When the doors finally opened, a tall man with grey hair accompanied by a short, stocky woman walked straight up to Brad. "I'm Dr. Savoy, and this is my sister Margaret," he said officiously.

"You're right on time," Brad said, and shook his hand. "Let me get that bag for you." Dr. Savoy started to hand Brad his bag, but Brad had been addressing his sister. He took the handle of her suitcase, turned and walked towards his car. "I'm Rose's husband, Brad," he said over his shoulder. "I think you've talked to her on the phone quite a bit, haven't you Margaret?"

"Yes, yes, we've had many conversations," she said as she struggled to keep up with the two tall, long-legged men.

Saturdays were usually the busiest travel day of the week for the airport.

The walkways were crowded and parking places were in demand, so they had a bit of a strut to get to Brad's car.

"Sorry to rush you," he said. "We're parked at the far end of the lot, which was all I could find. I have to come back in two hours to get the next group."

"Oh, we could've waited," offered Margaret sweetly.

"That's very nice, but there wouldn't have been enough room for everyone in my car, so it was just easier to plan on two trips." When they reached the car, Brad loaded their luggage in the back and unlocked the side doors. Harold sat in the front passenger seat.

As they drove through Cancun, Brad explained the arrangements. "I'm going to drop you off at the ferry. Someone is meeting you on the other side. You can't miss her; she's rather large and always wears brightly colorful muumuus." Harold looked out the window and said nothing, but Margaret kept up a steady conversation from the back seat, asking Brad about the buildings and places they passed. When they arrived at the ferry Harold never touched his bag. Brad handed it to the porter, and tipped him in advance. And then he turned right around and headed back to the airport for Dr. Don Grey, and his vet tech Jordan, and Dr. Belle. Luckily, their flights arrived within half an hour of each other.

Belle saw Brad and his sign right away and introduced herself. She had a friendly face surrounded by wavy dark blond hair, and looked to be in her late forties. She pointed Dr. Grey out in the next crowd that came through the doors, explaining that they'd worked together before. When Brad spotted him he was helping a young woman with her bags and heading in the wrong direction. Brad had to circle around the entire group of travelers in order to catch their attention. On the ride to the ferry it was quickly apparent that Jordan, though she looked half the doctor's age, was more than just Dr. Don's tech.

Jeannie Tull met each group at the ferry dock on the Isla Mujeres side and escorted them to their hotels. She chatted away about the island and put people at ease in her usual "mother-to-the-world" manner.

Cally had arrived the day before. She'd brought 4 bags of supplies, and she and Rose had been working steadily to get everything organized for transport to the mainland. The plan was to take the supplies to Rancho Viejo on Sunday morning after a group meeting.

"I'm feeling more prepared now, Cally, how about you?" Rose asked. She was sitting on her living room floor surrounded by plastic bins with labels like, 'syringes,' and 'catheters and IV lines,' and 'drapes and scrubs.' There were ten bins, all filled, and still more supplies were scattered about.

"I think we're in good shape but we're going to need time on the other side to set up properly," said Cally, who'd organized many clinics.

"I've got to get ready for the volunteer meeting. Are you okay with the rest of this?" Rose asked Cally. She didn't reply. She was completely absorbed in her task: organizing everything so that she knew what she had and where to find it. The minute that she arrived she'd changed into her hiking shorts, wrapped a bandana around her short brown hair, and insisted on getting to work.

Rose was nervous. Everything was going well, but the site was rustic and she hadn't met all the vets yet. She was prepared for things to go wrong. It was the not knowing what it would be that was the hard part.

The Sunday morning meeting was planned for nine thirty. Rose had bought muffins and borrowed a thirty-two-cup coffee maker. She'd asked her core group to arrive at nine so they could settle in before the out-of-towners arrived. By nine fifteen they were all there: Jennifer, Kat, Addy, Gretchen, Cally, and Rose. Jeannie Tull was bringing the rest. Brad was loading the car.

"Any first impressions?" Rose asked her group. But before anyone spoke she heard Brad talking in the driveway, and the sound of footsteps on the gravel.

"They're in the courtyard," Rose heard him say.

"Here we are," announced Jeannie, leading her guests through the front door. She looked tired. "I know we're a bit early but it just worked out that way." Two men and three women followed Jeannie into the courtyard.

"Let me do the introductions," she said. "This is Dr. Don Grey and his vet tech Jordan," and she pointed at a tall thin man in his fifties and the young blond woman standing beside him. "And here we have Dr. Harold Savoy and his sister Margaret. They're from LA. Don and Jordan are from Houston." Everyone nodded. "Oh, and this is Belle Fenn, sorry, Dr. Belle Fenn."

"Hi, everyone," said Belle, flashing a beautiful smile, "Just call me Belle." Rose had met Belle during a quick visit to a clinic in Cancun the year before, and she'd liked her immediately.

"And back there is Dr. Maria Rose, our vet from Mexico City. Poor Maria got in really late last night." Maria Rose bowed her head. Her black hair was pulled straight back in a ponytail, in the style of many Mexican woman. She was short, slightly overweight, and looked tired and uncomfortable. Jeannie had promised Rose that she would give Maria special treatment. Maria's English was limited and Rose wanted her to feel at ease, not outnumbered.

"Welcome, everyone," said Rose, "Please come on in and make yourselves at home. There's coffee over there and some muffins as well."

Almost every seat was filled after the group settled in. "Let me introduce our island crew. I'm Rose. I've spoken to most of you on the phone. This is Cally. You and Cally know each other from Houston, isn't that right, Dr. Grey?"

"Please, call me Don," he said, balancing a muffin on his plate. "Yes, Cally and I have crossed paths many times."

"Ha, too many times," said Cally and everyone chuckled.

"You've all met Jeannie Tull, and this is Jennifer, who owns the local bookstore with Gretchen." Jennifer and Gretchen smiled as they were introduced.

"We also have internet at the shop," Jennifer informed them, "so if you need to use it, please help yourselves. It's free for anyone who's here to help us with the animals." Again everyone smiled, relaxing a bit more on their hard benches.

"There will be more of us," continued Rose. "Dr. Esteban will join us once we are on the mainland, plus Mark and May, who run a rescue in Minneapolis, will be coming in tonight. You know them, don't you Belle?"

"Yes, they've brought a few of your rescue dogs into my clinic," said Belle.

"Also, we may have one other vet tech. Is that right, Kat?"

"I'm not sure about that. Let's not count on it." This is interesting, thought Rose. She'd ask Kat about it later.

"There will also be more volunteers coming from the island," Rose continued. "Most of them can only do a shift or two, so there'll be new people every day. Cally and I will be taking the ferry over this afternoon to set up. If any of you would like to go over with us today, you're welcome." Rose walked over to the table and poured herself a fresh cup of coffee. "Tomorrow," she continued, standing next to the table, "We want to get everyone there by eight a.m. As I'm sure you all know that first morning usually takes a while to get going. We're hoping to start surgery by ten."

"Even though I've already talked to all of you," Rose was addressing the vets now, "I've printed up sheets with our protocols." On cue, Cally walked around the courtyard and handed each vet a packet of notes. "We've all talked about this, but I thought you might like to have it on paper, and if you have questions talk to Belle, as these are her protocols. And as I've already explained to each of you, we're using injectable anesthesia. I'm afraid we aren't funded well enough to have our own gas machines. Someday, maybe. We'll also have weight charts for every drug. This will make it faster and easier to figure the doses."

While everyone was looking at their paperwork, Rose said, "If you have questions, or suggestions, we're not leaving for a couple of hours, so please talk to me about it. Help yourselves to coffee and muffins and thanks in advance for all of your hard work. I know this is going to be a wonderful clinic."

Afterwards, everyone broke up into smaller groups and chatted for a while. Rose was hoping this would happen. Better to get comfortable with each other before the clinic started. Margaret was the first person to approach her with questions.

"Rose, I have a list here of the things that Don wants at his table. I think I mentioned them before." Rose had noted that Margaret ran shotgun for her brother, who was showing very little interest in talking to anyone. Rose watched him approach Jeannie Tull, who must have been giving him directions to somewhere by the way she was moving her arms and pointing.

"I have that list, Margaret, you emailed it to me, and hopefully we'll have everything he needs. But as I said before, this is a poor area and our situation will be rustic. You assured me that it would be okay." Margaret looked nervous and held out the list until Rose finally took it. "Don't worry, we'll do our best," Rose assured her.

"One more thing, everyone," Rose said, raising her voice to get people's attention. "The volunteers from the island each have their own special responsibilities. If you have problems with your accommodations please talk to Jeannie; problems with the food, you can talk to Addy… or me. Cally is in charge of medical matters, and anything else you can discuss with Kat, Jennifer or Gretchen. We'll be having short meetings throughout the week and talk about any changes or problems that come up then. We're all here to make this work, so please come to me with anything that you need, no matter how small."

Rose was gathering her notes and paperwork up from the floor when Kat said her name.

"Can we go upstairs?" Kat asked.

"Of course," said Rose. They climbed the stairs to the kitchen and then Rose led Kat into the bedroom for privacy. She sat at her desk, and motioned for Kat to sit in one of the chairs next to the window. "What's up?" she said. "You don't look happy."

"I just feel like I've let you down," she said.

"Why, I think everything's going well, don't you?"

"It's not that. Greer isn't coming, and I know you were depending on him being here." Kat pulled the pillow out from behind her and wrapped her arms around it. Her body language was more revealing than her words. Rose rolled her office chair closer to Kat.

"It's not a big deal," Kat said. "Greer wanted to get serious; he started talking about a future together. I don't do that, at least not now." Kat pulled her hair behind her shoulders and looked out the window. "I watched my stupid mother morph into whatever she thought would keep whoever the man of the hour was around. She ended up being nobody, nothing." She put the pillow down and then picked it up again. "Anyway, I don't want to talk about that."

"Well, Kat, you are talking about it," Rose said gently. Kat tossed the pillow over onto the bed. "What I mean is that I don't give a shit about her. I'm just telling you that I'm not about to settle down with one guy and mold myself so he'll like me better and stay with me longer."

Rose sighed. The woman was always so hard on herself. "Kat, you're not that dumb. Greer likes you the way you are. What makes you think he wants you to be any different?"

"Really? The first thing he wanted was for me to move back to the States."

"He wants you with him." Rose stood up and walked over to sit at the end of the bed, it was closer to Kat. "If you don't want to move, why can't you just keep seeing each other the way you have?"

"He wants more," said Kat. She stood and faced the window. "He wants ME to move, ME to change my whole life. I told him he can come and see me if he wants. I mean, he's pretty cute. I'm just not going anywhere. I don't want just one guy, and I like the way things are now."

"Then you figured it out. Don't worry about him not being at the clinic. We'll be fine. Hell, I can tech if I have to."

"Thanks, Rose." Kat leaned forward in her chair so they were very close. "I just know how much this clinic means to you."

"No worries," said Rose. She reached for the pillow and handed it back to Kat.

"One more thing," Kat stuffed the pillow behind her, "I want to take Palomo home after the clinic. What do you think?"

"I think it's great." Kat stood up and Rose gave her a hug. "I think that Palomo is the perfect man for you."

"Yahoo," Kat said with a grin, and she spun around and walked out of the room.

Chapter 33
All The Working Parts

The afternoon set up went smoothly. Tents were erected with ease and the RV was parked next to them as protection from the road. People from the neighborhood kept stopping by, curious to see what was going on. Rose explained and then told them to pass the info on to anybody with animals. For further exposure they draped a large tarp over the side of the van. On it was painted the hours they'd be open and in extra-large letters the word "gratis".

During the clinic Cally would be living and sleeping in the RV. She was there for security, and once a clinic was going on, she never wanted to leave.

"We'll be here early," Rose told Cally. "Call us if you need anything or if you get nervous." Rose and Brad were walking towards their car, ready to head home, when Brad's cell phone rang. It was Mark and May.

"Hi, Brad," May said. "We're here at the airport."

"Hey May, I thought you had a ride." Brad said.

"Yeah, we had a ride, a voucher for a van from our last trip, but we have a bit of a problem." Brad handed his cell phone to Rose.

"Hi, May, how was your flight?"

"The flight was fine, but custom's a bitch." May said. "They want to take a lot of our supplies and I'm not leaving the airport without them." Rose's heart sank. The customs agents were in a constant state of reorganization. Sometimes they would confiscate dog shampoo and leave antibiotics. There was no method or reason or consistency to what they let through and what they said was not permitted.

"How much do they want to take?" Rose asked.

"Too much!" said May. "They want all the Frontline (a monthly tick and flea prevention) I brought, they want my sutures, but they don't care about the syringes. I just don't get it. It doesn't matter anyway. I worked too hard to get all of these supplies and I'm not leaving the airport without them."

"Listen," Rose said. "Brad and I are in Cancun with the car. We'll come to the airport now."

"Fine. I'll still be here until they decide to cooperate," grumbled May before hanging up.

"Oh, this is going to be great," Rose said, pulling on her seat belt. "Once May decides on something, there's no way around it. They want to take some of her supplies and she's adamant about keeping all of it. I can just see her sitting on her suitcase refusing to let them take anything." Rose took a deep breath, it had been a long day and a battle with customs was not part of their plan.

"Wish me luck." Rose said as she jumped out of the car. Brad nodded and headed to the parking lot. May was easy to spot through the glass walls of one of the offices bordering the luggage pick-up area. It was the only one with lights on.

Rose stood outside for a moment marveling at May's tenacity. Just as she had predicted, May was sitting on her suitcase, scowling at two officers who were trying to talk to Mark. She's a great player if she's on your team, thought Rose.

"Hola," Rose said as she entered the room. "I'm here to pick up my friends." Mark gave her a big hug and May, who was not in the mood for hugs, got right into it.

"They're not taking any of my supplies. We're using them to help the animals in their city and that's it. They don't have a list to show me, nothing." May crossed her arms firmly to illustrate her resolve.

"Do you have a list of things that people aren't allowed to bring into Mexico?" Rose asked the officers. One of them stepped forward. He'd obviously had enough of May.

"The lists that we have are not specific, they're general. We decide what looks suspicious or not. She," he gestured towards May, "has no papers, nothing to show us that she has permission to bring medical supplies into the country."

"Well," Rose said, looking at May. "Let's see what she's got." May reluctantly lifted herself off of the suitcase and opened it up. "These aren't any kind of special medical supplies," said Rose as she rummaged through its contents. "You don't need a doctor to have these things. I don't see what the problem is."

Rose actually did know what the problem was. It was all about saving face. The officer had said that the stuff couldn't come into the country and whether that was right or not he wasn't going to let a foreign passenger, especially a woman, tell him what he could or couldn't do. The items in the suitcase were not the sort of things that travelers usually arrived with and that had raised a red flag.

"Give me one reason why these things are any threat to national security," May snarled. Rose looked to Mark for help; he shrugged his shoulders.

At that moment Brad knocked on the door.

He introduced himself to the officer closest to Rose. "Long day, eh?" he said. The baggage claim area was empty but it was Sunday night, meaning that the men working at the airport were probably coming to the end of a long, busy weekend.

"Si," the officer replied.

"Rose, you make sure that Brad knows I'm not leaving without these supplies," reiterated May. Brad gave May a stern nod then asked the officer if he could speak to him privately. He was led into a smaller room next door leaving the other guard behind to keep an eye on the suitcases. "What else have you got in there?" Rose asked May so she would stop glaring at the other officer.

Five minutes later Brad reappeared, he was alone. The officer who had stayed behind passed Brad on his way to join his colleague. "Okay," Brad said, "this is what we're going to do. Both these guys go off-duty at nine thirty. When the next guys come on we'll have filled out these forms, stating that all of these supplies were donated and estimate their value at a hundred dollars. Then we're going to pay duty on that and we're free to go."

"Why couldn't we do that in the first place?" asked May, putting her hands on her hips.

"Because," Brad put the papers on the table. "You told him that the supplies were worth a lot more than that." He handed May a pen, "I've got the forms here. We'll fill them out and have them ready for the new guys to sign. The officers that you haven't pissed off yet." May made a face.

"Did you have to pay a bribe"? Rose asked.

"We can talk about it later," said Brad rolling his eyes in May's direction. "I did tell him to bring his dog to the clinic."

"So can I pack this suitcase back up?" asked May.

"Yeah," said Brad. If the new guy wants to see it he'll have to ask."

The new officers arrived on schedule. Brad told them he had a paper stating the value of the goods and had already paid the duty. They poked around in the suitcase for a while until Brad pointed out that it was all donated, and couldn't be used for resale. The officer signed the paper, ripped off a receipt for Brad and told them they could go. They all raced for the door, before anyone could change their mind.

Once in the car Rose gave each of them a beer. On the way to the ferry Brad pointed out that May could probably have just offered the guys a few of the supplies, like dog collars, and they might have backed off.

"It never occurred to me," she said, "We don't bribe customs agents in the US," her words dripping with sarcasm. She sat back and drank her beer for a while. When she finished that one Mark handed her another and she finally started to relax.

"Sorry you had to come and get us," she said. "I know how busy you must be. But really, ask Mark," May continued, "I just don't do bullshit well." Mark just gave a tired grin and opened his second beer.

The next morning everyone crossed over to Cancun on the same ferry. Brad had his car, and Mark was driving a borrowed truck. They were to be the gofers, in charge of transporting people, animals, and supplies when needed.

Rose had been preparing herself for everyone's reactions when they saw the tents. Though she'd known most of the people just a short time, she could already predict what each one would do and she was right on every count but one. Dr. Harold Savoy looked perturbed, his sister Margaret looked even more nervous, Belle just smiled and found something to do, and Marie Rose waited for instructions. The surprise was Dr. Don and Jordan. Dr. Don looked a bit concerned, but Jordan blurted out, "I can't work here. What are we, Boy Scouts?" Dr. Don led her away from the group, talking to her quietly. Rose wished she could be a fly on his shoulder and hear what he was saying.

There were three tents; two of them had been zipped together. The third was twenty feet away and had different sized kennels neatly stacked next to it. This tent was for prepping the animals for surgery. If it rained they would use it to check animals in, as well. Luckily there was no rain in the forecast.

The vegetation in Rancho Viejo was a mixture of low tangled bushes. The houses were wooden or corrugated metal or tar paper, and the roads were wide lanes of packed dirt and sand. Most people cooked outside over open fires and used wooden crates for chairs and old doors for tables. Rose hadn't seen any gardens, and the property lines were one or two strands of wire if there was any distinction at all. Most of the children had tattered clothes, no shoes, and ran about playing with things they'd found, probably something that had flown off of one of the many garbage trucks.

Droves of chickens waddled about. They were everywhere along the road, weaving in and out of the houses and for some reason neither the dogs nor the children ever chased them.

When Rose arrived, people were already lined up with their dogs. Some came on foot while others were delivered in the backs of trucks. The dogs were being dragged, carried, pushed, and in many cases, cursed at in an attempt to instantaneously leash train them so they could be transported. There were cats as well, brought in bags, tightly tied at the top.

Rose took special notice of a woman who brought her dogs in a wheelbarrow. But it wasn't just the wheelbarrow that made the woman stand out; she stroked her dogs and talked to them as she waited in line. When it was her turn at the check-in table she kept the wheelbarrow in front of her so she had to talk over the dogs. "These are my dogs," she said proudly in Spanish, then flashed a toothless grin. She was tiny, her clothes were dirty, and Rose noticed that she was missing two fingers on her left hand. "I've had enough puppies," she said, "I've got seven at home. No more!"

"Thanks for bringing the dogs," said Rose, who had posted herself at check-in. "You're doing them a favor. How old are the puppies?"

"They're little, but Frida doesn't want to feed them anymore," the woman explained while rubbing the dog's ears. "This is Frida and this is Paco." The dogs sat obediently in the wheelbarrow, seemingly unperturbed by the goings-on around them. "I can't have any more puppies," she said. "My husband doesn't like them."

"Okay," said Rose, "let's fill out the paperwork." While she wrote down the information, Kat tried to tie a string around Frida's neck. The dog backed away from her and almost fell out of the wheelbarrow. The woman smiled, took the string and easily looped it around Frida's neck. Then she did the same for Paco.

Rose was wondering about the next part of the check-in procedures. How was this tiny woman going to lift up each dog to be weighed? But the woman surprised her and hefted the dogs with ease. Kat read off each weight and then asked the woman to step back on the scale alone. The dogs weighed eighteen and twenty-two kilos and the woman only weighed forty-nine.

After the check-in was complete, Rose explained that there could be some risk involved with the surgery. Rose pushed the permission slip forward. "It'll be okay," Rose said. "We just need to warn you in case something goes wrong, but it rarely does." The woman continued to stand there until Rose realized she wasn't reading the paper. "I'll read this to you and then you can just put any mark you want at the bottom?" she said. The woman relaxed and took the pen. Holding it awkwardly she made two squiggly lines. "Are you going to leave the dogs or wait for them?" Rose asked.

"I'll wait," she said.

"It's going to take hours." Rose explained.

"I'll wait," she said again.

Surgery started at ten thirty. It took a while to get the tables situated and all the right supplies at each station. Mark and Brad had brought in cinder blocks to get the tables to just the right height for each vet.

Four operating tables filled the back room of the zipped-together tents. Surgery times varied for each vet based on experience and animal gender, so there was one volunteer just for flow. The flow person had the animals removed as soon as the vets were finished, and arranged to bring in the next one. If this wasn't done well the veterinarian would be standing there wasting valuable time, so the flow person had to be sharp. It took a while to 'knock an animal down,' meaning sedated, anesthetized, shaved and scrubbed. If they were considered "at risk," they would have a catheter put in one leg and if the owners couldn't say when the dog had last eaten, they would be tubed so that if they vomited they wouldn't aspirate it.

Rose had arranged for strong volunteers to transport the dogs to and from the operating tables. The medium and small sized dogs and cats were carried by their paws, the transporter holding the two front paws in one hand, and back paws in the other. When Rose had first seen this method she was horrified, but found out it had a purpose. The animals were out cold, and their heads would flop around no matter how they were carried and carrying them this way made it easier to situate them on the operating table. They were lowered between two rolled up towels with their feet straight up in the air, then each leg was tied to each leg of the table, and they lay there like a human stretched out on their backs exposing the part of the body that was going to be worked on.

The other considerations for the flow person were the vet's specialties. Some were especially good with nursing mothers. Some were more experienced at spaying puppies and the least experienced vets usually liked to do neuters. The flow person had to know all of this. It was very important that the right vet was given the right animals.

After surgery, the animals were laid on tarps or towels on the ground in the first tent. People who were working recovery had to acknowledge "the taking on of a patient" before the transporter would pass on the responsibility. Because there were two rooms together and the transporters had to travel through one to get to the other, it was crucial that the people doing recovery in the first room left an open passage for the animals being carried in and out of surgery.

After the operations had been going on for a while, the recovering animals and volunteers would start to take up too much space. It would get noisier and hotter so these were the times the flow person had to watch out for.

Rose was still doing check-in. Cally was doing flow and Jordan was doing surgery prep with a volunteer in the separate tent. They had planned to cut the intake off at thirty-five. The first day was exhausting. They were still a group of individuals getting used to one another in a new environment. But by the end of the week, if things went well, they would become one synchronized body.

Rose had checked in thirty-five cats and dogs and was instructing people to return the next day. The next in line was a boy carrying a small box under his arm. When he got to Rose he put it on the table. "I found it this morning," he said. Rose opened the box and discovered three puppies so young their eyes were still closed. She picked one up, it fit in the palm of her hand. When she looked up to ask the boy some questions, he'd disappeared. The puppies needed immediate attention. She scanned the crowd, looking for a volunteer to replace herself at the table but ended up making a sign telling people to come back the next day.

She took the puppies to the wheelbarrow lady. Her male dog must have gone in for surgery. Only the female was left in the wheelbarrow. She was lying down in a shady spot where the tiny lady had placed her. "How long is it since your female fed her babies?" Rose asked. Her Spanish had been improving, but only because she was no longer afraid to try. Most of the time she got her point across but would definitely have been sent to the back of the class if she were in school.

"They still nurse a little if they catch her lying down. She doesn't let them feed for long."

"So she still has milk?" Rose asked. The woman nodded. "Do you think she would feed these pups?" Rose opened her box and the woman's eyes widened in wonder. She lifted one out and placed it next to Frida's belly. The puppy had no trouble figuring out what to do and latched on immediately. Frida didn't move so they placed all three pups with her. Frida sniffed at the pups, pushed them with her nose, but couldn't dislodge the hungry little things so she lay back while Rose rubbed her ears.

Sitting beside the wheelbarrow on an overturned bucket, Rose had time to look around and noticed Brad talking to a policeman. The men shook hands and the policeman left.

"What was that all about?" Rose asked as Brad walked towards her.

"Remember that guy? He used to work on the island. He was always really grumpy with the tourists." Rose lifted her shoulders. She didn't recognize him. "Well, I guess they reassigned him over here," Brad said. "When I first saw him I thought we were in trouble but I've got this handled." Brad looked very pleased with himself.

"What happened?" asked Rose.

"He pulled up while I was delivering lunch to Addy. He said he'd come by earlier and a dog had peed on his tires. He wanted money to wash his police car."

"Are you kidding me?" said Rose. Brad held up his hand and explained that because the RV and tents were taking up space on a wide street, the cop made it clear that he could cause trouble but that he would let it pass for money. Brad had given him two hundred pesos and then another hundred to watch over Cally and the supplies when no one else was there.

"The guy was completely on board when he left," Brad said with pride. "I think he may actually help us out and watch over Cally when she's alone here." Rose gave her husband a hug.

"You're amazing," she told him. "I think things are going well for the first day, don't you?" The wheelbarrow lady was watching them curiously, so Rose told her that he was her husband, and then showed Brad the puppies.

"I can't take them home," the woman said, "my husband's mean to the dogs." Rose understood. Judging by her missing teeth, Rose figured the husband was probably mean to everyone.

"What are you going to do with them?" Brad asked.

"I don't know. Maybe I can find someone to take them home at night. I know another nursing mom was brought in. I bet we can keep them here during the day and just plug them into every mom that comes along."

Rose spotted Addy setting lunch up on a coke table in the shade. "Addy'll do it." She said. "She was wonderful with Rancho—remember, he was one of the puppies we brought home from here after the hurricane? Addy took great care of him."

On her way to talk to Addy, Rose heard Cally yelling for ice. She pushed her way through the crowd around the door to the surgery tent and found Cally on the ground next to a big black dog that was thrashing form side to side. "Espacio, por favor," Rose told the crowd, and gestured for them to clear some space. "Addy," she yelled over to the lunch table, "have you got ice in that cooler?" Addy looked up, surprised to hear her name. Rose asked again, "Have you got ice in that cooler?" Addy nodded. "Let's get this dog outside," Rose said to Cally. "You," she said to the man next to her, "ayudarnos, por favor?" Cally picked up the front of the dog and the man tried to pick up the other end but the dog kept squirming out of their arms. At that moment Belle showed up with a big blanket.

"Roll him onto this," she instructed, "And then fold it around him. Then you can each take an end." It worked perfectly. They laid the dog down outside next to the food table. "Addy can you fill some smaller bags with ice?" Belle asked, taking charge.

In less than three minutes they had bags of ice under the dog's front legs, next to his stomach and along his back.

"Keep taking his temperature, Cally. When it gets back down give him a sedative and dry him off." After that Belle walked calmly back towards the surgery tent where she explained to the staring people by the door that everything was fine, he just had a bit of a fever. Belle's Spanish was a lot better than Rose's. She talked to them for a little longer and then disappeared under the tent flap.

"Wow, she's great," said Cally when she sat back for a minute. "She's the calmest one in surgery. But I'm going to kill that Harold. What an asshole."

"It's the first day. Everything will be better tomorrow," Rose assured her.

"Not a chance. He's going to be an asshole every day," said Cally angrily. Rose left it there. She didn't know what was going on inside the tents but she made a mental note to keep an eye on that doctor.

Chapter 34
Personalities

At the end of the first day, Rose stayed with Cally while Brad and Mark drove everyone to the ferry. "Thanks for staying," said Cally. "I need to blow off some steam." She was resting on the couch in the RV. "Ahhh," she groaned with relief as she took off her running shoes.

"There wasn't enough room in the car for me anyway," Rose said, plopping down beside her. "Brad'll come back and get me."

"Oh, my god, that Dr. Savoy. He's more like Dr. Dread. And his sister Margaret is so afraid of him that she keeps taking things out of other people's supply bins. Then no one can find anything. I asked her to stop, but she's definitely more afraid of her brother getting pissed off than she is of me."

"You should have heard her on the phone before the clinic," said Rose, rubbing her neck. "I'm so stiff I can't even turn my head to look at you. I have to look straight ahead." Rose moved to the front of the RV and started to struggle with the release bar on the back of the passenger seat.

"Let me," said Cally. She easily lifted the bar that Rose was trying to push, allowing the chair to swivel smoothly around to face the couch.

Rose sat down and laid her head back. "Oh yeah, Margaret," she said. "She went on and on about getting the right things for her brother. I had to keep reminding her that we were working in Mexico and things aren't the same. At one point I even asked her if her brother really wanted to work in such a rustic area."

"Too bad he decided to come anyway," said Cally.

"Why don't we get Jordan to check with each vet a couple times a day, see if they need anything? That way she can take it from the general supplies," said Rose.

"Forget that," Cally said. "Jordan's hopeless. She can't adjust to the environment. She's always running to Dr. Grey and disrupting his surgery. Honestly, he deserves her. What a pedophile. I mean, how old is he?"

"He's in his fifties, I know that," said Rose.

"Well shit, Jordan's twenty-eight. I met his last girlfriend in Houston. She was in her late twenties too. Baby Jane's much more trouble than she's worth as a tech." Rose smiled. Cally had a funny habit of giving everyone nicknames, and they were rarely complimentary.

"Dr. Pedophile stops what he's doing right in the middle of surgery," said Cally. "And talks to Baby Jane every time she whines."

"Why can't he talk to her while he's doing surgery?" said Rose, massaging her shoulder.

"Because he always takes her to the side so no one else can hear what he's saying," said Cally.

"Maybe Jordan will get used to the circumstances," Rose said. "How's the Mexican vet Marie Rose doing?"

"She's fast," said Cally. "But I keep catching her taking her gloves off." Rose knew that Cally couldn't stand any vet that didn't use proper sterile protocols. "Holy shit, she told me that she isn't even used to doing surgery in sterile gloves. Unbelievable. Oh, and then Dr. Dread went off on me because one of his dogs started to wake up during surgery. I gave the dog more anesthesia. It only happened once but the guy told me that it was unacceptable. As if I thought it was acceptable." Pausing to rub her eyes, Cally rolled her neck from side to side and then stared at the ceiling. "I don't know if I can last the week with that shithead. What an ego." Cally got up and rooted in the fridge for a beer, opened it and took a long drink. "On the plus side," she said, "Mark and May are great. They learn fast. I'm going to put them in charge of recovery tomorrow, unless you want to do it."

"That's okay, give it to them," Rose said. "I think I should stick to check-in. That way I can float a bit and keep an eye on things. I may do a little bit of the food prep, you know, help Addy out."

Rose suddenly sat upright in her chair, "I forgot to tell you. Someone broke into Jennifer's and Gretchen's bookstore early this morning. They made a huge mess."

"What was stolen?" asked Cally, completely unfazed.

"That's the mystery," said Rose. "So far they can't find anything missing. Gretchen called me this afternoon and told me she thinks it was done by a guy that Jennifer just broke up with, but they don't know anything for sure." Rose switched to her other shoulder.

"The bad news for us is that they won't be coming over because they have a huge mess to clean up." Rose stood up and pulled her schedule out of her back pocket. "I had them down to work tomorrow so we'll be a bit short on volunteers."

"We'll be fine," said Cally. "Getting this first day out of the way is always the biggest hump for me. I'll keep my eyes open to see if anything's being neglected."

"When don't you watch everything?" said Rose. "Do we have any dogs staying overnight?"

"I'm watching the female wheelbarrow dog," Cally said, offering Rose some of the chips she'd retrieved from the snack box. "She's resting in a crate now, she was in surgery for a long time. But we sent the male home. That reminds me, you should talk to the wheel barrel lady about her puppies. Her adult dogs are really skinny. How do you feel about taking some of her pups?"

Rose saw Brad drive up. "I'll talk to her tomorrow," Rose said, slipping into her sandals. "Are you going to be okay here by yourself?"

"Are you kidding? I'm in heaven," said Cally. "Just dogs, no people."

"And look at that," Rose said, pointing out of the window. "That cop's doing what he said he would." Cally followed her gaze.

"Is that a good thing, I mean that he's there?" said Cally. "He isn't going to arrest me for trespassing, is he?"

"No, it's a good thing," said Rose. "He's here to make sure you're okay. Brad knows him from the island and asked him to keep an eye on things. I guess he decided to help out. Originally he was pissed off because a dog peed on the wheel of his car."

"You're kidding."

"Nope! By the way, if May is going to do recovery, talk to Mark about keeping her away from your Dr. Dread. Just a precaution. You know how she is." Cally agreed and Rose left the RV before Brad came in.

The next morning started earlier than the previous day. They had the first animal on a table by nine o'clock. Rose was doing check-in again and kept an eye out for nursing mothers. At eleven o'clock someone showed up with a mother and her puppy. The owner wanted to know if they could spay the mother. Rose reached over the table and took the pup in her arms. She had a sweet face and soft brown fur, but when Rose rubbed her tummy she discovered what she thought might be a hernia.

"Hey Kat, can you do check-in for a minute?" she asked. Poor Kat was on a break but agreed to take over. After asking the owner's permission, Rose took the pup into the surgery tent to ask Belle about the hernia. Belle was just doing the last bit of suturing on a small dog.

"Can I show you this puppy?" Rose asked Belle.

"Just two secs and I'll be done," Belle replied. Rose didn't mind waiting. She loved to watch. Belle picked up one side of the incision with long tweezers and pushed her curved needle just under the skin, then repeated the procedure on the other side, and after that she knotted the suture four times. She blotted the incision with gauze to check for bleeding, and then spread surgical glue over her stitches. "There, now what've you got?" she said, looking up at Rose. Rose held the pup out so Belle could have a look. "Wow," Belle said. "That's a big hernia for such a little pup."

"The owner wants us to fix the mother if we can."

"No problem," said Belle. "The puppies old enough, the mom should be fine and then let's see what we can do about this hernia."

Rose took the hernia pup to the prep tent and explained the situation then returned to the check-in desk to explain the same thing to the owner and fill in the paper work. Kat said that she was okay doing check-in for a while, so Rose went to find Addy and the nursing pups. Every time Rose walked from one station to another she had to wade through a mob of local kids who were hanging around. They got in the way but most of the volunteers put up with it because this was part of the whole picture, educating the children and spreading the word.

"Hey Rose," called one of the volunteers, "Belle says she needs you."

"Something the matter?" Rose asked, but the volunteer had already walked off, so Rose went back into the operating tent. "What's up, Belle?" she said.

"You have to help me with this." Rose looked down at the surgery table and saw that it was crawling with ticks. "They don't like the anesthetic," said Belle. "I've never seen so many come off of one dog. I want to use the sticky drape I brought. Otherwise I'm afraid some of the ticks will crawl into the incision. Can you grab it for me please?" Rose found the adhesive drape and a Dixie cup on the way back to the table. She filled the cup with rubbing alcohol and then proceeded to push the ticks together and shove them off the table into the cup. They were small ticks, the little round black kind, and they were slow, but the sheer number of them made things difficult. Belle stuck the drape, which was really just a sterile sticky piece of clear plastic, on the dog's stomach positioning the precut oval hole over the incision site. The ticks kept emerging and the only way Rose could keep up as they fell off of the anesthetized dog was to stand behind Belle, reaching around one side or the other to grab them and drop them in her cup. Belle couldn't touch even one of the ticks because it would soil her gloves and she'd have to change them. As she worked on the dog she kept saying things like, "check my left leg, I'm sure there's one crawling there," or "arm, check my arm."

She finished the surgery in fourteen minutes and then said she needed a break. Athough she was used to ticks and fleas, an army of them all heading in her direction was a challenge. Rose called for a transport for the dog and took Belle over to the food table, settled her in a chair and brought her a soda. Belle definitely needed time to compose herself.

The day passed quickly and Rose was thrilled to get through another day without incident.

The wheel barrel lady

Chapter 35
Sedgewick

A boy and his dog were first in line the next morning. As Rose asked him questions he started to cry. He didn't want his dog to have any more puppies but was afraid that she would die. Rose took him to talk to Belle, who explained the procedure and offered to let him watch her do a surgery. Nervously, he agreed.

After putting the boy's dog in a kennel, Rose took him to the prep tent and introduced him to Kat.

"Hey, Juan," Kat said, smiling her most friendly smile.

"He's nervous about getting his dog spayed, so we want him to watch a procedure before we do his dog. Belle's going to do the surgery."

"Okay, Juan," said Kat. "Give me a hand here."

"Si," said Juan shyly. After Rose left Juan in Kat's hands, she heard someone calling her name. It was coming from the check-in table. It was always that way. She was the first person that people called for help.

"What's up?" she asked the volunteer stationed there.

"This guy wants us to kill his dog," she told Rose. "He says that he doesn't want it." Rose looked at the man and then at the dog. The whole thing struck her as too silly to be true---to think that the guy had stood in line to get his dog killed. Rose knew it wasn't funny, in fact it was tragic but she had trouble keeping a straight face.

"Let me talk to him," Rose said, and sat down at the table. The man was short and stocky and wore a cowboy hat set low on his forehead. The lines on his face looked like they had been etched by a permanent frown. Rose bent over the table to take another look at his dog. He was white with an under bite and sat obediently on the ground next to his owner. There was a thick rope tied around his neck and he was panting. Rose put on her best smile. "You don't want this dog?"

"No, es malo." The man said loudly.

"What has he done?" Rose asked.

"Es malo y viejo," the owner said.

"Can I have him?" asked Rose. The man looked confused. "I mean can I have him as my own dog?"

"No," then the man loudly repeated, "Es malo,"

"I think he's cute," Rose said, taking another look over the table at the dog.

"It's my dog and he's bad," the man said for the fourth time." He was getting angry.

"Well I want a new dog, bad or good." Rose told him, trying to look serious as she sat back down.

"A hundred pesos," he said suddenly.

Rose couldn't hide her surprise. "You want to sell him now?"

"A hundred pesos," the man repeated.

"You wanted us to kill him," she said. "Why should I pay you?"

"A hundred pesos," was all he said.

Rose stood up again and looked at the dog as if she was trying to figure out what he was worth.

"I'll give you fifty," she said. The offer was against all of her rules, but there was a long line behind the owner and the situation was so ridiculous. She took fifty pesos out of her pocket, handed it to the man and reached for the end of the rope. The man shoved the rope at her and walked off in a huff. Kat was looking at Rose like she was out of her mind.

Rose just shrugged. "There's always an exception to every rule," she said, walking around the table to get her new dog.

After inspecting him she decided that he was only three or four years old. This was old for a dog in Mexico but young for a dog with a good home. She named him Sedgewick and asked one of the volunteers to clean him up.

When Cally heard the story, she was appalled. "Great," she said. "Now we're going to have everyone showing up with dogs to sell."

"Oh, come on," Rose said. "He wanted us to kill the dog. I didn't want him to see Sedgewick after we cleaned him up and then decide he wanted him back. I've had that happen, you know." Cally was still disgusted.

Sedgewick became the clinic mascot. Everyone had a hand in helping him along. Unfortunately, he was in worse shape than Rose first thought. He was covered with ticks and lethargic. The vets were sure that he had Ehrlichia and started him on antibiotics. Volunteers took turns picking the ticks off of him and he got a soothing bath for his mange. He never resisted a thing. He didn't eat much, so they hand fed him bits of chicken. After that his appetite slowly improved along with his energy level but he was still too sick for surgery. Rose kept him at the clinic with Cally, just in case he improved enough by the end of the week.

One of the volunteers picked out a handsome plaid collar for him but Sedgwick didn't need to be tied up; he lay quietly in the shade near the food table. People sat with him during their breaks. Everyone kept saying, "I know someone who would love to have him," but his short-term destiny depended on his health.

The three tiny pups were also a special case. Everyone knew about them and were on the watch for nursing females. Addy sometimes needed help getting the dogs to accept the babies. Two people would hold the momma, stroke her as the third person positioned the puppies but stayed close, ready to grab them if the female dog became too annoyed.

In the entire week, there was only one nursing mother that refused to cooperate. "I saw a nursing female in line," Addy whispered in Rose's ear. "When you check her in can you ask the owner if it's okay?" The owner was a man, which was too bad. The women were much more enthusiastic about helping to feed the puppies. They would encourage the dog to accept the babies, whereas the men just stood there.

Juan, the little boy who'd been nervous about having his dog spayed, had finally agreed to it after watching Belle do surgery. His dog had been spayed that morning and was in recovery. As he waited, he helped at the clinic wherever he was needed. One of his jobs was to assist Addy with the tiny puppies.

After the man agreed to let his dog feed them, a volunteer led him over to Addy and Juan. Juan asked the owner if he could make his dog lie down. The man nodded, bent over and yanked the dog's head to the ground with the rope around her neck. Addy could see the fear in the dog's eyes as the man pinned her head to the ground. She asked Juan to tell the man to stroke the dog's head so she would be calm. Juan asked but the man didn't do it. Addy felt sorry for the dog as it lay there pinned to the ground, but she needed to get her puppies fed. She pulled a pup out of the box and positioned it in front of one of the dog's tits. The momma dog leapt up, knocking the owner on his back and kicking the puppy a few feet away. The owner jumped to his feet and smacked the dog on the head. "No," yelled Addy, but the man was already walking off, dragging the cringing animal behind him. Addy yelled for Rose.

Rose, who had witnessed the whole episode, followed the man down the dirt road. When she caught up to him, she apologized for the inconvenience. She said they'd made a mistake and could he please bring the dog back so she could be spayed. He was angry, and it took some convincing to get him to stay.

After that they decided to assess the owners a little more carefully before asking them to help and fortunately, there were lots of nursing mothers. The female dogs in this area were in heat, pregnant or nursing most of their short lives. Rose went straight to the food table after checking the angry dog owner in and was relieved to hear that the tiny pup was okay.

Juan went back to sit by his dog in the recovery area, which was getting very crowded. There was barely room to walk through to the surgery tables, so Rose decided to send some of the male dogs home early, but only if they could walk and the owner lived nearby. She asked the wheelbarrow lady to help. She had returned with Frida, who'd chewed her stitches out. Kat lined the bottom of the wheelbarrow with towels and cleared out a few of the larger dogs that Rose picked. Then she followed the wheelbarrow until she could see where each animal lived. That way she could check on them later.

"Okay, everyone," Rose announced, standing in the doorway to the surgery and recovery tents. "Let's take a break after you're finished with the animal you're working on now." Nobody looked up but Belle. "We're getting stacked up in recovery," Rose continued. "Tomorrow we'll try to create another shady area outside so this doesn't happen again."

Overcrowded, hot, and tired is not a good idea, thought Rose.

Cally and Rose continued to check the dogs in recovery to see if they were ready to go home. They had to assess the owners as well as the dogs. Sending a sleepy dog home with a bad owner was not an option.

"Who's watching this dog?" Rose heard Cally ask. She was sitting next to a large, very skinny white male.

"I am," said Mark.

Cally lifted the dogs lip, "Were his gums always this pale?"

"Not that I noticed, but I haven't checked for a while. I'm watching four other dogs."

"But you don't remember thinking they were pale when he first came out of surgery?" asked Cally.

"No," he said. "Nothing that caught my attention, and I always check their gums as soon as they come out of surgery."

"Rose," Cally called, "this dog's gums are really pale and his breathing is shallow. Can you get a vet to check this out?" Rose walked quickly back into the adjoining tent to find an available vet. The only one between surgeries was Dr. Dread.

"Harold," she said, "We've got a dog here with white gums and shallow breathing. Can you have a look, please?" Harold was going through the box of supplies that was taped to the side of his table.

"Get a tech," he said without looking up. "Margaret," he called. Rose looked around the room for Jordan and then realized that Cally was a tech and she was asking for a vet. Belle wasn't in the room and the two other vets were in the middle of surgery.

"Harold, please," Rose said more adamantly.

"Rose!" Cally was calling from the other room.

"Harold, please could you have a look?" Rose said again. Harold turned around and leaned over the table so he could see into the other tent where Cally was on the floor.

"I'm surprised that dog survived the surgery," he said coldly.

"Rose, he's stopped breathing, get a vet!" Cally looked upset.

"That dog'll never make it," said Harold. "Forget it." Cally started mouth-to-mouth resuscitation through the dog's nose, using a thick piece of gauze over his nose and holding his mouth shut.

"Forget it. The dog won't make it," said Harold again. By now everyone was watching, and Cally was crying as she tried to keep up the mouth to nose respiration. Harold had gone back to looking through his supplies. Another volunteer was helping Cally by checking for a heartbeat. Everything got quiet as Cally labored over the dying dog. Someone offered to take over but she pushed them away. Finally, the volunteer with the stethoscope reached over and touched Cally's arm.

"Cally, stop, stop. He's gone," he said.

"It hasn't been that long," she said, her face wet with tears and sweat. After she blew into the dog's nose a few more times she finally sat back on her heels, lowered her head to her knees and sobbed quietly. This was the only death they'd had at the clinic so far.

"The dog was a stray," said Harold. He'd turned around again and was watching them on the floor.

Cally sat up and looked directly at him. "What the fuck has that got to do with anything?" she hissed. Rose knew that she had to get Cally out of the tent. It was hot, and who didn't want to kill Dr. Dread at that moment? Margaret joined them on the floor and apologized. Someone else might have thought it was for the death of the dog but Rose knew she was apologizing for her brother.

Sedgewick after he gained some weight

Chapter 36
Hope

The last day of the clinic was scheduled to end at three in the afternoon. There would be hours of cleaning-up work, and Rose wanted everyone to have time to go home and wash for dinner. She was having them over that night to celebrate. Gretchen and Jennifer were making the meal. They'd never returned to the clinic after the break-in at the bookstore and wanted to do something to help.

The day's intake was set for thirty animals. They'd been averaging fifty-five surgeries a day and that had kept them busy until six or seven each afternoon. The veterinarians were done by five, but the rest of the crew would be needed in recovery until at least seven.

Juan and the wheelbarrow lady had joined them as daily volunteers. The wheelbarrow lady's name was Rosalinda but everyone continued to refer to her as the wheelbarrow lady. She'd been an enormous help, shuttling animals back to their homes or picking them up if necessary. Juan had helped with puppies and walking dogs when they were ready to go. Due to the overcrowding in recovery they'd created a shaded area with a tarp suspended between four poles. The dogs that had already woken up spent their last hours of recovery there. The cats were recovered in crates.

Midmorning on that last day, Juan raced up to Rose at the check-in table dragging a post-op dog behind him. Rose was going to say something about running the dog around so soon after surgery but she could see how upset he was and held her tongue. "They're going to tie her to a tree," he said, out of breath.

"Juan, what are you talking about? They just need more room in recovery," said Rose in a soothing voice.

"No," said Juan, waving his free hand, "the boys are going to tie her to a tree in the jungle."

"Okay, sit'" Rose said, and pulled out the chair next to her. She waved over a volunteer and asked her to take Juan's dog. "Okay Juan, tell me what's going on," she said.

"So there's this family," he began, "and they have this dog, Rincon, she keeps having puppies and they don't want her. They keep taking her to other places and leaving her there, but she always finds her way home. So the mother told her boys to take the dog into the jungle and tie her to a tree, to leave her there." As the meaning of his words sunk in, Rose's upper lip lifted unconsciously, like she'd smelled something disgusting. "To die," Juan said, in case Rose didn't understand.

She understood. She was worm out and Juan's story made her feel unbearably exhausted. She'd been slowly unwinding, letting go of the hypervigilant state she'd maintained since the beginning of the clinic. The barefaced reality of what Juan described spread slowly, gradually pushing the air out of her lungs and then holding tight, not letting any back in. The mother, she thought, asked the boys to do this. A mother whose job it is to teach her children kindness? Finally Rose managed to suck enough air back into her lungs to ask Juan if they'd already done it.

"I just saw them when I was walking that dog," he said. "They're going to do it now."

Rose stood up. "Can you take me to them?" she said. She felt lightheaded but her feet were already on the move.

They walked quickly back in the direction he'd come from. He led Rose down some streets she hadn't seen before and then he turned onto a path that disappeared into the jungle. As they walked through the thick foliage, her anxiety grew. What if we can't find them? she thought. What if they hurt the dog? Rose tried to focus on Juan's back, or things that she had to do at the clinic.

The path forked and Juan wasn't sure which way to go until they heard voices. Two boys appeared out of the thick foliage, without a dog. "Donde esta?" Juan asked his friends. They laughed and shrugged their shoulders.

"Tell them what they did was wrong," urged Rose angrily.

"No," said Juan quietly. Rose realized immediately what a bad idea that would be. Juan asked them again where the dog was and again they shrugged their shoulders.

"This lady wants the dog," explained Juan. The boys just started to walk past them until Juan said a word Rose recognized as "brother." That got one boy's attention. Juan said something else in an angry voice and then said, "vamanos". One of the boys paused, kicked the dirt a few times and then turned around and started to walk back into the jungle. "Everyone's afraid of my brother," Juan told Rose.

"Why?" Asked Rose.

"He can be mean but he told me he's only mean to bad people."

"Do you believe him?" Rose asked.

"Yes," Juan said. "He's my brother." Rose nodded, realizing what a stupid question that was.

A long way from where the paths divided they found an emaciated brown dog bound to a tree on a short chain. "Aqui," she heard one boy say. Rose was the last one to enter the clearing where the dog was tied. The dog was wagging her tail and leaping against the end of the chain at the sight of the two boys.

It was the dog's tail wagging at the cruel boys that struck Rose with such force. She stumbled backwards, barely making it out of the clearing before she had to stop. She steadied herself with her hands on her knees and she threw up. Still stooping, Rose wiped her chin with her t-shirt and tried to clear her head.

The complete disregard. The lack of distinction between a dog's life and that of a rodent. She and the whole volunteer crew were there with a solution, just minutes from this place. The people didn't want a solution and they didn't want this dog. But if a puppy wandered into their yard the cycle would begin again.

Rose finally sat down. The two boys walked around her as they headed back to the street. Juan settled onto jungle floor and quietly waited. After a few minutes and with great effort she stood up, kicked loose debris over her vomit and wiped her face again. To avoid looking at Juan she kept her eyes on the dog which was resting peacefully on the ground, totally unaware of the fate she'd so narrowly escaped.

Rose was impressed by Juan who sat there, patiently. He didn't ask anything or say anything. How could Juan and these boys grow up in the same neighborhood and see things so differently?

Rose turned and headed back down the path. Once at the clinic, it was a relief to get busy. She asked Juan to take the dog to Cally, and then poured herself into the "tear-down" part of the last day. As she was packing the check-in materials Cally joined her by the table.

"So that new dog's in bad shape," she said. "What's the story on that?"

"It's not a good one," said Rose; she really didn't want to talk about it.

"Are we keeping her?"

Rose looked at Cally for the first time. She knew that some of what she'd just been through would show. "Yeah, she's ours, and I think we should name her Hope."

"Okay," said Cally. "You can tell me about it later." Rose saw an uncharacteristic amount of sympathy and understanding in Cally's eyes. Feelings that she usually saved for the animals. I must look really bad, thought Rose. She was about to say more but then heard someone calling her name.

"Rose, the wheelbarrow lady wants to see you." It was a volunteer standing next to the recovery tent.

"Her name's Rosalinda," said Rose, stepping out of the shade. The afternoon sun stung her tired eyes. Rosalinda was standing by the road with her wheelbarrow. This time there was a box in it and from a distance Rose could see little heads bobbing inside.

"Can you take them?" Rosalinda asked. "My husband doesn't like them. Sometimes he kicks my dogs and…"

"I would love to have them," she told her. "Let's get them into one of our animal crates, so we can take them across on the boat." Rosalinda helped put the pups into two crates with food and water. They were skinny, clearly dehydrated, and covered with ticks and fleas. After that Rosalinda stayed with them until it was time to go, obviously reluctant to say goodbye.

It took many hours to pack up, and when it was done there was still one dog in recovery. When the family came to collect their dog, they asked if Rose would take the puppies they had. Rose agreed. She knew this was going to happen. Earlier in the week she'd instructed Addy to tell the owners of the nursing mothers that if they couldn't find homes for their puppies, Rose would take them. Addy carried a stack of Rose's cards and had handed them out.

Finally it was time to go to the ferry. Kat had taken Sedgwick when she left for the island and Cally was arranging to get Hope in a crate so she could ride on the ferry. Bit by bit, people and things had dwindled down to just what could fit in the RV. The last ones to leave were Rose, Cally, and Brad.

The volunteers were tired but relaxed at dinner that night, and luckily Dr. Dread and Margaret and Dr. Pedophile and Baby Jane had taken a pass. They'd stopped by ahead of time to say goodbye. She thanked them for coming with sincerity. They were both good surgeons. It was their people skills that had come into question, and Dr. Dread definitely had compassion issues.

Rose watched her guests. She could see how bonded they were. Clinics did that, but this evening, Rose felt detached. She wanted to talk to Rudi. She was used to having him with her. Often she felt that he was the only one who truly understood, and she'd missed his quiet strength and personal support. But he'd had to stay home with the dogs at the house

She sat quietly with her Princes lying next her, unable to come to terms with the day's events. She wanted to be alone with her thoughts and she needed their inspiration as she wrestled with the idea that she could make a difference. That was the gift that Itzamna offered her and she definitely needed the comic relief that Ek Chauh so brilliantly supplied. They still believed they were making a change but Rose was feeling too small. She longed to empty her head, just for a little peace, just for a while.

Chapter 37
Trying To Compensate

Rose ended up with a total of 18 puppies from the clinic. They were put into three different sections of the house and Sedgwick was given his own dog bed in the kitchen. Rose wanted to keep him close until he felt better. Hope, the jungle dog, had her own place in the garage until they could do some blood tests and spay her.

The eighteen puppies were a lot to manage. Rose was overwhelmed and in heaven at the same time. Fortunately, the puppies had come straight from their mothers. They were still below the norm in general health, but had not yet wandered the streets unprotected from injury, starvation, and disease.

The exception was Rosalinda's litter, which was older and skinny, with mange and infected eyes. Rose kept that family in the most isolated part of the house. For the other litters, she had five separate areas to fill before she had to start creating more spaces.

The three tiny pups they'd plugged into all the nursing mothers were put in a laundry basket on the dryer which kept them warm and gently rocked them when it was in use, which it was, constantly, laundering the towels from the clinic. Rose was sad when one of them died but felt lucky every day that the other two survived. She was feeding them with a 10 cc syringe every four hours. The last two were both males. One was all white and one was completely black. The black one's body was way too small for his head or maybe it was the other way around. They called him Big Head Fred and it stuck. The white pup was smaller and needed a stronger name so they called him Rocky. Rose was looking forward to the time they could eat on their own, although once she sat down to feed them she was always grateful for the rest. She weighed them constantly and carefully monitoring everything that went in and came out of their tiny little bodies.

And then even more puppies arrived. During the week after the clinic, one of the Cancun rescues had a barbecue for their local volunteers.

"This is great," Rose told Angie, who ran the rescue. She was a beautiful young woman with a smile that could light up a room. Rose had liked her from the moment they'd met. The way she talked and how she handled her dogs made it obvious that her heart was deeply connected to every animal in her care.

Rose and Angie walked over to a table crowded with different platters of colorful snacks. She was spooning several things onto her paper plate but none of it really appealed to her. She hadn't been hungry for days, but didn't want to be rude.

Angie had been asking her about the clinic, and expressed a desire to help at the next one. "If we can get a better location, I'd do a clinic every month." Said Rose. "Not as many animals of course, but just to keep hitting the same area over and over."

"I agree," Angie said. "I'll work on finding a location, maybe a school. We could do it on the weekends. Is it worth it to set everything up and tear it down again for just two days? Can we be that mobile?"

"We can try it. I'll talk to people in other areas of Mexico, ask how they do it. Although I don't think I can handle the constant onslaught of puppies." Rose and Angie found two chairs and sat down.

"Hey," said Angie, "after a few clinics in the same area, there won't be any, or at least a lot less, right?"

"Right," said Rose.

"Maybe we should work near the pound," said Angie. "I was there yesterday and they have so many puppies. Really, I've never seen so many there."

"Are they taking good care of them?" asked Rose, looking around for a place to put her plate.

"What do you think?" Angie replied sarcastically.

Rose stood up and put her plate on the nearest table, just the smell of it was making her nauseous. "Have you got a car?" she asked.

"No, but Jesika does," Angie said, discarding her plate as well.

"Do you think she'll take me?" Rose was scanning the crowd, looking for Jesika.

Angie spotted her and waved her over. "Right now?" Angie asked.

Rose said, "Absolutely, why wait?"

"I shouldn't have told you," said Angie, trying to keep up with Rose.

"Why? Should we let them die?" Rose regretted saying it the moment the words came out of her mouth. It just wasn't like her to talk to people like that. Angie looked wounded. "I'm so sorry," Rose said and gave her a hug. "I don't know, what's the matter with me? Really, I'm so sorry."

"Don't worry about it," said Angie, "that's exactly why we have to do as many clinics as we can. Come on. Let's see if Jesika will give you a lift."

It was an easy twenty-minute ride. Vincente, the pound's manager, was thrilled that Rose wanted to take the puppies. She'd found them huddled together at the back of a cement kennel with hard kibble spilled on the floor amongst their watery feces. They were skinny and scared. The workers at the pound had no interest in putting in the amount of effort that was required to keep them alive. Euthanasia by neglect, thought Rose. If the pups couldn't eat kibble or ever needed special medicines, they didn't make it. Rose knew it would be impossible to take them all, so she made a deal with herself. She'd take the youngest and the weakest, and that added up to eighteen.

Jesika helped her put them in boxes. When they returned to the barbecue, everyone gathered around to see. The more experienced rescuers shook their heads. They knew what it would take to save these pups. And the newer rescuers couldn't believe that the pound had puppies that were in such bad shape. Rose was relieved when one rescue worker from Playa del Carmen offered to take eight of them. Somehow ten seemed more manageable.

"You're kidding, right?" Brad asked when he saw how many puppies were in the boxes.

"I only took half of them," Rose said defensively. "These are all the weakest and youngest. I know some of them won't make it but at least they'll be with us." Brad rolled his eyes. He knew that she could never completely protect herself from the heartbreak of losing a puppy and would have to put in many more hours every day to save this new batch. But he also knew that he couldn't stop her.

"Let's hire Lizzy," he suggested. Lizzy was an Irish woman whose son had married a Mexican. She was in Mexico to visit her grandchildren. She'd been working at a rescue on the mainland until it closed, and had already asked them for a job.

So, Lizzy came on as puppy assistant. She was a strong, hard worker with an uncontrollable mop of black curly hair and a pretty face. When she was working she wore an old pair of black rubber boots with wide rims that made her legs look like tiny sticks in comparison. Kat, of course, had made the comment that Lizzy was just a dot between her huge black hair and her huge black boots. Rose tried not to think about it when she looked at Lizzy, it made her laugh.

They now had thirty-two puppies: three litters from the clinic, including Rosalinda's and Big Head Fred and Rocky, and now ten new ones from the pound. They had no way of knowing which of the pound pups were litter mates but it didn't matter since they'd all been together in one kennel. If any of them had Parvovirus or Distemper, they'd would have all been exposed so Rose divided them into two groups by size.

After she arranged new spaces and settled them all in, there was still one more pup out there that Rose had to have. She remembered Rosalinda saying that she had eight puppies and she'd only brought seven to the clinic. It had bothered her ever since she'd discovered what bad shape the others were in. Lizzy lived on the mainland so she asked her to check it out.

Lizzy arrived with the pup the following morning. She'd already named him Garcia. "This fellow's really bad," she said when she presented him to Rose. Rosalinda's other pups had been at the house for a week and were already twice the size of Garcia. He was obviously the runt but the difference was surprising. "Rosalinda was glad to see me this morning," said Lizzy. "She wanted help. She's sure Garcia is dying."

"God, he looks terrible," Rose said when she saw him. "Can he hold his head up?"

"He can, but he's really dehydrated." Lizzy pinched his skin away from his bony frame to illustrate. It took a while to settle back into place—proof of a lack of fluids in the pup's tissues.

"Let's bathe him upstairs in warm water," said Rose. It was easier for her to get right to work rather than agonize over his chances of survival. "We'll keep him in a separate crate in the laundry room. I'll start poaching some chicken and send Rudi out for rice. But we can't get our hopes up on this one." Lizzy nodded sadly.

"I need you to bring me the supplies I will need to put him on IV fluids." Said Rose. She took Garcia upstairs and slowly lowered him into a tub of warm water. He hardly reacted. "And here's the part you'll love," she said as she wrapped him up in a towel and gently rubbed him dry. He shivered slightly so she warmed the towel with the low setting on her hair dryer. He was all bones except his big wormy belly.

"I have everything you asked for," said Lizzy as she came into the bathroom. "But you didn't ask me to bring any fluids."

"I've already got a bag hanging from the clothes line," said Rose.

She was relieved that she managed to get a catheter into Garcia's small dehydrated vein. IV fluid made the biggest difference.

Lizzy brought in a wire crate and they settled him on the towel inside.

By the next morning Garcia had definitely improved. He could stand up and he wanted out of his crate. Rose unhooked him so he could walk around the room. Then she brought in one of his littermates to keep him company.

She found Lizzy sitting in the pen with the larger group of puppies from the pound. They were doing well—all skinny but manageable. The smaller group was another story. Rose had divided them again, by putting five of the weakest ones in another large crate in her laundry room, which was now considered the hospital. It was home to Rocky and Big Head Fred, who still lived on the dryer, Garcia in a smaller crate, and then five new patients. Rose didn't think they would all make it, but was determined to do everything she could to help them survive.

"There are people here," called Rudi, coming around the corner of the house. "They're in the driveway."

"I'll come out," she told him, annoyed at the interruption. They had so much to do. Rose had that uncomfortable feeling of never quite keeping up. "If they want to see puppies we can bring one of the healthy litters out there." This place is looking ridiculous, she thought, as she walked through the courtyard. The never-ending poop and puppy-packed pens were giving her claustrophobia. "Rudi, would you mind cleaning up the two bench areas for me?" she said. "We could spend the whole bloody day cleaning up shit."

There were three of them at the gate, two women and a man. They looked related, all stocky and sun burnt with blond hair. "Hi Rose, do you remember me?" one woman said. "We were here last year. I'm Donna."

"Yes, how are you?" Rose lied. This was the second group of tourists to visit that day and it was still morning. Brad had told her to put a sign on the door with visiting hours. It hadn't seemed right to her, but she was starting to reconsider.

"This is my brother Trevor and his wife Mimi," Donna said, turning to her companions. "I've told them all about you. They wanted to come and see," she continued.

"How long have you been here?" asked Mimi. This was the part that Rose didn't like. The same questions every time. What made you move here? Did you come here to save the dogs? Did you build this place? People were just curious, but it all got so tiresome.

"You want to see some of our new puppies?" Rose asked, ignoring the questions. Somehow, she just couldn't force herself to answer today.

First she introduced them to the older dogs. There were only eight.

"You wouldn't believe the change in the number of dogs, in the streets, I mean," said Donna, talking to her brother and his wife. "When we first came here there were packs of them on the beach. Rose has made an incredible difference."

"Thanks, Donna. I'm sure it's not all me." Things were better. Rose knew it. But she often wondered if the number of strays were down because of her efforts or if it was because of the Government round ups.

Donna and her family gave Rose forty dollars and told her she was doing a great job. Rose thanked them for the donation.

"Rose," Lizzy called from the courtyard. Her voice sounded anxious. "Are you coming in here?" Rose got up but she knew that it probably wasn't a crisis. Lizzy was fantastic but she worried and handled each dilemma like it was new and unique.

"I'm in the driveway."

"You better get in here," Lizzy yelled. Rose sat down and stared at the forty dollars she held. She thought about the puppies she'd left behind at the pound in Cancun. She thought about the five in the laundry room, and then focused on the forty dollars again and wondered how far she'd be able to stretch it. Then she slowly got up and headed inside.

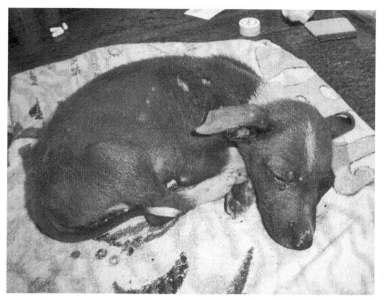

Garcia when he came in after the clinic.

Garcia healthy just before he was adopted

Chapter 38
Big Head Fred, Rocky And Garcia

Rose was tired the next morning. She'd been tired the morning before. She was finding it difficult to get past that first feeling when she woke up. The one that wanted to go back to sleep. She got up anyway but had to lean into it.

The puppies from the pound were a challenge. She'd known the risk. But what else could she do? Rose was doing as much as she could and then some, but her resolve had been jeopardized. She was afraid that it would never be enough. She'd started to feel this way ever since she found Hope tied to the tree.

The spay and neuter clinic had been in the same neighborhood. That family must have known about it. So, the truth was that they didn't care. Would they have given thought to the dog waiting for them, or slowly weakening from hunger and thirst? Rose could only see it as disconnected. Their empathy didn't step outside of their own human dilemma.

Rose felt like each incident was gnawing away at her. She was haunted by the pups that she'd left behind at the pound and worried about the ones that she hadn't found yet and other dogs, heartlessly tied to trees. There were always more in the street, moms having pups at that very moment. The worrying gave her a constant headache. She knew she needed rest but could never seem to get enough sleep.

She'd begun to dread the mornings when it was time to check on the litters. There had been a time when she couldn't wait to see them. Now, she forced herself into the laundry room knowing those pups were least likely to have made it through another night.

Rose was scaring herself, slowly losing the resolve needed to believe she could make a difference. She was no longer sure that one starfish at a time would be enough. Big Head Fred, Rocky, and Garcia were all on the edge of survival, so as her energy waned, she gave them to Itzamna. It helped to imagine him in the laundry watching over them. When she placed them on a towel to clean their cages she'd picture him nuzzling them with his nose. It was a strong image. Itzamna cared as much as she did, and like Rose, he noticed the tiniest heartbeat-skipping nuances that implied an improvement or decline. Ek Chauh, she willed outside with the older dogs. She wanted him there, giving them love and hope.

Rose had developed coping mechanisms. When a dog died of neglect she told herself that he didn't have to be a dog in Mexico anymore. When a puppy died, she drew comfort from the idea that the puppy had died in her loving care. In fact, if Rose knew a pup was past the point of recovering, she would wrap it up and carry it with her so it wouldn't die alone. But lately the weight of each loss wasn't diminishing with time, it was adding up. What if there were too many starfish?

Two of the weakest Pound Puppies had died. Realizing a pup wasn't sleeping but dead was a heart-skipping jolt. She had simply gotten to them too late. One of the three remaining pups was cold, but still breathing. She pulled her out of the crate and rushed into the bathroom. Using the hair dryer for warmth, Rose gently massaged her tiny body.

"Rudi," Rose called out the window. "Rudi." She could see him next to the driveway cleaning one of the kennels.

"Si."

"Can you come up and help me?"

"Ahora?" Rudi said with, tilting his head towards the dirty kennels.

"Si, ahora," replied Rose. Rudi came in through the outside door to the laundry room. He didn't look surprised to see Rose trying to save one of the small pups.

He hadn't complained, but Rose knew he was annoyed that she'd taken in so many. So much of the responsibility fell on him.

"I need a new twenty-two-gauge needle on the IV line and a pot of hot water, just from the tap. You don't need to heat it up. Okay?"

Rudi said, "Si," on his way to the kitchen.

"And bring me some corn syrup," she yelled. The puppy was motionless but Rose could feel her little heart beating.

When Rudi returned Rose instructed him to put the bowl of hot water on the shelf and place the bag of IV fluids in it. Then he attached the new needle to the end of the line.

"Let's call her Sunshine," Rose said as she rubbed. Sometimes she didn't name the weaker puppies. It didn't mean she wouldn't try everything she could to save them, but it kept it less personal. Why was she swinging that door wide open?

"It's pretty warm in here already," said Rose. "It shouldn't take long to raise the fluids a degree or two. Did you bring the corn syrup?" Rudi rolled his eyes before handing her a small bottle. Rose opened Sunshine's mouth and rubbed a drop of the syrup on her tongue.

"I think she has warmed up a bit but she's still dehydrated." Rudi nodded.

Rose placed Sunshine on the end of the table in patch of sunlight coming through the window, then lifted up the pup's skin and inserted the needle. She repeated this in four different places, creating small pockets of fluid. Rudi closed the IV line while Rose manipulated the bumps, helping them to absorb into Sunshine's body. Then more hair dryer, more rubbing, another drop of syrup until Rose sensed some movement. She knew this didn't mean that Sunshine would survive; it only meant that it wasn't over yet.

"I think I'll take her into my room now," she told Rudi. "Could you take care of the rest of them or call Lizzy to do it?" Rudi was staring at the pup. He'd seen it move too.

"You saved her," he said. "I thought she'd die."

"She's still here," said Rose proudly, although she was surprised too.

She lay down on her bed, wrapped her arm around the pup, and fell asleep that way.

When she woke, Sunshine looked better, her gums were pinker. She was going to live another day.

Later, while putting tiny bits of softened kibble on Rocky's tongue, Rose saw Gretchen come through the gate with Pepe. She rarely arrived without him. Gretchen tried to talk Rose into a walk on the beach, but instead Rose coaxed her into the laundry room.

"How are you feeling?" asked Gretchen.

"I'm tired," Rose confessed. Even though the nap had helped, her feelings of heaviness had returned quickly. "Actually, if you wouldn't mind, maybe you could just help Lizzy while I lie down. Do you have the time?" Gretchen agreed and then called Jeannie who came right over.

Rose didn't get out of bed again that day. An ache had spread like a chill through her body. The next morning wasn't any better so Gretchen suggested Addy take some of the laundry room pups to the bed and breakfast. Rose agreed and stayed bed.

Kat, Palomo, and Gretchen and Pepe came over midday to see how things were going. Palomo kept chasing Pepe around the driveway, so Kat put him in with the bigger dogs.

"I'm worried," said Lizzy, when they walked into the courtyard. "Rose is still in bed."

"Oh shit," said Kat and then called Jeannie. "I think you might be right."

"Right about what?" asked Gretchen, but Kat was still on the phone.

When she finished the call, she turned to Gretchen and Lizzy. "Dengue fever. Brad and Rose drove to Puerto Morelos during the clinic to pick up some donated supplies, and there have been eight cases reported there. Jeannie told me that Rose had mentioned aching, but didn't think it was a cold or the flu and it had reminded her of the way she'd felt. Jeannie had it last year."

"Are there any cases on the island," asked Lizzy, "people having it here?"

"Not that I've heard of," said Gretchen.

The next day Brad couldn't stay on his feet either. Jeannie finally shared her thoughts of Dengue with them and arranged for the doctor to come to the house to take blood samples. Then she rounded up all the people she knew who had offered to assist with the dogs. She made a schedule so they would be spread out appropriately to cover each day. She even moved the healthiest litter of puppies to a rescue on the mainland. Everyone was more than happy to do whatever they could.

Lizzy took over the hospital in laundry room with Rudi's help.

"How's it going?" asked Gretchen when she arrived the next day. Lizzy was sitting on a bench in the courtyard and when she turned around, there were tears streaming down her face. She was holding a small bundle in her lap.

"I don't know how she does it. I found this puppy dead, just a minute ago. It's awful. I just went in to change the paper."

"I'm sorry," Gretchen said, sitting next to Lizzy. "Is it one of the pound pups?"

"Yeah," said Lizzy, wiping her nose with her sleeve. "Now there's only two left in this group."

Gretchen pulled the towel open. "Is this the one that Rose called Sunshine, the one she saved the other day?"

"I don't know," Lizzy said. "It's a little male."

"Then it can't be Sunshine," said Gretchen. "Listen I don't want you to tell Rose when any of the puppies die."

"I haven't even seen Rose," said Lizzy, wiping her whole face with the front of her t-shirt. "I've seen Brad a few times, but Rose hasn't left her room."

"I'm not surprised. Did you know that they call Dengue brokebone fever? Jeannie's had it. She said it's incredibly painful. You just lie there feeling like every bone in your body is broken. She told me the islanders sometimes call it malaria's little brother. You can be laid up for weeks." Gretchen saw fear in Lizzy's eyes. "Don't worry, it's not contagious. You get it from mosquitoes. So," Gretchen paused, "if they have it, they may be sick for a while. Can you handle it?"

Lizzy slumped forward, elbows on her knees, "I don't know," she said.

"Sometimes it's hard to be here. I can hear them arguing," Lizzy pulled at some loose strands of hair.

"Who?"

"Rose and Brad, and I heard Rose crying. It's like everything has changed." Lizzy started to cry again. They're like different people." Gretchen leaned in and wrapped her arm around Lizzy.

"They're just sick," she said. "You know how everything feels bad when you're sick."

"But she's still upset about the dog that was tied to the tree," said Lizzy. "I heard her talking about it."

"It was pretty awful. I've tried not to think about it myself. She worries about all the dogs."

Lizzy pulled away and turned to face Gretchen. "This morning, when I was in the laundry room, I heard Brad say something about it being too much. I didn't hear what Rose said, but she was crying. I wasn't trying to eavesdrop. It's just all so sad." Fresh tears ran down Lizzie's cheeks. "This rescue is Rose. She's the one who keeps everything going. I can't do this without her."

When Gretchen left the house, she walked straight to Jeannie's bed and breakfast. Jeannie always seemed to know what to do.

"I've got the test results!" said Jeannie, the minute Gretchen stepped through the door. "The doctor wasn't going to tell me but then he got called away on an emergency, so I offered to take the results to them and he said 'okay.'"

"Well?" Gretchen leaned on Jeannie's check-in counter.

"They both have dengue fever, but Rose's is much worse. She also has salmonella poisoning; can you believe that?" Jeannie walked around the counter and they sat in the stuffed chairs opposite the check-in desk. Jeannie leaned her head back and stared at the ceiling.

It was Gretchen who spoke first. "That's why I came over." Gretchen told Jeannie what Lizzy had heard.

"I'd better talk to Brad," Jeannie said. She took a deep breath and pulled out her cell phone.

Chapter 39

Edges

Jeannie was about to hang up when Brad finally answered the phone. "I'm so glad that you answered," she said.

"Sorry, it took me a while to find it." He was speaking so quietly Jeannie had to strain to hear him.

"I'm sure you're a little slow on your feet. I got the results of the blood tests and you both have dengue."

"No shit," said Brad. "Well, that explains a lot.

"And Rose has it bad, along with salmonella poisoning."

"I'm not surprised," said Brad. "I've never seen her so down. I mean, the timing couldn't be worse."

"Listen," Jeannie said, "I can get everything handled until you two are feeling better." Jeannie talked quickly, so Brad couldn't object. "I'll arrange extra volunteers and I'm sure Rudi can tell them what to do. And," Jeannie hesitated, "I'm coming over now, if you don't mind, and even if you do."

There was a pause and then Brad said, "I'll get Rudi to open the gate for you."

Brad was in the kitchen when Jeannie arrived. He was up and dressed but he looked pale. After saying hello, Jeannie asked him how it was going. He didn't answer her at first, just looked out the window at the waves beating the coral shore. "I don't know," he said finally. "Rose is a mess. She can't stop talking about that dog in the jungle being so happy to see those fucking kids who left her there to die. That one thing just kind of pulled her plug." Brad ran his fingers through his hair. "And she should never have gone to the pound."

"I know, unbelievable, right." Said Jeannie.

"That's Rose," said Brad. "She could hardly walk away once they told her about it."

"But wasn't it a lunch for dog rescues?" Brad nodded. "Why didn't they rush over and grab the pups if they knew about it?"

"That's just it, isn't it?" Brad turned to watch the ocean again. "That's Rose, she can't leave a puppy. If they'd just said there was a bunch of dogs I don't think she would have gone."

Jeannie got up and helped herself to a beer out of the fridge. "Can I get you anything?"

"I think there's a ginger ale in there. That would be great."

"Ice?"

Brad shook his head. "Can's just fine, thanks." He popped it open and took a long drink. "She's just so tired, I think it bothers her more than the aching. I know how everything seems harder when you're tired."

"Then there's nothing to do. We'll just have to wait it out," said Jeannie. "I've had Dengue, it knocked me down for weeks. I had to get someone to run the B&B and even when I went back to work I had to take it easy."

"But how did you feel?" Brad asked. "She's so distraught. Half the time, when she's awake she can't stop crying." Brad sat back to his stool. "I can't stand to see her this way."

Jeannie sat down across from Brad, "How do you feel?"

"I feel like thing's are falling apart." Brad slapped his hands on the counter. "I feel like we've made bad decisions, but mainly I worry about Rose. I know people think she's strong, and she is, but she's also feels things very deeply."

Jeannie checked Brad's ginger ale and then pushed it closer to him. "Drink," she said.

He drained the can and set it down. "It's such a fine balance," he continued. "The crying could be Dengue fever or it could just be that she's had enough."

"Well, before she gives up on dog rescue, she needs to know that she's not alone. She's never been alone." Jeannie sipped her beer. "I've been inundated with calls," she said. "You know how news travels on this island. Everyone knows you're both sick. People want to help, and oh my god, the stories they tell." Jeannie pulled a tissue from her pocket and blew her nose loudly. "I put out a call for help with the rescue—"

"I know," said Brad. "We can't thank you enough,".

"But that isn't what I'm saying. I'm trying to tell you how much people care and how much they appreciate what Rose does. They bring food every day, and everyone has a story to tell me about her. One woman told me Rose had bathed and vaccinated her poodle, and ever since then, her husband has let her keep the dog in the house. Then she handed over a warm pot of lime soup and asked me to deliver it. Another woman arrived with a flan, telling me that her dog had been sick and Rose gave her all the medicine she needed, never asked for a dime. A basket of empanadas came with a woman whose dog had been hit by a car and Rose had driven her and the dog to the vet and stayed there until she knew everything was going to be okay. A man with a cake said that Rudi had been bringing him dog food for years. It goes on and on. I've written it down so I can remember the people and their stories to share with Rose when she's better."

Brad stood up and walked to the fridge, opened the door, pushed a few things around, and pulled out another ginger ale. "I think it's the doubt that's getting to her. What's the point? For her I mean, if she can't do enough? How will she live with that?"

Jeannie lowered herself off the stool and stood to face Brad. "What you've done is incredible. Maybe you have done enough. But I don't think that either Rose or you should decide anything until you're both healthy again." She put her hands on her hips. "Honestly, Brad, she's made it through tough times and needy puppies before. I can't imagine this island without her."

Brad stood up and wrapped Jeannie in an uncharacteristic hug. "I'm going to check on Rose," he said.

Jeannie joined Lizzy in the courtyard, she was cleaning one of the corrals while the puppies ran around outside.

"Hey Lizzy," she said. "Those pups are looking good."

"They're doing better," Lizzy said, smiling. "The group under the bench over there is still having tummy problems, but we haven't lost a pup for a while. Gretchen and Kat have been amazing."

"How are you doing?"

"I'm okay," Lizzy said, leaning on her mop handle. "It's all depends on the pups. If they're sick I worry, if they're better, I'm happy."

"I'm so glad that you're here," Jeannie said, bending down and scooping up a scruffy black pup. "I've got a big crew coming into the Inn, so I'll probably be busy for a few days, but call me if you need anything."

"Okay." Lizzy rinsed her mop and squeezed it over the bucket. "I'm sure Kat will let you know if we run into any trouble."

It was a week before Jeannie had time to go back to Rose's house. Kat had been reporting to her every day when she showed up to clean the rooms. The last report was that Brad was up more and Rose was better, although still, no one had seen her. Jeannie walked to the house, taking the route that passed by the orange juice stand where she purchased a large jug of fresh juice.

"Why don't you take some of this juice to Rose?" Brad suggested when Jeannie arrived. "I'm sure she'd love to see someone other than me for a change."

Jeannie filled a glass and took it into the bedroom. Rose was laying against a stack of pillows. She had dark circles around her eyes, her hair was dull and flat, and her skin was pale, but she greeted Jeannie with a smile.

"You've been so wonderful," said Rose, pushing herself into a sitting position. "Brad told me you've been coming by."

"Here, try some of this orange juice. It's fresh," said Jeannie, holding out the glass.

"No, that's okay." Rose turned her head as if to avoid a bad smell.

"Drink it!" insisted Jeannie, holding the glass out.

"Okay, okay." Rose raised her hands in defeat, then took the glass and sipped from it. "Oh, my god, that's good," she said. She took another drink. "That may be the best thing I've ever tasted." She drank again. "I mean it, wow." Rose drained the glass. "Is there more?"

"All you want," said Jeannie. "How are you feeling?"

"I'm doing better, but if I get up and move around I'm just exhausted. It's not as bad as the aching, luckily that's almost gone."

"You and Brad are the only cases on the island, so I'm sure you got this in Puerto Morelos," said Jeannie, sitting on the edge of the bed.

"Bit of bad timing on that one, eh? And with all these puppies," said Rose.

"We've got people lined up to help you." Jeannie moved closer and patted Rose's leg. "Addy has Big Head Fred and Rocky eating on their own, and the last two-pound pups in the laundry room are almost well enough to go down to the courtyard." Rose noticed that the pound puppy number had gone down but she'd been expecting that.

She hesitated. "Is Sunshine alive?"

"Do you want me to find out?" Jeannie said.

"Yes," Rose said, "I do."

Jeannie opened the bedroom window. Lizzy was in the courtyard cutting an older dog's nails. "Did Sunshine survive?" she called to her. "She's one of the pound pups in the laundry room."

"Yes," Lizzy called back. "Sunshine is still with us. I think we should call her Milagre."

Rose smiled, "How about Garcia?" she asked.

Jeannie knew the answer to this one. Kat had been taking care of him. "He was doing better until he started to vomit after eating. He's lost the weight he'd gained and Kat told me he seems uncomfortable."

"Does he have diarrhea?" asked Rose.

"I asked, she said no."

"Does he have a fever?"

"No, she would have told me."

"Is he still lethargic?"

"He has more energy than he did but Kat says the vomiting has worn him out."

Rose thought about this for a minute.

"Is he still in the laundry room?" Jeannie nodded yes. "Can you bring him in here?"

"Are you up to that?"

"Of course I am. I feel better every day. I'm just a little tired, that's all." Jeannie shook her head and then went to get Garcia. When she didn't return right away, Rose started to panic. She was just about to get out of bed when Jeannie reappeared with Garcia wrapped in a hand towel. His tail was hanging out of the open end and it was wiggling ever so slightly. Rose started to cry.

"I'll take him back," said Jeannie. "This is too soon."

"No! I'm just so happy to see him. Did you see his tail wag?" Jeannie shook her head. "Well it did, he wagged his little tiny tail. Can I have him?" Rose reached up and gently pulled Garcia from Jeannie's arms. She laid him on her lap and opened the towel. "He looks better, don't you think?" Jeannie didn't respond.

"Look at you." Rose lifted his skin and watched it settle back quickly. "Oh yeah, he's better, look at the difference."

"I haven't been taking care of him. I don't know what he looked like before," said Jeannie.

"Oh, I can tell. Look at his eyes. They're so clear. I've seen it when they give up. Their eyes tells you everything." Rose looked down at skinny little Garcia. "Such a cutie," she crooned to him. "You feel better, don't you?" There was another wiggle of the tail. "Oh, I think he's going to make it. Ask Lizzy if she's dewormed him lately."

"Hey Lizzy," Jeannie called down again. "Have you dewormed Garcia lately?" Lizzy scrunched up her face in thought.

"Garcia, no," she finally said.

"She says no," Jeannie reported.

"That's it then, that's all he needs. Look, his eyes are better, he's not dehydrated. Sometimes the worms can make them vomit. He just needs to be dewormed. You'll see, he'll be fine." Rose got out of bed still holding Garcia and went to the window. "Hey, Lizzy, he's fine. He just needs to be dewormed, that's all. Don't you think he looks better?"

"I did think he was looking better but then he started to vomit and it scared me to death," said Lizzy, shielding her eyes from the sun.

"Oh, he's going to be fine. In fact, I think he's going to be incredibly handsome. I can't wait to get down there with you. Is everything good?"

"Everything's good," Lizzy said, smiling up at Rose's happy face. "You better get down here; I'm tired of cleaning up poop by myself."

"I can't wait," Rose said. "I miss them all. There's so much to do."

"You should get back in bed," said Jeannie. "You're not cleaning up any poop today."

"I know," said Rose, "but I could." After Rose climbed back into bed, Jeannie reached for Garcia.

"Let him stay" she said. "Brad will be in soon. I need Garcia here with me for a little longer." Jeannie leaned over and laid her cheek on the top of Rose's head.

"I have so much to tell you. All the people who have helped and brought food and are so grateful for everything you've done." Rose could see the tears in Jeannie's eyes as she picked up Rose's empty juice glass and turned for the door.

"Thanks, Jeannie. Thanks for everything." Rose let her go. She wanted to be alone with Garcia.

Itzamna was lying beside her and Ek Chauh was at the end of the bed. You see this, she said to Itzamna, Garcia made it. We can do this. Just don't ever leave me. Itzamna looked just like King to her now. He'd faded while she was sick. She'd dreamt of him as a ghost and woke up sweating and miserable. Today he and Ek Chauh were solid, lounging on the bed beside her. They're excited about Garcia too, thought Rose.

Rose knew she could work with the dogs. It was the people that made it so difficult. She hadn't planned on this life; she wasn't following a ten year plan that could map out or comparatively monitor her progress. I've had no expectations, she thought. It all just happened, she told Itzamna, I should have had a strategy, but who can prepare themselves for what goes on here.

She asked Itzamna, could I go back? She confessed, I considered giving up. I've been so tired. I mean, we can't get the overwhelming happiness of Garcia's small wagging tail without the overpowering horror of Hope tied to a tree. Can we?

Over the next week Rose got up and worked in the courtyard a bit longer each day. She let the dogs that were being cared for by other people stay where they were. She had decisions to make, and it did her no good to think about it when she was worn out. Everyone wanted to help and she let them.

Hope was improving. She was a friendly dog to begin with. Jeannie especially seemed to enjoy sitting with her. When Rose started to work more, Jeannie arrived with food. "You must be getting your appetite back by now," she said. "And I have to get this food out of my freezer."

Jeannie put a container on the kitchen counter where Rose was making notes. "I told Brad about this, and I've written everything down. Each meal comes with a story, and you're going to love them. The food probably isn't as good as it was originally, I've had to freeze all of it. I'll put this in the fridge for you."

Rose read the story that came with the soup and what struck her the most was how happy the people were for their dog. They'd cared and they'd wanted the help.

Jeannie continued to bring food every day and every day there was another story. Reading them gave her strengh. She didn't always remember the people but she always remembered the dogs.

Taking a nap each afternoon was one of the rules laid down by Brad. If she wanted to work with the pups she had to do what he said. He was watching her closely. If she wasn't tired, she would lie down and talk to the Princes. She wanted to consider her future rather than joining in as it rolled on by. I can never seem to put into words how I got so deeply involved in this, she said to Itzamna. I think it should be more obvious, at least to myself.

Giving up on sleep, Rose rolled onto her back and stared at the ceiling. When a new puppy is left outside the door, all I want to do is help him.

It doesn't matter if I'm busy, hungry, or tired. It fills me up, but then look at me now.

Itzamna was watching her with his handsome head resting on his paws. "If you described this life to me ten years ago," said Rose aloud, "I would have thought you were crazy." Ek Chauh crawled up next to his brother; they were both looking at her.

I know what you're waiting for, she thought. Am I still the dog lady? She let her head sink back into her pillow and didn't realize she'd fallen asleep until she woke with a start. Her feet were cold and she was tired of being in bed. The princes were still waiting.

So pushy, she thought as the questions she'd fallen asleep with came back. She slid her legs off of the bed, raised her arms above her head and stretched them towards the ceiling. Every joint in her body felt stiff.

When she turned back to the bed, Itzamna was still there, but Ek Chauh was gone. She'd brought Garcia in from the laundry room. The de-worming had been hard on him but he was getting stronger. Such a small, bedraggled-looking creature, she thought. He reminded her of the rat that Rudi had tied to a post all those years ago. The rat had run when the line was cut. He got a break and took his life back. Just like Garcia. Rose was sure the puppy would live.

I have to move on, she thought, massaging her forehead. Too much thinking. She walked to the window and saw that Itzamna and Ek Chauh were in the courtyard. They were surrounded by her dogs.

Kat was holding a puppy. Her hair had fallen forward, and when she turned to flip it back over her shoulder she saw Rose watching her. "Hey Rose," she called. "You're looking good!"

Rose smiled. Just seeing Kat there sent a warm rush through her stiff bones.

"I feel much better," she said, leaning a little farther out of the window. "What are you doing to that puppy?"

"What does it look like?" Kat replied. "I'm cleaning his stupid ears."

The puppy on her lap was squirming as she held his head.

"Well, could you be a little gentler?" Rose said.

Kat made a face. "It's lucky to get its ears cleaned at all while I'm on duty." She put the pup on the floor and stood up, turning to face the window. "Did you hear that Jeannie took Hope home yesterday?"

The thought of Hope wrapped in Jeannie's loving care made Rose's eyes tear. From a possible slow death tied to a tree, into Jeannie's arms. One dog, she thought…just one. And then another dog and another.

Kat was still watching her.

"You can't stop," Kat said, and swept an arm across the courtyard crowded with dog pens and kennels. "Fat chance."

"What are you, a mind reader?" said Rose. Of course I can't.

A mischievous grin spread across Kat's face. "Welcome back."

About the Author

Alison Sawyer Current was born and raised in Toronto, Ontario. Her passion for pottery started at 18. She was a successful artist for many years while married to her husband Jeff and raising her three children in Boulder, Colorado. In 2000, they built a home on Isla Mujeres to exchange their view of the mountains for a view of the ocean.

By 2004, she founded Isla Animals, a nonprofit organization that sponsors spay and neuter clinics, vaccinations and animal care. She won *The Doris Day Animal Kindred Spirit Award* in 2005. With the help of her husband, she has expanded the shelter to include other parts of Mexico. She created the *Dog Gone Foundation*, an adoption program that has placed thousands of pups into homes all over North America.

She is a regular speaker at *We Move Forward*, a women's conference on Isla Mujeres. She speaks at special interest groups internationally raising funds for Isla Animals. In 2010 Alison was featured in the Amazon best-selling book, *How Did You Do That* by Gail Kingsbury. Alison's first novel, *No Urn for the Ashes* was published in 2008. The *Dog Lady Of Mexico* is her second novel.

Connect with Alison at www.islaanimals.org

The beginning of puppy camp

Appreciation

This story shares the struggles of all the incredible people who put their heart and time into animal rescue. There is no one 'dog person', It's a community of like minded, hard workers who are making a difference all over the world.

I would like to thank Michele McCutchen and Peggy Sue Davis for being the first people to read and comment on the book. Helen Bryce who has read every version over the years. Thank you Janeen Halliwell for your support and for introducing me to a wonderful group of women – Teresa Kruze, Janet Rouss and Terry Macdonald who have helped me get the book out.

I'm so grateful to all the volunteers and supporters of Isla Animals who have made this possible. A special thanks to Trina Noakes, Anna Krallis, Dr. Arturo Dzul Leon, Steve Ferree and Marrien Neilson, Jeannie Johnson, Amanda Schaffer, Marcelino Velazquez, Letty Garrido, and Tiffany and Brad Waring who have all been steady and generous in helping the animals in any way they can.

Made in the USA
San Bernardino, CA
04 February 2020